DEVELOPING THE FRUIT OF THE SPIRIT
A JOURNEY THROUGH THE HEART OF CHRIST

SUZANNE PHILLIPPA MARCELLUS

Copyright © 2016 by Suzanne Phillippa Marcellus
Published by Suzanne Phillippa Marcellus
www.suzannemarcellus.com
Printed in the United States of America

All rights reserved. No part of this publication may be reproduced, stored in a retrieval system, or transmitted in any form by any means, for example, electronic, photocopy, recording, scanning, or other -without prior written permission of the publisher. The only exception is brief quotations in printed reviews.

Scripture taken from the New King James Version®. Copyright © 1982 by Thomas Nelson. Used by permission. All rights reserved.

Scripture marked KJV is taken from the King James Version of the Bible.

Editor: Phillip Washington Fender
Cover Design: Teodore Thomas
Photo on Back: Jeaneane Swaby of ThruJensEyes
ISBN: 978-0-9976864-0-1

DEDICATION

This book is dedicated to my husband, children, parents, grandparents, and siblings. Thank you for your love and support!

ACKNOWLEDGEMENTS

My heart is filled with gratitude for all those who have prayed me through the writing process, listened to my thoughts and ideas and shared Godly wisdom over the last ten years.

I would like to thank my husband, Jacob Marcellus, and our children, for their patience, prayers and support as I took this journey.

I would like to thank my father, Phillip Fender, for all of his editing and advice. Since the beginning, you have invested hundreds of hours in assisting me to make this vision a reality.

To my mother, Francine Abrahams, thank you for your prayer support, your presence, encouraging talks and inspiring me to be greater.

I would like to thank my grandmother, Mommy Kitty, for her prayers and support. You are Blessed and Highly Favored. Thank you for assisting in the raising and caring of my four children, because of your presence I can do all that I was made to do.

I am grateful for my grandmother, Avril Brown, who is now home with the Lord. She always believed in me and encouraged me to do what God created me to do.

PREFACE

This book is designed to be read over a period of weeks, perhaps even months, no need to rush through it. There are times I will ask you to set the book aside and evaluate some areas of your life, for this reason I suggest you have a journaling pad and pen on hand. Throughout this manuscript, I have chosen to use the Hebrew transliteration of the name of our Heavenly Father, YHWH, translated as Yahweh (normally translated in English as Jehovah or "the Lord"). I have also included the Hebrew name for Jesus our Messiah, Yahshua.

*Sing to God, sing praises to His name; extol Him who rides on the clouds, By His name **YAH**, and rejoice before Him. - Psalm 68:4*

*Behold, God is my salvation, I will trust and not be afraid; 'For **YAH**, the LORD, is my strength and song; He also has become my salvation.'"- Isaiah 12:2*

*Trust in the LORD forever, for in **YAH**, the LORD, is everlasting strength. - Isaiah 26:4*

*I said, "I shall not see **YAH**, The LORD in the land of the living; I shall observe man no more among the inhabitants of the world.- Isaiah 38:11*

TABLE OF CONTENTS

INTRODUCTION		7
CHAPTER 1	What type of soil are you?	11
CHAPTER 2	A Cry of Repentance	17
CHAPTER 3	A Call to Forgiveness	22
CHAPTER 4	What Kind of Fruit Are We Developing?	28
CHAPTER 5	Developing: Love	36
CHAPTER 6	Developing: Joy	54
CHAPTER 7	Developing: Peace	74
CHAPTER 8	Developing: Patience/Longsuffering	93
CHAPTER 9	Developing: Kindness	112
CHAPTER 10	Developing: Goodness	121
CHAPTER 11	Developing: Faithfulness/Faith	139
CHAPTER 12	Developing: Gentleness/Meekness	169
CHAPTER 13	Developing: Self-Control	181
CHAPTER 14	Developing: Righteousness	193
CHAPTER 15	Developing: Justice	218
CHAPTER 16	Developing: Mercy	227
CHAPTER 17	CONCLUSION	236

INTRODUCTION

Feb. 17, 2008 at 9:40AM (A page from my journal.)

"It has been 5 months, now, since I have moved to Miami Florida, a few miles south of where I grew up. I was so excited to find a Naseberry Tree, along with many other tropical fruit trees, in our back yard. But this one was particularly special to me; it was a fruit from my country, my homeland, Jamaica. Oh the sweet smell of ripening fruits in the country, there is none other like it. The aroma is so sweet, the scents awake you in the early morning, as they relax and motivate you to enjoy another day of life. Oh, the life giving gift of a succulent fruit. King Solomon describes it so well in the following passages of scripture.

Song of Solomon 2:13 *-The fig tree puts forth her green figs, and the vines with the tender grapes give a good smell. Rise up, my love, my fair one, and come away!*

Song of Solomon 4:16 *- Awake, O north wind; and come, O south! Blow upon my garden, that its spices may flow out. Let my beloved come to his garden and eat its pleasant fruits.*

The aromas are as a love song from our Lord, wooing us to come nearer, closer, to have an encounter with our Maker, the One who created our souls.

Upon arriving at our new home, there were so few fruits on the Naseberry tree, that I could count them on two hands. There was only one that was ripened, so my grandmother and I excitedly picked it and gave it away. I was so looking forward to my next fruit, oh how I longed to taste the sweet fruit of the Naseberry. Yet here I am five months later, and not even one is ripened on the tree. I didn't think I would be waiting this long. Over the last few months, more fruits have grown on the tree, but they manage to stay the same size, seemingly forever. I am so tempted to pick it early before the squirrels get to it, yet I must wait, because I will only find a bitter taste, that will stain my very sensitive tongue. **I can only imagine how God must feel with His children, waiting patiently for just one fruit to be produced in us, yet there are nine we should be developing."** *(End of journal entry)*

Throughout Scripture, there are references of God's people being likened to trees planted by water. Psalm 1:3 (KJV) declares, *"And he shall be like a tree planted by the rivers of water, that bringeth forth his fruit in his season; his leaf also shall not wither; and whatsoever he doeth shall prosper."* The Lord spoke through the Prophet Jeremiah in Jeremiah 17:8 (KJV), *"For he shall be as a tree planted by the waters, and that spreadeth out her roots by the river, and shall not see when heat cometh, but her leaf shall be green; and shall not be careful in the year of drought, neither shall cease from yielding fruit."*

We find reference to another type of tree planted by water, a heavenly tree that never dies and is always fruitful. In Ezekiel's vision recorded in Ezekiel 47:12, he was told, *"Along the bank of the river, on this side and that, will grow all kinds of trees used for food; their leaves will not wither, and their fruit will not fail. They will* **bear fruit every month***, because* **their water flows from the sanctuary***. Their fruit will be for food, and their leaves for medicine."* John records what the angel shows him in his visit to heaven, in Revelation 22:1-2 (KJV), *"And he shewed me a pure river of water of life, clear as crystal, proceeding out of the throne of God and of the Lamb. ² In the midst of the street of it, and on either side of the river, was there the* **tree of life, which bare twelve manner of fruits, and yielded her fruit every month***: and the leaves of the tree were for the healing of the nations."* What a breathtaking site this must be!

April 18, 2009 (A section from my journal)

"A mango was waiting for me under the tree today. For weeks I have been anxiously awaiting even one. All of them that have fallen from the wind were green, but not this one, it was waiting there just for me. I couldn't help but to think about spiritual fruit while enjoying it in the natural. Immediately, the trees in heaven spoken of in Revelation 22:1-2, came to my mind. As I ate my ripened mango I thought that this tree of life planted by the <u>river in heaven bears twelve fruit and we are to bear 9 according to Galatians 5:22 these fruit are as follows: LOVE, JOY, PEACE, LONGSUFFERING, GENTLENESS, GOODNESS, FAITH, MEEKNESS, TEMPERANCE.</u> I have to ask, are there twelve fruit we should be bearing? Are there three others we have overlooked all this time, or do we stop at nine?"

What do you think? Is it possible that we are to be a reflection of the Tree of Life in Heaven to a dying world? I say, "YES, WE ARE!" Notice that the leaves on the Tree of Life are for healing and the fruit are for eating. People should experience Christ's healing power through our lives and be able to eat of the Fruits of the Spirit in our lives daily. When they come in contact with us, they should be able to taste and see that the Lord is good (Psalm 34:8). No matter the seasons we go through in our lives, whether high or low, we have the ability to produce fruit in spite of our circumstances as Paul stated in 2 Timothy 4:2, "…Be ready in season and out of season…"

Along with the nine fruits of the Spirit we will focus on developing: Righteousness, Justice and Mercy.

Philippians 1:11(KJV) - "Being filled with the fruits of righteousness, which are by Jesus Christ, unto the glory and praise of God."

Isaiah 5:7 - "For the vineyard of the LORD of hosts is the house of Israel, and the men of Judah are His pleasant plant. He looked for justice, but behold, oppression; for righteousness, but behold, a cry for help."

James 3:17 - "But the wisdom that is from above is first pure, then peaceable, gentle, willing to yield, full of mercy and good fruits, without partiality and without hypocrisy."

Come with me on this *Journey Through the Heart of Christ,* as we partake of Yahweh's Word and allow Holy Spirit to produce the necessary Fruit in our lives.

CHAPTER ONE
What Type of Soil Are You?

Often times we don't consider how important soil is to our everyday lives. Quite frankly we would not be able to survive without it. We use it for a countless number of things, for example we cannot grow food or build without it. Did you know that it supplies most of the antibiotics used to fight diseases? Interestingly enough, Yahweh formed Adam from the soil. According to Genesis 2:7 (KJV), *"And the Lord God formed man of the dust of the ground, and breathed into his nostrils the breath of life; and man became a living soul."* In order to grow as healthy believers we must know the current condition of the soil of our souls. In Matthew 13:1-23, Yahshua shares a parable of a farmer who plants seeds in various types of soil.

On the same day Jesus went out of the house and sat by the sea. ² And great multitudes were gathered together to Him, so that He got into a boat and sat; and the whole multitude stood on the shore. ³ Then He spoke many things to them in parables, saying: "Behold, a sower went out to sow. ⁴ And as he sowed, some seed fell by the **wayside***; and the birds came and devoured them. ⁵ Some fell on* **stony places***, where they did not have much earth; and they immediately sprang up because they had no depth of earth. ⁶ But when the sun was up they were scorched, and because they had no root they withered away. ⁷ And some fell among* **thorns***, and the thorns sprang up and choked them. ⁸ But others fell on* **good ground and yielded a crop: some a hundredfold, some sixty, some thirty.** *⁹* **He who has ears to hear, let him hear!"** - Matthew 13:1-9

Each of us are represented by one of these types of soil; if we are anything less than the fertile soil that is described in verse 8, then we have some work to do and we must allow the Holy Spirit to assist us in this work.

As you read Matthew 13:18-23, consider your own life and examine your current situation.

"Therefore hear the parable of the sower: 19 When anyone hears the word of the kingdom, and does not understand it, then the wicked one comes and snatches away what was sown in his heart. This is he who received seed by the wayside. 20 But he who received the seed on stony places, this is he who hears the word and immediately receives it with joy; 21 yet he has no root in himself, but endures only for a while. For when tribulation or persecution arises because of the word, immediately he stumbles. 22 Now he who received seed among the thorns is he who hears the word, and the cares of this world and the deceitfulness of riches choke the word, and he becomes unfruitful. 23 But he who received seed on the good ground is he who hears the word and understands it, who indeed bears fruit and produces: some a hundredfold, some sixty, some thirty."

Which soil are you?

Are you a wayside, who doesn't understand what a relationship with Christ is about or why it's necessary?

Perhaps you identify with the stony places. You were excited when you first heard the Gospel of Christ, but your roots are not deep in Him, you think it's too hard to live by, believe and spread the Word of God.

Could your soil be full of thorns? You know Yahweh's word, but you have too many distractions, and they have become more important than living a life like Christ.

Are you producing fruit that portrays the goodness of Christ and help to expand Yahweh's Kingdom in the earth?

For most of my relationship with Yahshua, the soil of

my soul was the thorny ground. According to Christ, these thorns represent the worries of life and the deceitfulness of wealth. No fruit is produced. I must confess that although I have always wanted wealth, my thorns were mostly made up of worries and the desire for things other than Christ. In the Gospel of Mark, he records it this way, **"And the cares of this world, and the deceitfulness of riches, and the lusts of other things entering in, choke the word, and it becometh unfruitful."-Mark 4:19 (KJV).**

CHALLENGE: Let us not lie to ourselves or pretend any longer. It is imperative that we examine ourselves in the light of Yahweh's holiness.

As Christians, we each have some evidence of the fruit of the Spirit being developed in our lives. However, we must be careful. Although we may have baby fruit on the tree of our lives, our job is still not complete. Baby fruit that have not come to their full maturity, leave much to be desired on our taste buds. Unfortunately, we as a whole have left a bad taste in the mouths of each other and the world. We must recognize our sin, ask for forgiveness, repent, and GROW together on this journey.

To grow we must build on the proper foundation. In Luke 6:47-49, Yahshua shares, *"Whoever comes to Me, and hears My sayings and does them, I will show you whom he is like: ⁴⁸ He is like a man building a house, who dug deep and laid the foundation on the rock. And when the flood arose, the stream beat vehemently against that house, and could not shake it, for it was founded on the rock. ⁴⁹ But he who heard and did nothing is like a man who built a house on the earth without a foundation, against which the stream beat vehemently; and immediately it fell. And the ruin of that house was great."* In Proverbs 10:25, Solomon writes, *"When the whirlwind passes by, the wicked is no more, but the righteous has an everlasting foundation."*

So what is this deep and lasting foundation on Solid Rock? <u>It is obedience to the Word of God.</u> Paul in 1 Corinthians 3:11, clarifies that <u>the foundation is Yahshua the Christ</u>. Remember the seeds that fell on rocky soil did not last long, because their roots were not deep. We must deepen our roots in Christ by obeying His words.

1 Corinthians 3:8-15

Now he who plants and he who waters are one, and each one will receive his own reward according to his own labor. ⁹ For we are God's fellow workers; you are God's field, you are God's building. **¹⁰ According to the grace of God which was given to me, as a wise master builder I have laid the foundation, and another builds on it. But let each one take heed how he builds on it. ¹¹ For no other foundation can anyone lay than that which is laid, which is Jesus Christ.** *¹² Now if anyone builds on this foundation with gold, silver, precious stones, wood, hay, straw, ¹³ each one's work will become clear; for the Day will declare it, because it will be revealed by fire; and the fire will test each one's work, of what sort it is. ¹⁴ If anyone's work which he has built on it endures, he will receive a reward. ¹⁵ If anyone's work is burned, he will suffer loss; but he himself will be saved, yet so as through fire."*

Before we move forward, let's take this opportunity to rededicate our hearts and lives to Christ. Salvation occurs when we understand that sin separates us from Yahweh. To be reunited with Him we need a bridge, and this bridge is Yahshua the Christ. Our Heavenly Father sent His only son to live among us, so He could relate to us on a human level. He showed us that it is possible to live in a flesh body and be Holy before Yahweh and men. He came to teach us, heal us, and give us a second chance to have a relationship with our Creator. To do this Christ had to die, and when He was crucified He took on Himself my sins and yours, and through the shed blood of Yahshua, we have a way to have forgiveness of our sins. And through His resurrection we are raised from death to life and have a guaranteed eternity with Him. All you have to do is believe that Christ came for you because of Yahweh's overwhelming love for you, and whisper a prayer, saying,

Heavenly Father, I recognize that the soil of my soul is not right, I know that I have sinned against you, and I am asking for your forgiveness. Remove the stones and thorns from my heart. I believe that You sent Jesus to die for me. Please take away my sin, come into my heart and change me. I surrender to you Lord. Have your way in my life, allow me to fulfill the purpose for which I was created, and fill me with your Holy Spirit, in Yahshua's name, Amen.

If you prayed this prayer for the first time, Welcome to the Body of Christ!

If you are a Christian that has not had a right relationship with our Savior and you said this prayer to rededicate your life to Yahshua, Welcome Home!

The angels in heaven are rejoicing! *"Likewise, I say to you, there is joy in the presence of the angels of God over one sinner who repents."* (Luke 15:10)

As you read Isaiah 55:6-13, hear and receive the Lord as He is speaking to each of us.

<u>*Seek the* L<small>ORD</small> *while He may be found, call upon Him while He is near.*</u> *⁷ Let the wicked forsake his way, and the unrighteous man his thoughts; let him return to the* L<small>ORD</small>, *and He will have mercy on him; and to our God, for He will abundantly pardon. ⁸ "For My thoughts are not your thoughts, nor are your ways My ways," says*

the LORD. ⁹ "For as the heavens are higher than the earth, so are My ways higher than your ways, and My thoughts than your thoughts. ¹⁰ "For as the rain comes down, and the snow from heaven, and do not return there, but water the earth, and make it bring forth and bud, that it may give seed to the sower and bread to the eater, ¹¹ <u>So shall My word be that goes forth from My mouth; it shall not return to Me void, but it shall accomplish what I please, and it shall prosper in the thing for which I sent it.</u> ¹² "For you shall go out with joy, and be led out with peace; the mountains and the hills shall break forth into singing before you, and all the trees of the field shall clap their hands. ¹³ Instead of the thorn shall come up the cypress tree, And instead of the brier shall come up the myrtle tree; and it shall be to the LORD for a name, for an everlasting sign that shall not be cut off."

CHAPTER TWO
A Cry of Repentance
"Now, therefore," says the LORD, *"Turn to Me with all your heart, With fasting, with weeping, and with mourning."*
Joel 2:12

Matthew 4:17 records, *"From that time Jesus began to preach and to say, "Repent, for the kingdom of heaven is at hand."* Over the last few years I have developed a further understanding on repentance as it relates to the sorrow one should experience before the act of turning away from sin. Repentance happens before the turn; it is the driving force that propels the turn. James 4:8-10(KJV) describes it this way, *"Draw nigh to God, and he will draw nigh to you. Cleanse your hands, ye sinners; and purify your hearts, ye double minded. ⁹ **Be afflicted, and mourn, and weep: let your laughter be turned to mourning, and your joy to heaviness.** ¹⁰ Humble yourselves in the sight of the Lord, and he shall lift you up."*

Repentance is **an important key to developing the Fruit of the Spirit in our lives**. Without repentance we become spiritually dead and bear no good fruit on our trees. Paul writes in Acts 20:21, *"testifying to Jews, and also to Greeks, repentance toward God and faith toward our Lord Jesus Christ."* We must realize that **repentance is a privilege**. Acts 11:18 states, *"When they heard these things they became silent; and they glorified God, saying, "Then God has also granted to the Gentiles repentance to life."*

Throughout scripture we find examples of Yahweh's wrath directed to the unrepentant and His mercy towards those who repent. It is important that we do not become like those written about in scripture. No matter how much Yahweh tried to get their attention through judgment after judgment, they refused to repent. Jeremiah prays in Jeremiah 5:3(KJV), *"O* LORD, *are not thine eyes upon the truth? Thou hast stricken them, but* *they have not grieved; thou hast consumed them, but they have refused to receive correction: they have made their faces harder than a rock; they have **refused to return**.*" Unfortunately, for those who refuse to repent, they will face eternal consequences. Asaph writes in Psalm 50:16-22, *"But to the wicked God says: "What right have you to declare My statutes, or take My covenant in your mouth, 17 Seeing you hate instruction and cast My words behind you? 18 When you saw a thief, you consented with him, and have been a partaker with adulterers. 19 You give your mouth to evil, and your tongue frames deceit. 20 You sit and speak against your brother; you slander your own mother's son. 21 These things you have done, and I kept silent; you thought that I was altogether like you; but I will rebuke you, and set them in order before your eyes. 22 "Now consider this, you who forget God, lest I tear you in pieces, and there be none to deliver:"*

Those of us with repentant hearts experience God's mercy, as can be seen in the following passages:
Hosea 6:1 (KJV) - Come, and let us return unto the LORD: for he hath torn, and he will heal us; he hath smitten, and he will bind us up.
Luke 15:7 (KJV) - I say unto you, that likewise joy shall be in heaven over one sinner that repenteth, more than over ninety and nine just persons, which need no repentance.
2 Peter 3:9 (KJV) - The Lord is not slack concerning his promise, as some men count slackness; but is longsuffering to us-ward, not willing that any should perish, but that all should come to repentance.

The proof that we are genuinely remorseful for our sins results in a positive change in our lifestyle.
Ezekiel 14:6 (KJV) - Therefore say unto the house of Israel, Thus saith the Lord GOD; Repent, and turn yourselves from your idols; and turn away your faces from all your abominations.

Acts 26:20 (KJV) - But shewed first unto them of Damascus, and at Jerusalem, and throughout all the coasts of Judaea, and then to the Gentiles, that they should repent and turn to God, and do works meet for repentance.

In Chapter 1, we evaluated the soil of our lives which is the foundation of our faith in Yahshua our Messiah. We identified our weaknesses and surrendered ourselves completely to our Heavenly Father. At this time, I would like to lead us through repentance. Paul writes in Acts 17:30, *"Truly, these times of ignorance God overlooked, but now commands all men everywhere to repent,"* Yahweh instructs us in 2 Chronicles 7:14, *"if My people who are called by My name will humble themselves, and pray and seek My face, and turn from their wicked ways, then I will hear from heaven, and will forgive their sin and heal their land."* And the Apostle Peter is recorded in Acts 3:19, *"Repent therefore and be converted, that your sins may be blotted out, so that times of refreshing may come from the presence of the Lord,"*

When your child, parent, spouse, closest friend or trusted relative betrays, hurts, insults or abuses you in anyway, what type of pain do you feel? When your offender approaches you with a general, "I'm sorry." Does this suffice?

What if he/she approaches you with a visible and genuine sign of sorrow for causing suffering to you? For example, "I am so sorry that I allowed my hands that are here to protect you to hurt you." The heartfelt remorse is evident as your offender continues with tears, "The hurt that I caused you was selfish and inconsiderate of me, I will never cause you that pain again." Your offender's words and tone makes a difference as to how you respond.

As you pray a prayer of repentance, don't do it out of obligation or out of fear of negative consequences, do it from a position of deep love for God and the realization of the pain you've caused to Him and others.

Father God, I come to you through your precious son Yahshua. I am sorry that my disobedience, rebellion, idolatry, perversion, adultery (add whatever you need to...) has caused you great pain and that my sins have brought shame to your name. I am sorry for hurting You with my lifestyle. I cry out to you today, committing myself to change, to turn from my selfish, prideful ways. Please forgive me Father and help me not to desire to do things that are sinful in your sight and to take the way of escape that you make me for me when I am tempted by my own sinful desires. In Yahshua's name, Amen.

David models repentance for us in Psalm 51.

To the Chief Musician. A Psalm of David when Nathan the prophet went to him, after he had gone in to Bathsheba. *Have mercy upon me, O God, According to Your lovingkindness; According to the multitude of Your tender mercies, blot out my transgressions. 2 Wash me thoroughly from my iniquity, and cleanse me from my sin. 3 For I acknowledge my transgressions, and my sin is always before me. 4 Against You, You only, have I sinned, and done this evil in Your sight— that You may be found just when You speak, and blameless when You judge. 5 Behold, I was brought forth in iniquity, and in sin my mother conceived me. 6 Behold, You desire truth in the inward parts, and in the hidden part You will make me to know wisdom. 7 Purge me with hyssop, and I shall be clean; Wash me, and I shall be whiter than snow. 8 Make me hear joy and gladness, that the bones You have broken may rejoice. 9 Hide Your face from my sins, And blot out all my iniquities. 10 Create in me a clean heart, O God, and renew a steadfast spirit within me. 11 Do not cast me away from Your presence, and do not take Your*

Holy Spirit from me. ¹² *Restore to me the joy of Your salvation, and uphold me by Your generous Spirit.* ¹³ *Then I will teach transgressors Your ways, And sinners shall be converted to You.* ¹⁴ *Deliver me from the guilt of bloodshed, O God, the God of my salvation, And my tongue shall sing aloud of Your righteousness.* ¹⁵ *O Lord, open my lips, and my mouth shall show forth Your praise.* ¹⁶ *For You do not desire sacrifice, or else I would give it; You do not delight in burnt offering.* ¹⁷ *The sacrifices of God are a broken spirit, A broken and a contrite heart— These, O God, You will not despise.* ¹⁸ *Do good in Your good pleasure to Zion; Build the walls of Jerusalem.* ¹⁹ *Then You shall be pleased with the sacrifices of righteousness, With burnt offering and whole burnt offering; Then they shall offer bulls on Your altar.*

CHAPTER THREE
A Call to Forgiveness

The exercise of forgiveness is one of the most important facets of a believer's everyday life. We must partake in it every second of the day. Initially, it appears as one of the most difficult aspects of Christianity. There are times when our offenders don't seem worthy of our forgiveness. They seem like they could care less about whether we forgive them or not, so why should you or I waste the time, energy, and emotion going through the process of forgiving others.

The answer: We, ourselves, are in daily need of being forgiven.

Do you remember the adulterous woman the Pharisees wanted to stone in John 8? Jesus responded to them in verse 7 (KJV), *"...He that is without sin among you, let him first cast a stone at her."* He couldn't have said it better. Apostle Paul writes in Romans 3:23 (KJV), *"For all have sinned, and come short of the glory of God;"* God is rich in His mercy and love to forgive us of every one of our sins. We ask God and others for forgiveness when we are in error and God asks us to forgive others when they are in error against us.

To forgive or not to forgive, that is the question.

When Yahshua taught us how to pray in Matthew 6:12-15 (KJV), He says, *"and forgive us our debts, as we forgive our debtors. [13] And lead us not into temptation, but deliver us from evil: For thine is the kingdom, and the power, and the glory, forever. Amen. [14] For if ye forgive men their trespasses, your heavenly Father will also forgive you: [15] But if ye forgive not men their trespasses, neither will your Father forgive your trespasses."*

NOTE: We must first forgive to be forgiven.

GOD FORGIVES US AS WE FORGIVE OTHERS.
Mark 11:25 - "And whenever you stand praying, if you have anything against anyone, forgive him, that your Father in Heaven may also forgive you your trespasses."
Luke 6:37 (KJV) - Judge not, and ye shall not be judged: condemn not, and ye shall not be condemned: forgive, and ye shall be forgiven:
Colossians 3:13 (KJV) - Forbearing one another, and forgiving one another, if any man have a quarrel against any: even as Christ forgave you, so also do ye.

UNFORGIVENESS CREATES A PROBLEM FOR US, BECAUSE GOD WILL NOT FORGIVE US. When we choose not to forgive others we render the blood of Christ powerless thus denying our salvation. It was by the shedding of His blood that we have forgiveness of sins. When we choose not to forgive others we tie God's hands from forgiving us. God sent His only begotten son to be beaten, bruised, bloodied and murdered for us to receive forgiveness of our sins. Who are we that we would refuse that same grace to another?

I encourage you to read the entire story from Matthew 18, in verses 32-35 (KJV) Yahshua is ending a parable, *"Then his lord, after that he had called him, said unto him, O thou wicked servant, I forgave thee all that debt, because thou desiredst me:* 33 *Shouldest not thou also have had compassion on thy fellow servant, even as I had pity on thee?* 34 *And his lord was wroth, and delivered him to the tormentors, till he should pay all that was due unto him.* 35 *So likewise shall my heavenly Father do also unto you, if ye from your hearts forgive not everyone his brother their trespasses."*

There is a level of torment that we experience when we choose not to forgive others. And the truth is, we can never repay the debt we owe Christ for the cross, the empty tomb, and the home He is preparing for us in Heaven.

IT IS BECAUSE OF CHRIST'S BLOOD THAT WE RECEIVE FORGIVENESS.
Matthew 26:28 (KJV) - For this is my blood of the new testament, which is shed for many for the remission of sins.
Hebrews 9:22 (KJV) - And almost all things are by the law purged with blood; and without shedding of blood is no remission.

WE HAVE FORGIVENESS THROUGH JESUS CHRIST.
Acts 10:43 (KJV) - To him give all the prophets witness, that through his name whosoever believeth in him shall receive remission of sins.
Luke 23:34 (KJV) - Then said Jesus, Father, forgive them; for they know not what they do. And they parted his raiment, and cast lots.
1 John 1:9 (KJV) - If we confess our sins, he is faithful and just to forgive us our sins, and to cleanse us from all unrighteousness.

Please understand, that forgiveness is not saying that the wrong done to us is ok and that people have permission to do it again. Instead, forgiveness says your offender's penalty is pardoned; his/her debt is paid through Christ. It is choosing not to hold your offender hostage to your pain but releasing God's justice and mercy over him/her. **It does not mean trust has returned; trust must be earned.** Does this mean, you drop legal charges against your child's murderer, your rapist, or an individual who ravaged your home and stole from you? No, it absolutely does not, but there are two attitudes we can take when we seek Yahweh's justice through the earthly legal system.

Attitude One: About our offender, we say and we pray, "I hope you suffer as I did, I hope you die a slow and painful death, I hope you get every evil thing you deserve and on top of all of that I hope you rot in Hell!"

Attitude Two: "I am angry and deeply wounded at what you've done to my family and me, but I pray that you accept Yahshua as your Lord and Savior, as you serve the time you earned for your crime. I pray you experience God's love, grace, mercy and forgiveness. I choose to forgive you, I release you into Yahweh's hands!"

We allow God to bring healing to the broken areas of our life when we forgive our offenders.

The Apostle Paul writes in Romans 5:15, *"But the free gift is not like the offense. For if by the one man's offense many died, much more the grace of God and the gift by the grace of the one Man, Jesus Christ, abounded to many."*

Forgiveness is a gift that God gives to us that we are to pass along to others. It is the gift that keeps on giving.

FORGIVENESS SHOULD FLOW FREELY FROM US TO OTHERS.
Luke 17:4 - And if he sins against you seven times in a day, and seven times in a day returns to you, saying, 'I repent,' you shall forgive him."
Ephesians 4:32 - And be kind to one another, tenderhearted, forgiving one another, even as God in Christ forgave you.
2 Corinthians 2:7 - so that, on the contrary, you ought rather to forgive and comfort him, lest perhaps such a one be swallowed up with too much sorrow.

Do you remember the story of Joseph? His older brothers plotted to kill him because of their jealousy and hatred, but decided to sell him into slavery, instead. Their father, Jacob, mourned the loss of Joseph, believing the lies of his sons, who told him their brother was killed by an animal. Pay attention to the moment of forgiveness recorded in Genesis 50:14-21.

*"And after he had buried his father, Joseph returned to Egypt, he and his brothers and all who went up with him to bury his father.¹⁵ When Joseph's brothers saw that their father was dead, they said, "Perhaps Joseph will hate us, and may actually repay us for all the evil which we did to him." ¹⁶ So they sent messengers to Joseph, saying, "Before your father died he commanded, saying, ¹⁷ 'Thus you shall say to Joseph: "I beg you, please forgive the trespass of your brothers and their sin; for they did evil to you."' Now, please, forgive the trespass of the servants of the God of your father." **And Joseph wept when they spoke to him.** ¹⁸ Then his brothers also went and fell down before his face, and they said, "Behold, we are your servants." ¹⁹ **Joseph said to them, "Do not be afraid, for am I in the place of God? ²⁰ But as for you, you meant evil against me; but God meant it for good, in order to bring it about as it is this day, to save many people alive.²¹ Now therefore, do not be afraid; I will provide for you and your little ones." And he comforted them and spoke kindly to them."***

Forgiveness is POWERFUL! Psalm 130:4 says, *"But there is forgiveness with You, that You may be feared."* There is a Holy Reverence that arises in us, when we realize how horrible our sin is and how without Yahweh's mercy and grace we would be eternally hopeless.

Through our discussions on the necessity of salvation and repentance we have been tilling the soil of our lives. <u>Forgiveness is the next step in the process.</u>

It's time to make a list of those you know you have not forgiven. Those who may be on this list are: **God** (sometimes we blame Him for things) **others** (parents, siblings, spouse, friends, etc., whether living or deceased) and **ourselves**. How can we forgive others when we can't forgive ourselves of shameful things we have done, said and thought? Speak to God about each person on the list, even if it's you or Him. Be transparent with Him about the difficulty of setting this person or yourself free. Today is the day that you forgive and become free.

FORGIVENESS=FREEDOM.

Physical, emotional and mental healing come when we are forgiven and when we forgive. In David's song of Praise to our Heavenly Father, he sings in Psalm 103:2-3, *"Bless the L*ORD*, O my soul, and forget not all His benefits: ³ Who **forgives all your iniquities, Who heals all your diseases**,"* In 2 Chronicles 7:14 we are instructed, *" if My people who are called by My name will **humble themselves**, and **pray and seek My face**, and **turn from their wicked ways**, then **I will hear from heaven**, and will **forgive their sin and heal their land**."*

Let's say this prayer together,

Heavenly Father, I come to you recognizing that without your forgiveness I am lost and broken. I choose to forgive _____. I repent for holding onto unforgiveness and ask for Your forgiveness. Please heal every soul (mental and emotional) wound, physical wound, and spiritual wound that my offender(s) has caused me. I receive Your forgiveness and Your healing. I renounce all anger, bitterness, hatred, unforgiveness and resentment and invite you to replace these emotions with YOUR LOVE, in Yahshua's name I pray. Amen.

Blessed is he whose transgression is forgiven, whose sin is covered. - Psalm 32:1(KJV)

CHAPTER FOUR
What Kind of Fruit Are We Developing?
Examine Yourself.

How often do you take the time to evaluate yourself as a Believer and Follower of Yahshua the Christ? In 2 Corinthians 13:5, Apostle Paul writes, *"Examine yourselves as to whether you are in the faith. Test yourselves. Do you not know yourselves, that Jesus Christ is in you?—unless indeed you are disqualified."* He encourages us in 1 Corinthians 11:27-30 to examine ourselves before partaking of communion. He says if we take it unworthily we are guilty of sinning against the body and blood of Christ, which results in drinking God's judgment upon ourselves. He goes on to explain that this is the reason why many had become weak and sick and some had died. In vs. 31 (KJV) Paul continues, *"For if we would judge ourselves, we should not be judged."*

It is necessary that we pay attention to the types of fruit we are bearing in our lives. It is never enough for us to say that our inappropriate actions or words in public or in private are excusable because we didn't really mean to do or say something. These occurrences allow us to evaluate the type of fruit we are bearing. Everything that comes out of our mouth is flowing out of our hearts. We must take personal responsibility for our shortcomings and allow them to challenge us to do better. Yahshua says in Luke 6:43-45, *"For a good tree does not bear bad fruit, nor does a bad tree bear good fruit. 44 For every tree is known by its own fruit. For men do not gather figs from thorns, nor do they gather grapes from a bramble bush. 45 A good man out of the good treasure of his heart brings forth good; and an evil man out of the evil treasure of his heart brings forth evil.* **For out of the abundance of the heart his mouth speaks***."*

Our character is defined by the fruit we bear and the

fruit we bear are identified by what comes out of our souls. Whatever is in our heart is evident in our actions and our speech. In Matthew 7:15-20, Christ shares, *"Beware of false prophets, who come to you in sheep's clothing, but inwardly they are ravenous wolves. 16 You will know them by their fruits. Do men gather grapes from thornbushes or figs from thistles? 17 Even so, every good tree bears good fruit, but a bad tree bears bad fruit. 18 A good tree cannot bear bad fruit, nor can a bad tree bear good fruit.* **19 Every tree that does not bear good fruit is cut down and thrown into the fire 20 Therefore by their fruits you will know them.*"*

God describes any tree that does not produce good fruit as being chopped down and thrown into fire. **Our Heavenly Father takes fruit bearing seriously; therefore we need to take it just as seriously.**

Let's take a look at the difference between the fruit of our sinful nature and the fruit of the Spirit.

Paul writes in Galatians 5:16-26, *"**I say then: <u>Walk in the Spirit, and you shall not fulfill the lust of the flesh</u>**. 17 For the flesh lusts against the Spirit, and the Spirit against the flesh; and these are contrary to one another, so that you do not do the things that you wish. 18 But if you are led by the Spirit, you are not under the law. 9 Now the works of the flesh are evident, which are: adultery, fornication, uncleanness, lewdness, 20idolatry, sorcery, hatred, contentions, jealousies, outbursts of wrath, selfish ambitions, dissensions, heresies, 21 envy, murders, drunkenness, revelries, and the like; of which I tell you beforehand, just as I also told you in time past, that those who practice such things will not inherit the kingdom of God. 22 **But the fruit of the Spirit is love, joy, peace, longsuffering, kindness, goodness, faithfulness, 23 gentleness, self-control.** Against such there is no law. 24 And those who are Christ's have crucified the flesh with its* *passions and desires.* ²⁵ *If we live in the Spirit, let us also walk in the Spirit.* ²⁶ *Let us not become conceited, provoking one another, envying one another.*

FRUIT OF THE SINFUL NATURE	FRUIT OF THE SPIRIT
Adultery	Love
Fornication	Joy
Uncleanness	Peace
Lewdness	Longsuffering/Patience
Idolatry	Kindness
Sorcery	Goodness
Hatred	Faithfulness
Contentions	Gentleness/Meekness
Jealousies	Self-Control
Outbursts of Wrath	
Selfish Ambitions	
Dissensions	
Heresies	
Envy	
Murders	
Drunkenness	
Revelries	

Examine yourself, which of the above fruit have you bourn lately?

THERE IS A COST FOR NOT BEARING THE FRUIT OF THE SPIRIT

Luke 13:6-9 records, "He also spoke this parable: "A certain man had a fig tree planted in his vineyard, and he came seeking fruit on it and found none. ⁷ Then he said to the keeper of his vineyard, 'Look, for **three years** I have come **seeking fruit** on this fig tree and **find none. Cut it down**; why does it use up the ground?' ⁸ But he answered and said to him, 'Sir, let it alone this year also, until **I dig around it and fertilize it.** ⁹ **And if it bears fruit, well. But if not, after that you can cut it down.**"

The planter is Father God, the gardener is Yahshua and we are the fig tree in this parable. Yahshua intercedes for us, willing to gently dig around the soil of our soul. He provided the fertilizer, LOVE, by His Broken Body and Shed Blood. What will the Father say about you? Will you bear figs, by the time you take your final breath? Or will you be the tree that is cut down, because you had just taken up space in the Kingdom of God, producing nothing good for others to taste and see that the Lord is good?

In Mark 11:13-14, Yahshua approaches a tree, *"And seeing from afar a fig tree having leaves, He went to see if perhaps He would find something on it. When He came to it, He found nothing but leaves, for it was not the season for figs. ¹⁴ In response Jesus said to it, "Let no one eat fruit from you ever again." And His disciples heard it."*

I read this scripture over and over again and couldn't understand, I said, "Lord, why did you curse the fig tree, when it was not its season to bear fruit?" The first thought that came to me was that when a fig tree is in full leaf it's a sign that there is fruit on the tree. Yahshua saw this, was hungry and expected to eat. This tree had the appearance of having fruit but it had none. It had a form of godliness but denying its power (2 Timothy 3:5). Let's examine ourselves some more, do you and I have the appearance of bearing fruit? We say all of the right things to others, we don't forsake fellowshipping with the saints, we pray daily, and on the outside we look clean but on the inside we are filthy. We walk around wearing masks, and may fool the people of God, but the world and Yahweh see right through us. Christ spoke to the Pharisees in Matthew 23:25-26, and it still applies to us, *"Woe to you, scribes and Pharisees, hypocrites! For you cleanse the outside of the cup and dish, but inside they are full of extortion and self-*

indulgence. ²⁶ Blind Pharisee, first cleanse the inside of the cup and dish, that the outside of them may be clean also." One of the many beautiful things about having the Holy Spirit is that as we study the Word of God and allow Him to cleanse us, we begin to change.

The second thought that came to me about this fig tree, was 2 Timothy 4:1-2 (KJV), *"I charge thee therefore before God, and the Lord Jesus Christ, who shall judge the quick and the dead at his appearing and his kingdom; ²Preach the word;* **be instant in season, out of season***; reprove, rebuke, exhort with all long suffering and doctrine."* As followers of Christ we need to be ready in season and out of season. Remember our goal is to be a reflection of the trees of life in heaven which bear a fresh crop of fruit each month.

"In the middle of its street, and on either side of the river, was the tree of life, which bore twelve fruits, each tree yielding its fruit every month. The leaves of the tree were for the healing of the nations." Revelation 22:2

Many unbelievers and believers in Christ, believe they will go to Heaven because they are good people; they do nice things for people, animals and the environment. But let me be very clear, outside of Christ, no one is good! **According to John 16:9 the world's sin is unbelief in Jesus.** The fruit that are produced in us are Spiritual and they will never die, they cannot be bought or sold for a price. They are developed only in the Presence of God, in the fertile soil of our lives, bearing a harvest from the seed, who is Christ, the WORD OF GOD.

PRODUCE GOOD FRUIT
For those who bear good fruit, Psalm 92:12-15 states, *"The righteous shall flourish like a palm tree, he shall grow like a cedar in Lebanon. ¹³ Those who are planted in the house of the L*ORD *shall flourish in the courts of our*

God. ¹⁴ They shall still bear fruit in old age; they shall be fresh and flourishing, ¹⁵ to declare that the L̲ord *is upright; He is my rock, and there is no unrighteousness in Him."*

Bearing good fruit has many benefits, for we as children of God and for those around us. To produce the fruit of the Spirit in our lives we must pay attention to what we are planting and allowing to be planted in the soil of our souls. Paul writes in Galatians 6:7-10, *"Do not be deceived, God is not mocked;* **for whatever a man sows, that he will also reap**. ⁸ <u>For he who sows to his flesh will of the flesh reap corruption, but he who sows to the Spirit will of the Spirit reap everlasting life.</u> ⁹ *And let us not grow weary while doing good, for in due season we shall reap if we do not lose heart. ¹⁰ Therefore, as we have opportunity, let us do good to all, especially to those who are of the household of faith."*

What type of harvest do you prefer, one of death and decay or one of blessing and everlasting life from the Spirit? Will you live to only satisfy your sinful nature or will you live to please God? It is a choice made moment by moment; the positive or negative choices made become seeds planted and these seeds will bear a harvest. It is only the development of the attributes of the Fruit of the Spirit that will cause us to develop character that is like Christ, outside of Him we are nothing, only dried up branches. As Believers we must check ourselves daily and observe if the bad fruit in Galatians 5:19-21 are the abundant fruit in our lives. If so, then WOE UNTO US, less we consider ourselves in Christ, only to find that we never knew Him and He doesn't know us. In Matthew 7:21-23 Jesus warns, *"Not everyone who says to Me, 'Lord, Lord,' shall enter the kingdom of heaven, but he who does the will of My Father in heaven. ²² Many will say to Me in that day, 'Lord, Lord, have we not prophesied in Your name, cast out demons in Your name, and done many wonders in Your name?'*

²³ And then I will declare to them, 'I never knew you; depart from Me, you who practice lawlessness!'"

I challenge each of us to examine ourselves **DAILY** against the Word of God. We must not compare ourselves to another individual in order to gage how righteous or unrighteous we are. We must only compare ourselves to our Holy God who commands us to be Holy because He is Holy (Leviticus 11:44-45, 1 Peter 1:16). This self-examination will produce desperation in us for Yahweh to cleanse us through His Word and produce in us fruit that are appealing to Him and those around us. As we stay joined to Yahshua, allowing His words to remain in us, we will produce fruit that will last!

John 15:1-17
*"I am the true vine, and My Father is the vinedresser. ² Every branch in Me that does not bear fruit He takes away; and every branch that bears fruit **He prunes**, that it may **bear more fruit**. ³ You are already clean because of the word which I have spoken to you. ⁴ Abide in Me, and I in you. As the **branch cannot bear fruit of itself, unless it abides in the vine, neither can you, unless you abide in Me.** ⁵ "I am the vine, you are the branches. He who abides in Me, and I in him, bears much fruit; for without Me you can do nothing.** ⁶ If anyone does not abide in Me, he is cast out as a branch and is withered; and they gather them and throw them into the fire, and they are burned. ⁷ If you abide in Me, and My words abide in you, you will ask what you desire, and it shall be done for you. ⁸ **By this My Father is glorified, that you bear much fruit; so you will be My disciples.** ⁹ "As the Father loved Me, I also have loved you; abide in My love. ¹⁰ If you keep My commandments, you will abide in My love, just as I have kept My Father's commandments and abide in His love. ¹¹ "These things I have spoken to you, that My joy may remain in you, and that your joy may be full. ¹² This is My commandment, that you love one another as I have*

loved you. ¹³ Greater love has no one than this, than to lay down one's life for his friends. ¹⁴ You are My friends if you do whatever I command you. ¹⁵ No longer do I call you servants, for a servant does not know what his master is doing; but I have called you friends, for all things that I heard from My Father I have made known to you. ¹⁶ **You did not choose Me, but I chose you and appointed you that you should go and bear fruit, and that your fruit should remain, that whatever you ask the Father in My name He may give you.** ¹⁷ These things I command you, that you love one another.

CHAPTER FIVE
Developing: Love
But above all these things put on love, which is the bond of perfection. Colossians 3:14

In writing this book, I had a clear picture in my heart that each spiritual fruit was to connect with a specific fruit in the natural. I only sought out fruits that grow on trees, and what better fruit to represent love than the Pomegranate. In Exodus 28, Yahweh included it in the design instruction to Moses of the priestly garments. Because of the hundreds of juicy red seeds, called arils, during the annual celebration of Rosh Hashanah, the Jewish New Year, a sweet pomegranate is eaten, to represent one's desire to fulfill all of Yahweh's 613 commandments found in the Torah (the first five chapters of the Old Testament). The Apostle Paul teaches us in Romans 13:8-10 to, **"Owe no one anything except to love one another, for <u>he who loves another has fulfilled the law</u>**. ⁹ *For the commandments, "You shall not commit adultery," "You shall not murder," "You shall not steal," "You shall not bear false witness", "You shall not covet," and if there is any other commandment, are all summed up in this saying, namely,* **"You shall love your neighbor as**

yourself." ¹⁰ *Love does no harm to a neighbor; therefore <u>love is the fulfillment of the law</u>."*

King Solomon describes love in *Song of Solomon 8:7, "Many waters cannot quench love, nor can the floods drown it. If a man would give for love all the wealth of his house, it would be utterly despised."*

While the word love stirs sweet passionate thoughts in many, it rouses very bitter undesirable memories in others. How can sweet love leave a bitter taste in anyone's mouth? This answer is realized as you converse with a person who has been abused, abandoned, cheated on, lied to or betrayed by someone who claimed to love him/her. Those with unhealed wounds from "love" use phrases like, "love is for fools", "love is blind", "love stinks" and "love hurts". The majority of humans, including Yahshua our Messiah, have had a negative experience at the hand of someone who confessed their love for us.

The truth is, GOD is LOVE and outside of Yahweh there is no true love. We may think that we know love, show love, and are in love, but unless we know God, show God and are in God, we have never truly loved. 1 John 4:7-8, 15-16 implores, *"Beloved, let us love one another, for love is of God; and everyone who loves is born of God and knows God. ⁸ He who does not love does not know God, for **God is love**. ¹⁵ Whoever confesses that Jesus is the Son of God, God abides in him, and he in God. ¹⁶ And we have known and believed the love that God has for us. <u>God is love, and he who abides in love abides in God, and God in him.</u>*

Our goal in this chapter is to allow Holy Spirit to produce and mature the fruit of LOVE in our lives so as not to leave a bitter taste in the mouths of our family, friends, co-workers, and enemies. Our love for others is evidence that Christ lives in us. Galatians 5:6 explains

that when our faith is placed in Christ, it is important that that **faith is expressed in love**. Yahweh explains what love is through Paul in 1 Corinthians 13:4-7,
LOVE...
Suffers Long
Is Kind
Does Not Envy
Does Not Parade Itself (Boastful)
Is Not Puffed Up (Proud)
Does Not Behave Rudely
Does Not Seek Its Own
Is Not Provoked
Thinks No Evil
Does Not Rejoice in Iniquity
Rejoices in Truth
Bears All Things
Believes All Things
Hopes All Things
Endures All Things

When cultivating a garden at home, your productivity and crop quality is based on the health of your soil. The soil must be fertilized. Our SOUL is the SOIL, the WORD of Yahweh is the SEED and LOVE is the FERTILIZER (Luke 13:8) needed for all other fruits to grow. **EVERY FRUIT OF THE SPIRIT IS DEVELOPED IN LOVE.** For the Word to be fruitful and multiply, it must be planted in healthy ground. That good ground represents those whose *understanding of the WORD causes them to apply it in their lives* (Matthews 13:23). We must ask our Heavenly Father, to root and ground us in His love, so we will be filled with His fullness, through our faith in Yahshua as in Ephesians 3:17-19, *"that Christ may dwell in your hearts through faith;* **that you, being rooted and grounded in love**, [18] *may be able to comprehend with all the saints what is the width and length and depth and height—* [19] *to know the love of Christ which passes knowledge; that you may be filled with all the fullness of God."*

By experiencing Yahweh's great love for us, we are able to model His love to others. Everything our Heavenly Father does is an example of how we should live. Remember, everything Yahshua heard Father say, that's what He would say (John 12:49), and everything He saw Father do, that's what He did (John 5:19). Yahshua's love for us is unfailing. He shows us His love through the cross, the grave, our hope of eternal life by His resurrection and the gift of Precious Holy Spirit. John 13:1(KJV) tells us, *"Now before the Feast of the Passover, when Jesus knew that his hour was come that he should depart out of this world unto the Father, having loved his own which were in the world, **he loved them unto the end**."* Romans 5:5 declares, *"Now hope does not disappoint, because **the love of God has been poured out in our hearts by the Holy Spirit who was given to us**."* 1 John 4:13 convinces us, *"By this we know that we abide in Him, and He in us, because **He has given us of His Spirit**."* Jude 1:20-21 teaches, *"20 But you, beloved, building yourselves up on your most holy faith, praying in the Holy Spirit, 21 **keep yourselves in the love of God**, looking for the mercy of our Lord Jesus Christ unto eternal life."*

When we live in Christ and Him in us, there is no need to fear. Fear does not exist in the atmosphere of Yahweh's love.

On October 24, 2013, I had one of the most incredible dreams. *In this dream, I was speaking on the phone with my husband, Jacob, discussing a variety of doctrines that different denominations in Christianity have not come to agreement on. Suddenly, as I peered through a window, I saw Yahshua as a bright light in the form of a man, coming in the clouds. The sky was a magnificent crystal blue and I began to say to Jacob, "He's here!" "He's here!" As Christ came nearer, I dropped my phone, stared into His eyes and said, "It's you, it's really you". I specifically remember that everything I was worrying about such as my children and ministry, all disappeared from my mind. I forgot everything and everyone, I was lost in His Love. I experienced a love that was the warmth of liquid gold flowing in the innermost part of my soul. There were no fears or feelings of insecurity. As I said, "You're going to take me aren't you?" I felt my spirit separate from my earthly body and went up with Him as in a blink of an eye.*

Later in the book I will share with you the rest of my encounter with Yahshua, as of now, it is important to understand that there was no fear. I was not afraid of what I would be leaving behind, neither was I afraid of where I was going. I knew that everything coming from Him was only good. This experience took away my fear of dying. Fear hinders us from living an enjoyable life in Christ and stops us from stepping out in faith, when He speaks to us. The Apostle Paul tells young Timothy in 2 Timothy 1:7 (KJV), *"For God hath not given us the spirit of fear; but of power, and **of love**, and of a sound mind."* Our inheritance is not fear, but POWER, not fear, but LOVE, not fear but our SANITY! 1 John 4:17-19 says, *"Love has been perfected among us in this: that we may* **have boldness in the day of judgment***; because as He is, so are we in this world.* [18] **There is no fear in love; but perfect love casts out fear, because fear involves torment***. But he who fears has not been made perfect in love.* [19] *We love Him because He first loved us."* Let's ask our Heavenly Father to make us perfect in His love as evidenced with living a life free from fear.

LOVE IS SACRIFICIAL.
<u>**Yahweh sacrificed His only begotten son for us, therefore love may at times require us to sacrifice for others.**</u>
John 3:16 (KJV) - For God so loved the world, that he gave his only begotten Son, that whosoever believeth in him should not perish, but have everlasting life.

Romans 5:8 - But God demonstrates His own love toward us, in that while we were still sinners, Christ died for us.

Ephesians 5:2 - And walk in love, as Christ also has loved us and given Himself for us, an offering and a sacrifice to God for a sweet-smelling aroma.

1 John 4:9-10 - In this the love of God was manifested toward us, that God has sent His only begotten Son into the world, that we might live through Him. ¹⁰ In this is love, not that we loved God, but that He loved us and sent His Son to be the propitiation for our sins.

LOVE TEACHES AND CORRECTS.
Yahweh teaches and corrects us, therefore our love for others should edify lives and bring correction when there is error.
Often times, out of fear of offending others, we do not bring correction when we see them going down a path that will lead to spiritual death. We live in a society and culture that gives us permission to give into every fleshly craving with no regard for Yahweh's boundaries that He has set for our lives. The reality is, if I genuinely love you, I am compelled to share God's truth with you in love, not in condemnation.

John 5:20 - For the Father loves the Son, and shows Him all things that He Himself does; and He will show Him greater works than these, that you may marvel.

Hebrews 12:6 - For whom the LORD loves He chastens, and scourges every son whom He receives."

Revelation 3:19 (KJV) - As many as I love, I rebuke and chasten: be zealous therefore, and repent.

LOVE IS UNCONDITIONAL.
Yahweh allows nothing to separate us from His love, our love for others should be unconditional.
Romans 8:35-39 (KJV) - Who shall separate us from the love of Christ? Shall tribulation, or distress, or persecution, or famine, or nakedness, or peril, or sword? ³⁶ As it is written, for thy sake we are killed all

the day long; we are accounted as sheep for the slaughter. ³⁷ Nay, in all these things we are more than conquerors through him that loved us. ³⁸ For I am persuaded, that **neither death, nor life, nor angels, nor principalities, nor powers, nor things present, nor things to come,** ³⁹ **nor height, nor depth, nor any other creature, shall be able to separate us from the love of God, which is in Christ Jesus our Lord**.

Now that we have a deeper understanding of Yahweh's Love for Us, let's take a look at some practical examples in scripture which teach us how to put love in action.

<u>STEP ONE</u> - LOVE THE LORD

"And you shall love the L<small>ORD</small> *your God with all your heart, with <u>all your soul, with all your mind, and with all your strength</u>.' This is the first commandment.* ³¹ *And the second, like it, is this: 'You shall love your neighbor as yourself.' There is no other commandment greater than these."*- Mark 12:30-31

Obedience Proves Our Love
Goose bumps, happy feelings, tears, etc. is not proof of our love for Yahweh, it is **doing what He says, it is obedience**. John 15:9-10, 16-17 (KJV) Yahshua says, "*As the Father hath loved me, so have I loved you: continue ye in my love. If ye **keep my commandments**, ye shall abide in my love; even as I have kept my Father's commandments, and abide in his love. ...*¹⁶ *Ye have not chosen me, but I have chosen you, and ordained you, that **ye should go and bring forth fruit, and that your fruit should remain**: that whatsoever ye shall ask of the Father in my name, he may give it you.* ¹⁷ *These things **I command you, that ye love one another**.*"

During the times that we desire to do things our way instead of His way, LOVE will compel us to obey.

1 Samuel 15:22 - So Samuel said: "Has the LORD as great delight in burnt offerings and sacrifices, as in obeying the voice of the LORD? Behold, to obey is better than sacrifice, and to heed than the fat of rams.
John 14:15 (KJV) - If ye love me, keep my commandments.
John 14:21 (KJV) - He that hath my commandments, and keepeth them, he it is that loveth me: and he that loveth me shall be loved of my Father, and I will love him, and will manifest myself to him.
John 14:23-24 (KJV) - Jesus answered and said unto him, if a man love me, he will keep my words: and my Father will love him, and we will come unto him, and make our abode with him. 24 He that loveth me not keepeth not my sayings: and the word which ye hear is not mine, but the Father's which sent me.
John 14:31 (KJV) - But that the world may know that I love the Father; and as the Father gave me commandment, even so I do. Arise, let us go hence.
1 John 2:5 (KJV) - But whoso keepeth his word, in him verily is the love of God perfected: hereby know we that we are in him.
1 John 3:20-24 (KJV) - For if our heart condemn us, God is greater than our heart, and knoweth all things. 21 Beloved, if our heart condemn us not, then have we confidence toward God. 22 And whatsoever we ask, we receive of him, because we keep his commandments, and do those things that are pleasing in his sight. 23 And this is his commandment, that we should believe on the name of his Son Jesus Christ, and love one another, as he gave us commandment. 24 And he that keepeth his commandments dwelleth in him, and he in him. And hereby we know that he abideth in us, by the Spirit which he hath given us.
2 John 1:5-6 - And now I plead with you, lady, not as though I wrote a new commandment to you, but that which we have had from the beginning: that we love one another. 6 This is love, that we walk according to His

commandments. This is the commandment, that as you have heard from the beginning, you should walk in it.

As we choose to love daily; it will grow from an action of obedience into an action of compassion. Paul teaches that love comes from a <u>pure heart</u>, a <u>good conscience</u> and <u>sincere faith</u> (1 Timothy 1:5).

<u>STEP TWO</u> - LOVE YOUR NEIGHBORS AS YOURSELF

*Jesus said to him, "'You shall love the L*ORD *your God with all your heart, with all your soul, and with all your mind.' This is the first and great commandment. And the second is like it: 'You shall love your neighbor as yourself.' On these two commandments hang all the Law and the Prophets." (Matthew 22:37-40)*

Let's take one minute and meditate on this truth. Loving your neighbor as yourself is **equally important** to loving Yahweh with all of your heart, soul, mind and strength.

DO YOU LOVE YOURSELF?
This is a hard question for so many to answer. It is not possible to genuinely love yourself until you love Yahweh. In our relationship with Him, we come to know who we are and why we were created. We see His reflection when we look in a mirror and the beauty of how He crafted every part of us.

An instinctual aspect of loving ourselves, is to make sure our basic needs are met. When we are hungry we eat, thirsty we drink, and we make sure we are clothed and have shelter. Therefore, we should be concerned about providing for the needs of others in an equal manner as we are about providing for ourselves and our families. Yahshua simplifies it for us in Matthew 7:12, *"Therefore, whatever you want men to do to you, do also* to them, for this is the Law and the Prophets." We must always treat others with the same level of respect, kindness, and empathy we hope to be given. Think of your last stormy day... would a warm smile, an encouraging call, a prayer, a hug, a meal, an outfit, or a monetary gift have made a difference in your countenance and level of hope in that moment? Of course it would have! Let's ask our Heavenly Father to soften our hearts, so we will be more aware of the needs of those around us and give us the wisdom and provision to help in whatever capacity He equips us to.

WHO IS OUR NEIGHBOR?
Yahshua answers this question in the Parable of the Good Samaritan found in Luke 10:29-37 (KJV).
*But he, willing to justify himself, said unto Jesus, and who is my neighbour? ^{30} And Jesus answering said, A certain man went down from Jerusalem to Jericho, and fell among thieves, which stripped him of his raiment, and wounded him, and departed, leaving him half dead. ^{31} And by chance there came down a certain priest that way: and when he saw him, he passed by on the other side. ^{32} And likewise a Levite, when he was at the place, came and looked on him, and passed by on the other side. ^{33} But a certain Samaritan, as he journeyed, came where he was: and when he saw him, he had compassion on him, ^{34} and went to him, and bound up his wounds, pouring in oil and wine, and set him on his own beast, and brought him to an inn, and took care of him. ^{35} And on the morrow when he departed, he took out two pence, and gave them to the host, and said unto him, Take care of him; and whatsoever thou spendest more, when I come again, I will repay thee. ^{36} **Which now of these three, thinkest thou, was neighbour unto him that fell among the thieves? ^{37} And he said, He that shewed mercy on him. Then said Jesus unto him, Go, and do thou likewise.***

Our neighbors are our relatives, people living next door, the homeless beggar on the roadside, the elderly lady in the grocery store, your co-worker, and fellow brother/sister in the faith. We are all each other's neighbors, your neighbor is not limited to your zip code, state or country.

Love One Another.
1 John 5:1-2 - Whoever believes that Jesus is the Christ is born of God, and everyone who loves Him who begot also loves him who is begotten of Him. [2] By this we know that we love the children of God, when we love God and keep His commandments.
John 13:34-35 (KJV) - A new commandment I give unto you, that ye love one another; as I have loved you, that ye also love one another. [35] By this shall all men know that ye are my disciples, if ye have love one to another.
John 15:12 (KJV) - This is my commandment, that ye love one another, as I have loved you.
John 15:17 (KJV) - These things I command you, that ye love one another.
1 Peter 1:22 - Since you have purified your souls in obeying the truth through the Spirit in sincere love of the brethren, love one another fervently with a pure heart,
1 Peter 2:17 - Honor all people. Love the brotherhood. Fear God. Honor the king.
1 Peter 3:8 - Finally, all *of* you be of one mind, having compassion for one another; love as brothers, be tenderhearted, be courteous;
1 John 4:11-13 - Beloved, if God so loved us, we also ought to love one another. [12] No one has seen God at any time. If we love one another, God abides in us, and His love has been perfected in us. [13] By this we know that we abide in Him, and He in us, because He has given us of His Spirit.

Love Your Family.
Matthew 19:19 - 'Honor your father and your mother,' and, 'You shall love your neighbor as yourself.' "
Ephesians 5:25 - Husbands, love your wives, just as Christ also loved the church and gave Himself for her,
Ephesians 5:28 - So husbands ought to love their own wives as their own bodies; he who loves his wife loves himself.
Ephesians 5:33 - Nevertheless let each one of you in particular so love his own wife as himself, and let the wife see that she respects her husband.
Colossians 3:19 (KJV) - Husbands, love your wives, and be not bitter against them.
Titus 2:4 (KJV) - That they may teach the young women to be sober, to love their husbands, to love their children,

What Does Loving Our Neighbors Look Like?
Not being hateful, abusive violent, or murderous.
- 1 John 4:19-20 (KJV) - We love him, because he first loved us. [20] If a man say, I love God, and hateth his brother, he is a liar: for he that loveth not his brother whom he hath seen, how can he love God whom he hath not seen?
- 1 John 3:14-15 (KJV) - We know that we have passed from death unto life, because we love the brethren. He that loveth not his brother abideth in death. [15] Whosoever hateth his brother is a murderer: and ye know that no murderer hath eternal life abiding in him.

Not being envious and jealous when good things are happening in their lives.
- John 3:11-12(KJV) - For this is the message that ye heard from the beginning, that we should love one another. [12] Not as Cain, who was of that wicked one, and slew his brother. And wherefore slew he him?

Because his own works were evil, and his brother's righteous.

Sacrificing
- John 15:13-14(KJV) - Greater love hath no man than this, that a man lay down his life for his friends. ¹⁴ Ye are my friends, if ye do whatsoever I command you.
- 1 John 3:16-19 - By this we know love, because He laid down His life for us. And we also ought to lay down our lives for the brethren. ¹⁷ But whoever has this world's goods, and sees his brother in need, and shuts up his heart from him, how does the love of God abide in him? ¹⁸ My little children, let us not love in word or in tongue, but in deed and in truth. ¹⁹ And by this we know that we are of the truth, and shall assure our hearts before Him.

Sharing the Gospel and our Lives with Others
- 1 Thessalonians 2:8 - So, affectionately longing for you, we were well pleased to impart to you not only the gospel of God, but also our own lives, because you had become dear to us.

Serving
- Galatians 5:13-14 - For you, brethren, have been called to liberty; only do not use liberty as an opportunity for the flesh, but through love serve one another. ¹⁴ For all the law is fulfilled in one word, even in this: "You shall love your neighbor as yourself."

Caring for Others, Helping When They Are in Need
- Hebrews 6:10 - For God is not unjust to forget your work and labor of love which you have shown toward His name, in that you have ministered to the saints, and do minister.
- Hebrews 10:24(KJV) - And let us consider one another to provoke unto love and to good works:

Honoring Each Other
- Romans 12:9-10 - Let love be without hypocrisy. Abhor what is evil. Cling to what is good. [10] Be kindly affectionate to one another with brotherly love, in honor giving preference to one another;

Forgiving Faults
- Luke 7:47 - Therefore I say to you, her sins, which are many, are forgiven, for she loved much. But to whom little is forgiven, the same loves little."
- Ephesians 4:2 - with all lowliness and gentleness, with longsuffering, bearing with one another in love,
- 1 Peter 4:8 - And above all things have fervent love for one another, for "love will cover a multitude of sins."

Not Causing Others To Stumble
- 1 John 2:10 - He who loves his brother abides in the light, and there is no cause for stumbling in him.

Speaking the Truth
- Ephesians 4:15-16 - but, speaking the truth in love, may grow up in all things into Him who is the head— Christ— [16] from whom the whole body, joined and knit together by what every joint supplies, according to the effective working by which every part does its share, causes growth of the body for the edifying of itself in love.

STEP THREE - LOVE YOUR ENEMIES

Who is your enemy?
Take a moment and write a list of individuals that you classify as your enemies. As you recall your offender(s), if you are experiencing rage, anger, hate, hurt or any other displeasing emotions or thoughts, that is your clue, that you still have unforgiveness. Ask our Heavenly Father to remove the hate, bitterness and

unforgiveness in your heart for each person you have listed.

We may consider some strangers and acquaintances as our enemies. This list may include politicians, entertainers, and individuals who appear to have no love or conviction in their heart for Yahweh. We often make the mistake of equating people who do not believe in Christ as our enemies, because we rightfully detest the sin they participate in. <u>1 John 2:15-17</u> (KJV) states, *"Love not the world, neither the things that are in the world. If any man love the world, the love of the Father is not in him. 16 For all that is in the world, the lust of the flesh, and the lust of the eyes, and the pride of life, is not of the Father, but is of the world. 17And the world passeth away, and the lust thereof: but he that doeth the will of God abideth forever."* It is possible to hate sin in our own lives and in the lives of others, while maintaining love for ALL people, without compromise.

Having the ability to love our enemies is what separates us from the world. We were once Yahweh's enemies (ungrateful and wicked), yet in His loving kindness, He extended grace and mercy towards us. It is His desire that we love like He loves. To fulfill this, we must not only love those whom we desire to love but we must also love our enemies. Yahshua says in Luke 6:32, *"But if you love those who love you, what credit is that to you? For even sinners love those who love them."*

As a believer and follower of Christ, it is challenging to forgive our more serious offenders, and then be expected to love them. Although it is uncomfortable to walk this out each day, our hearts' desire must be to please our Creator and King. Let this be our prayer, *"Teach me, how to love my enemy, not just in words, but genuinely from my spirit and in action, in Yahshua's name, Amen."*

What Does Loving Our Enemies Look Like?

<u>Bless and Pray for our enemies.</u>
- Matthew 5:43-45 (KJV) - Ye have heard that it hath been said, Thou shalt love thy neighbour, and hate thine enemy. ⁴⁴ But I say unto you, **Love your enemies, bless them that curse you, do good to them that hate you, and pray for them which despitefully use you, and persecute you**; ⁴⁵ *That ye may be the children of your Father which is in heaven*: for He maketh his sun to rise on the evil and on the good, and sendeth rain on the just and on the unjust.

<u>Do good things for them; be kind to them.</u>
- Luke 6:27-30 (KJV) - But I say unto you which hear, **Love** your enemies, **do good** to them which hate you, ²⁸ **Bless** them that curse you, and **pray** for them which despitefully use you. ²⁹ And unto him that smiteth thee on the one cheek offer also the other; and him that taketh away thy cloak forbid not to take thy coat also. ³⁰ **Give** to every man that asketh of thee; and of him that taketh away thy goods ask them not again.

<u>Lend to them without expecting to be repaid.</u>
- Luke 6:35-37 (KJV) - But **love** ye your enemies, and do **good**, and **lend**, hoping for nothing again; and your reward shall be great, and **ye shall be the children of the Highest**: *for he is kind unto the unthankful and to the evil.* ³⁶ Be ye therefore merciful, as your Father also is merciful. ³⁷ **Judge not**, and ye shall not be judged: **condemn not**, and ye shall not be condemned: **forgive**, and ye shall be forgiven:

Are the above scriptures as hard to swallow for you as they are for me? We have to remember that our Heavenly Father's thoughts and ways are higher than ours (Isaiah 55:8-9). Our way looks like rage and

revenge. Yahweh constantly stretches us; encouraging us to be like him. Think about this, most parents do not train their children as follows:
- If a bully hits you, let them hit you again.
- If an aggressor curses at you and spreads lies about you, speak blessings over their life.
- When people hate you, go out of your way to do kind things for them.
- Pray for everyone who takes advantage of you and persecutes you.
- If someone is stealing from you, let them take everything they want from you.
- If anyone asks you to borrow anything, lend it to them, without expecting it back.

I'll be the first to say, I have always taught my children that they should not initiate fights but that they need to be ready to finish one. Yet Apostle Paul instructs, in Romans 12:17-21, *"Repay no one evil for evil. Have regard for good things in the sight of all men. [18] If it is possible, as much as depends on you, live peaceably with all men. [19] Beloved, do not avenge yourselves, but rather give place to wrath; for it is written, "Vengeance is Mine, I will repay," says the Lord. [20] Therefore "If your enemy is hungry, feed him; if he is thirsty, give him a drink; for in so doing you will heap coals of fire on his head." [21] Do not be overcome by evil, but overcome evil with good."* **There is an eternal reward when we are courageous enough to walk in love like this, but it requires a circumcision of our hearts.**

1 Corinthians 13

Though I speak with the tongues of men and of angels, but have not love, I have become sounding brass or a clanging cymbal. 2 and though I have the gift of prophecy, and understand all mysteries and all knowledge, and though I have all faith, so that I could remove mountains, but have not love, I am nothing. 3 And though I bestow all my goods to feed the poor, and though I give my body to be burned, but have not love, it profits me nothing. 4 Love suffers long and is kind; love does not envy; love does not parade itself, is not puffed up; 5 does not behave rudely, does not seek its own, is not provoked, thinks no evil; 6 does not rejoice in iniquity, but rejoices in the truth; 7 bears all things, believes all things, hopes all things, endures all things. 8 Love never fails. But whether there are prophecies, they will fail; whether there are tongues, they will cease; whether there is knowledge, it will vanish away. 9 For we know in part and we prophesy in part. 10 But when that which is perfect has come, then that which is in part will be done away. 11 When I was a child, I spoke as a child, I understood as a child, I thought as a child; but when I became a man, I put away childish things. 12 For now we see in a mirror, dimly, but then face to face. Now I know in part, but then I shall know just as I also am known. 13 And now abide faith, hope, love, these three; but the greatest of these is love.

All of our good deeds and intentions are meaningless if they are not done through LOVE.

> Everything we do must be done with love.
> (1 Corinthians 16:14).
>
> Love is our highest goal!
> (1 Corinthians 14:1)

CHAPTER SIX
Developing: Joy
Rejoice in the Lord always: and again I say, Rejoice.
Philippians 4:4 (KJV)

Have you ever eaten breadfruit? It is a starchy and highly nutritious fruit with a bread or potato like texture. When the Breadfruit matures and ripens, it can be eaten raw, but it is commonly eaten cooked while still green. As a Jamaican, my family has always roasted breadfruit on an open fire or in an oven, the skin is peeled, then the breadfruit is sliced, fried and sprinkled with salt, it's absolutely delicious. It can be eaten in countless other ways, used as an accompaniment to any meal as well as used to make desserts. It is a subsistence food, like boiled green bananas or potatoes. Breadfruit is increasingly being researched and used as an answer to the hunger epidemic across the globe. In Scripture, Yahshua is referred to as the WORD (John 1:1) and the Bread of Life.

John 6:30-35, 48-51 records, *"Therefore they said to Him, "What sign will You perform then, that we may see it and believe You? What work will You do?* [31] *Our fathers ate the manna in the desert; as it is written, 'He gave them bread from heaven to eat.'"* [32] *Then Jesus said to them, "Most assuredly, I say to you, Moses did not give you the bread from heaven, but* **My Father gives you the true bread from heaven.** *33* **For the bread of God is He who comes down from heaven and gives life to the world."** *34 Then they said to Him, "Lord, give us this bread always." 35 And Jesus said to them,* **"I am the bread of life. He who comes to Me shall never hunger, and he who believes in Me shall never thirst...48 I am the bread of life.** *49 Your fathers ate the manna in the wilderness, and are dead. 50* **This is the bread which comes down from heaven, that one may eat of it and not die.** *51* **I am the living bread which came down from heaven. If anyone eats of this bread, he will live forever; and the bread that I shall give is My flesh, which I shall give for the life of the world."**

Are you ready to eat and be filled with His Joy? Jeremiah 15:16 exclaims, *"Your words were found, and* **I ate them, and Your word was to me the joy and rejoicing of my heart***; For I am called by Your name, O L*ORD *God of hosts."*

YAHSHUA IS OUR JOY! In Matthew 2:10 the wise men rejoiced when they saw the star that led them to Baby Yahshua. The announcement of the birth of Yahshua to the shepherds is recorded in Luke 2:10-11, 20, *"Then the angel said to them, "Do not be afraid, for behold, I bring you* **good tidings of great joy** *which will be to all people." 11 For there is born to you this day in the city of David a Savior, who is* **Christ the Lord***.20 Then the shepherds returned,* **glorifying and praising God for all the things that they had heard and seen, as it was told them.**

On the third day when Mary Magdalene and Mary went to the tomb to find Yahshua, He was not there. Matthew 28:5-10 records, *"But the angel answered and said to the women, "Do not be afraid, for I know that you seek Jesus who was crucified. 6 He is not here; for He is risen, as He said. Come, see the place where the Lord lay. ⁷ And go quickly and tell His disciples that He is risen from the dead, and indeed He is going before you into Galilee; there you will see Him. Behold, I have told you." ⁸ So they went out quickly from the tomb with fear and* **great joy**, *and ran to bring His disciples word. ⁹ And as they went to tell His disciples, behold,* ***Jesus met them, saying, "Rejoice!" So they came and held Him by the feet and worshiped Him.*** *¹⁰ Then Jesus said to them, "Do not be afraid. Go and tell My brethren to go to Galilee, and there they will see Me."* At Yahshua's ascension, Luke 24:51-53 states, *"⁵¹ Now it came to pass, while He blessed them, that He was parted from them and carried up into heaven. ⁵² And they worshiped Him, and* ***returned to Jerusalem with great joy, ⁵³ and were continually in the temple praising and blessing God. Amen."***

Yahshua says in John 15:11(KJV), *"These things have I spoken unto you, that* ***my joy might remain in you****, and that* ***your joy might be full."*** Then in John 17:13 He prays to our Heavenly Father, *"But now I come to You, and these things I speak in the world, that they may have* ***My joy fulfilled in themselves****."* Our Messiah wants us to be filled with the joy of salvation!

<u>Isaiah 12:3</u> - Therefore with joy you will draw water from the wells of salvation.

<u>Psalm 20:5</u> (KJV) - We will rejoice in thy salvation, and in the name of our God we will set up our banners: the LORD fulfil all thy petitions.

<u>Psalm 40:16</u> (KJV) - Let all those that seek thee rejoice and be glad in thee: let such as love thy salvation say continually, The LORD be magnified.

<u>Psalm 51:12</u> - Restore to me the joy of Your salvation, and uphold me by Your generous Spirit.

<u>Psalm 70:4</u> - Let all those who seek You rejoice and be glad in You; and let those who love Your salvation say continually, "Let God be magnified!"

Psalm 95:1 - Oh come, let us sing to the LORD! Let us shout joyfully to the Rock of our salvation.
Psalm 118:15 (KJV) - The voice of rejoicing and salvation is in the tabernacles of the righteous: the right hand of the LORD doeth valiantly.
John 16:24 - "Until now you have asked nothing in My name. Ask, and you will receive, that your joy may be full."

Our joy comes in knowing that we have eternal life in Christ sealed with the gift of Precious Holy Spirit. If we **focus on what is eternal** and **not on what is temporary** then we never have to lose our joy. Joy should not be based on material things in this life, but rooted in our eternal hope. When the foundation of our joy is correct nothing can shake it. **Joy should be continual not conditional.**
Isaiah 26:19 - Your dead shall live; together with my dead body they shall arise. Awake and sing, you who dwell in dust; for your dew is like the dew of herbs, and the earth shall cast out the dead.
1 Thessalonians 4:13-18 (KJV) - But I would not have you to be ignorant, brethren, concerning them which are asleep, that ye sorrow not, even as others which have no hope. 14 For if we believe that Jesus died and rose again, even so them also which sleep in Jesus will God bring with him. 15 For this we say unto you by the word of the Lord, that we which are alive and remain unto the coming of the Lord shall not prevent them which are asleep. 16 For the Lord himself shall descend from heaven with a shout, with the voice of the archangel, and with the trump of God: and the dead in Christ shall rise first: 17 Then we which are alive and remain shall be caught up together with them in the clouds, to meet the Lord in the air: and so shall we ever be with the Lord. 18 Wherefore comfort one another with these words.
Acts 13:52 - And the disciples were filled with joy and with the Holy Spirit.

Psalm 144:15 - Happy are the people who are in such a state; Happy are the people whose God is the LORD!

Psalm 149:5 - Let the saints be joyful in glory; Let them sing aloud on their beds.

Psalm 16:11 - You will show me the path of life; In Your presence is fullness of joy; at Your right hand are pleasures forevermore.

Psalm 21:6 - For You have made him most blessed forever; You have made him exceedingly glad with Your presence.

Let's take a moment and tell the Lord THANK YOU!

Psalm 9:2 - I will be glad and rejoice in You; I will sing praise to Your name, O Most High.

Psalm 33:1 - Rejoice in the LORD, O you righteous! For praise from the upright is beautiful.

Psalm 33:3 (KJV) - Sing unto him a new song; play skillfully with a loud noise.

Psalm 43:4 - Then I will go to the altar of God, To God my exceeding joy; and on the harp I will praise You, O God, my God.

Psalm 63:5 (KJV) - My soul shall be satisfied as with marrow and fatness; and my mouth shall praise thee with joyful lips:

Psalm 66:1 (KJV) - Make a joyful noise unto God, all ye lands:

Psalm 68:3 - But let the righteous be glad; let them rejoice before God; yes, let them rejoice exceedingly.

Psalm 89:15 (KJV) - Blessed is the people that know the joyful sound: they shall walk, O LORD, in the light of thy countenance.

Psalm 98:4 (KJV) - Make a joyful noise unto the LORD, all the earth: make a loud noise, and rejoice, and sing praise.

Psalm 98:6 - With trumpets and the sound of a horn; shout joyfully before the LORD, the King.

Psalm 100:1-2 - Make a joyful shout to the LORD, all you lands! 2 Serve the LORD with gladness; come before His presence with singing.

Throughout the Old Testament, joy is found harmoniously with singing, dancing, shouting, and playing instruments. As Believers and Followers of Christ we must understand that **joy is a constant state of being**. Our goal in this chapter is to choose joy despite of our daily circumstances. As we continue to eat the Word of Yahweh, I pray that the Fruit of Joy will be developed in our lives.

In the book of Nehemiah, we learn that as Ezra read the Law of Moses to the Israelites, they became sorrowful, as they recognized how much they had disappointed Yahweh with their disobedience. Nehemiah 8:9-11 records, *"And Nehemiah, who was the governor, Ezra the priest and scribe, and the Levites who taught the people said to all the people, "This day is holy to the L*ORD *your God; do not mourn nor weep." For all the people wept, when they heard the words of the Law.* *10 Then he said to them, "Go your way, eat the fat, drink the sweet, and send portions to those for whom nothing is prepared; for this day is holy to our Lord.* **Do not sorrow, for the joy of the L**ORD **is your strength***."* *11 So the Levites quieted all the people, saying, "Be still, for the day is holy; do not be grieved."*

Our past sins, which are not limited to but may include: having an abortion, committing murder, stealing, lying, fornicating, or engaging in an adulterous relationship, have a way of making us prisoners to shame. Once we repent, forgive ourselves and others, then ask Yahweh for forgiveness, through Yahshua we are forgiven! Our joy is strengthened in Yahweh's forgiveness and help. He replaces our shame and turns it to everlasting joy! Isaiah 61:7 promises, *"Instead of your shame you shall have <u>double honor</u>, and instead of confusion they shall rejoice in their portion. Therefore in their land they shall possess double; <u>Everlasting joy</u> shall be theirs."*
<u>Psalm 32:1-2</u> (KJV) - Blessed is he whose transgression is forgiven, whose Sin is covered. ² Blessed is the man

to whom the LORD does not impute iniquity, and in whose spirit there is no deceit.
<u>Psalm 34:5</u> - They looked to Him and were radiant, and their faces were not ashamed.
<u>Isaiah 51:3</u> - For the LORD will comfort Zion, He will comfort all her waste places; He will make her wilderness like Eden, and her desert like the garden of the LORD; joy and gladness will be found in it, thanksgiving and the voice of melody.
<u>Isaiah 52:8-9</u> - Your watchmen shall lift up their voices, with their voices they shall sing together; for they shall see eye to eye when the LORD brings back Zion. ⁹ Break forth into joy, sing together, you waste places of Jerusalem! For the LORD has comforted His people, He has redeemed Jerusalem.

Having the JOY OF THE LORD profits our physical, mental and spiritual health. Several medical studies have proven that laughter benefits our health. Solomon teaches us in Proverbs 17:22 (KJV), *"A merry heart doeth good like a medicine: but a broken spirit drieth the bones."*
<u>Job 8:21</u> - He will yet fill your mouth with laughing, and your lips with rejoicing.
<u>Psalm 126:2-3</u> - Then our mouth was filled with laughter, and our tongue with singing. Then they said among the nations, "The LORD has done great things for them." ³ The LORD has done great things for us, and we are glad.
<u>Psalm 4:7</u> - You have put gladness in my heart, more than in the season that their grain and wine increased.

Heavenly Father we ask you to fill us with your joy as we meditate on Your Word. Let us overflow with laughter and be made well in our bodies, minds and spirits. Thank you for answering our prayer and for the many ways You bring joy to our lives. In Yahshua's name we ask these things, Amen.

YAHWEH'S WONDERFUL ACTS BRING JOY!

Psalm 63:7 - Because You have been my help, therefore in the shadow of Your wings I will rejoice.

Psalm 92:4 - For You, LORD, have made me glad through Your work; I will triumph in the works of Your hands.

Psalm 146:5 - Happy is he who has the God of Jacob for his help, whose hope is in the LORD his God,

Psalm 65:4 - Blessed is the man You choose, and cause to approach You, that he may dwell in Your courts. We shall be satisfied with the goodness of Your house, of Your holy temple.

YAHWEH'S RIGHTEOUSNESS BRINGS JOY

Isaiah 61:10 - I will greatly rejoice in the LORD, my soul shall be joyful in my God; for he has clothed me with the garments of salvation, he has covered me with the robe of righteousness, as a bridegroom decks himself with ornaments, and as a bride adorns herself with her jewels.

YAHWEH'S PROTECTION AND DELIVERANCE BRINGS JOY

Psalm 14:7 (KJV) - Oh that the salvation of Israel were come out of Zion! When the LORD bringeth back the captivity of his people, Jacob shall rejoice, and Israel shall be glad.

Psalm 90:14 - Oh, satisfy us early with Your mercy, that we may rejoice and be glad all our days!

Psalm 5:11 - But let all those rejoice who put their trust in You; let them ever shout for joy, because You defend them; let those also who love Your name be joyful in You.

Psalm 28:7 - The LORD is my strength and my shield; my heart trusted in Him, and I am helped; therefore my heart greatly rejoices, and with my song I will praise Him.

Psalm 71:23 - My lips shall greatly rejoice when I sing to You, and my soul, which You have redeemed.

Psalm 59:16 - But I will sing of Your power; yes, I will sing aloud of Your mercy in the morning; for You have been my defense and refuge in the day of my trouble.

YAHWEH'S COMMANDMENTS & CORRECTION BRINGS JOY

Understanding Yahweh's instructions while accepting His correction brings joy to our souls. Many hesitate to read His Word because they have little understanding of how to apply it in their lives. We must ask our Heavenly Father to give us His wisdom and understanding. He will give us clarity about our life's purpose, and we will be filled with joy knowing that we have a safe and trusted plan to follow.

Job 5:17 - "Behold, happy is the man whom God corrects; therefore do not despise the chastening of the Almighty.

Nehemiah 8:12 - And all the people went their way to eat and drink, to send portions and **rejoice** greatly, because **they understood the words** that were declared to them.

Psalm 19:8 - The statutes of the LORD are right, rejoicing the heart; the commandment of the LORD is pure, enlightening the eyes;

Psalm 94:12 - Blessed *is* the man whom You instruct, O LORD, and teach out of Your law,

Psalm 119:92 - Unless Your law had been my delight, I would then have perished in my affliction.

Psalm 119:143 - Trouble and anguish have overtaken me, yet Your commandments are my delights.

Proverbs 3:13 - Happy is the man who finds wisdom, and the man who gains understanding;

Luke 10:21 - In that hour Jesus rejoiced in the Spirit and said, "I thank You, Father, Lord of heaven and earth, that You have hidden these things from the wise and prudent and revealed them to babes. Even so, Father, for so it seemed good in Your sight.

TRUSTING IN YAHWEH BRINGS JOY

Is it easier for you to trust Yahweh, whom you cannot see, than it is for you to trust yourself? Many are plagued with anxiety because they feel more secure in trusting in what we can see and control. Joy replaces our fears and insecurities when we take the leap of faith to trust the Lord, to take care of all of our needs and desires.

Psalm 40:4 - Blessed is that man who makes the LORD his trust, and does not respect the proud, nor such as turn aside to lies.

Psalm 84:12 - O LORD of hosts, blessed is the man who trusts in You!

Proverbs 16:20 - He who heeds the word wisely will find good, and whoever trusts in the LORD, happy is he.

Romans 15:13 - Now may the God of hope fill you with all joy and peace in believing, that you may abound in hope by the power of the Holy Spirit.

1 Peter 1:8 - whom having not seen you love. Though now you do not see Him, yet believing, you rejoice with joy inexpressible and full of glory,

DOING YAHWEH'S WILL, BRINGS JOY

Psalm 1:1 - Blessed is the man who walks not in the counsel of the ungodly, nor stands in the path of sinners, nor sits in the seat of the scornful;

Psalm 40:8 (KJV) - I delight to do thy will, O my God: yea, thy law is within my heart.

Psalm 112:1 (KJV) - Praise ye the LORD. Blessed is the man that feareth the LORD, that delighteth greatly in his commandments.

Psalm 119:1-2 (KJV) - Blessed are the undefiled in the way, who walk in the law of the LORD. ² Blessed are they that keep his testimonies, and that seek him with the whole heart.

Psalm 128:1-2 (KJV) - Blessed is every one that feareth the LORD; that walketh in his ways. ² For thou shalt eat the labour of thine hands: happy shalt thou be, and it shall be well with thee.

Proverbs 29:18 (KJV) - Where there is no vision, the people perish: but he that keepeth the law, happy is he.

LOVING RIGHTEOUSNESS, JUSTICE AND PEACE BRINGS JOY

Psalm 32:11 - Be glad in the LORD and rejoice, you righteous; and shout for joy, all you upright in heart!
Psalm 45:7(KJV) - Thou lovest righteousness, and hatest wickedness: therefore God, thy God, hath anointed thee with the oil of gladness above thy fellows.
Hebrews 1:9 (KJV) - Thou hast loved righteousness, and hated iniquity; therefore God, even thy God, hath anointed thee with the oil of gladness above thy fellows.
Psalm 97:11 (KJV) - Light is sown for the righteous, and gladness for the upright in heart.
Psalm 67:4 - Oh, let the nations be glad and sing for joy! For You shall judge the people righteously, and govern the nations on earth. Selah
Proverbs 12:20 - Deceit is in the heart of those who devise evil, but counselors of peace have joy.
Proverbs 13:9 - The light of the righteous rejoices, but the lamp of the wicked will be put out.
Proverbs 21:15 - It is a joy for the just to do justice, but destruction will come to the workers of iniquity.

I am so grateful for all of the ways Yahweh has allowed for us to live in His JOY! As we trust and obey him, love what He loves and do what He does, we will experience a growth spurt in JOY.

Joy seems most difficult to access during hard times. There are many occurrences in our lives that cause us to be sad, dejected and depressed. It may be the negative report from a doctor, death of a friend or family member, the loss of a home or business, the end of a marriage or friendship, or a catastrophic event that causes countless lives to be changed in a moment. Consequently we experience the drying of our bones that comes with having a broken spirit (Proverbs 17:22).

During times of hopelessness, despair and grief, we physically do not feel like we have the STRENGTH to handle anymore blows that life may throw at us. In these moments we must stand (confess and believe) on our Heavenly Father's Promise to turn our mourning (grief, sorrow) to joy.

Psalm 30:5 - For His anger is but for a moment, His favor is for life; Weeping may endure for a night, but joy comes in the morning.

Psalm 30:11 - You have turned for me my mourning into dancing; You have put off my sackcloth and clothed me with gladness,

Psalm 126:5 - Those who sow in tears shall reap in joy.

Isaiah 35:10 and 51:11 - And the ransomed of the LORD shall return, and come to Zion with singing, with everlasting joy on their heads. They shall obtain joy and gladness, and sorrow and sighing shall flee away.

Isaiah 61:3 - To console those who mourn in Zion, To give them beauty for ashes, *The oil of joy for mourning, The garment of praise for the spirit of heaviness*; That they may be called trees of righteousness, The planting of the LORD, that He may be glorified."

Jeremiah 31:12-13 - Therefore they shall come and sing in the height of Zion, streaming to the goodness of the LORD— For wheat and new wine and oil, for the young of the flock and the herd; *their souls shall be like a well-watered garden, and they shall sorrow no more at all.* 13 "Then shall the virgin rejoice in the dance, and the young men and the old, together; *for I will turn their mourning to joy, will comfort them, and make them rejoice rather than sorrow.*

Jeremiah 31:25 - For I have satiated the weary soul, and I have replenished every sorrowful soul."

John 16:20-22 - Most assuredly, I say to you that you will weep and lament, but the world will rejoice; and you will be sorrowful, but your sorrow will be turned into joy. 21 A woman, when she is in labor, has sorrow because her hour has come; but as soon as she has given birth to the child, she no longer remembers the

anguish, for joy that a human being has been born into the world. ²² Therefore you now have sorrow; but I will see you again and your heart will rejoice, and **your joy no one will take from you**.
2 Corinthians 6:10 - As sorrowful, yet always rejoicing; as poor, yet making many rich; as having nothing, and yet possessing all things.

These are such beautiful promises from our Heavenly Father. I implore you, **do not allow sorrow and the worries of life to steal your strength and dry up your bones**. Solomon writes in Proverbs 14:10, *"The heart knows its own bitterness, and a stranger does not share its joy."* Only you and Yahweh know what you have been through, and only you and He know what He has brought you out of. When His joy fills you until it overflows, others may not understand, why you smile, laugh and love despite the struggles our Savior Yahshua has brought you through or is bringing you through right now. Encourage yourself like David did; call back to your remembrance all Yahweh has done for you. Count your past and present blessings and tell Him thank you. In this passage of scripture the Hebrew word translated as Bless is *barak*, meaning to kneel and show the Lord admiration.

Psalm 103 (KJV)

Bless the LORD, O my soul: and all that is within me, bless his holy name. ² Bless the LORD, O my soul, and forget not all his benefits: ³ Who forgiveth all thine iniquities; who healeth all thy diseases; ⁴ Who redeemeth thy life from destruction; who crowneth thee with lovingkindness and tender mercies; ⁵ Who satisfieth thy mouth with good things; so that thy youth is renewed like the eagle's. ⁶ The LORD executeth righteousness and judgment for all that are oppressed. ⁷ He made known his ways unto Moses, his acts unto the children of Israel. ⁸ The LORD is merciful and gracious, slow to anger, and plenteous in mercy. ⁹ He will not always chide: neither will he keep his anger for ever. ¹⁰ He hath not dealt with us after our sins; nor rewarded us according to our iniquities. ¹¹ For as the heaven is high above the earth, so great is his mercy toward them that fear him. ¹² As far as the east is from the west, so far hath he removed our transgressions from us. ¹³ Like as a father pitieth his children, so the LORD pitieth them that fear him. ¹⁴ For he knoweth our frame; he remembereth that we are dust. ¹⁵ As for man, his days are as grass: as a flower of the field, so he flourisheth. ¹⁶ For the wind passeth over it, and it is gone; and the place thereof shall know it no more. ¹⁷ But the mercy of the LORD is from everlasting to everlasting upon them that fear him, and his righteousness unto children's children; ¹⁸ to such as keep his covenant, and to those that remember his commandments to do them. ¹⁹ The LORD hath prepared his throne in the heavens; and his kingdom ruleth over all. ²⁰ Bless the LORD, ye his angels, that excel in strength, that do his commandments hearkening unto the voice of his word. ²¹ Bless ye the LORD, all ye his hosts; ye ministers of his, that do his pleasure. ²² Bless the LORD, all his works in all places of his dominion: bless the LORD, O my soul.

David not only encourages his own soul to bless the Lord but he begins to speak to all of Yahweh's creations in Heaven, and command them to bless Him. Although it often goes unnoticed by us, all of creation bursts with joy for our Creator. Creation knows how to rejoice in our Creator, therefore we must learn to do it as well. As you read the following passages of scripture, do not just think of them as metaphorical sayings, ALL of creation literally responds to Yahweh. When the Pharisees insisted that Yahshua rebuke His disciples for praising Him as he rode on a donkey, our Lord replied in Luke 19:40, *"But He answered and said to them, "I tell you that if these should keep silent, **the stones would immediately cry out**."*
Job 38:7 (KJV) - "When the morning stars sang together, and all the sons of God shouted for joy?"

1 Chronicles 16:32 - Let the sea roar, and all its fullness; let the field rejoice, and all that is in it.
Psalm 65:8 - They also who dwell in the farthest parts are afraid of Your signs; You make the outgoings of the morning and evening rejoice.
Psalm 65:11-13 - You crown the year with Your goodness, and Your paths rip with abundance. 12 They drop on the pastures of the wilderness, and the little hills rejoice on every side. 13 The pastures are clothed with flocks; the valleys also are covered with grain; they shout for joy, they also sing.
Psalm 96:12 (KJV) - Let the field be joyful, and all that is therein: then shall all the trees of the wood rejoice
Psalm 98:8 - Let the rivers clap their hands; let the hills be joyful together before the LORD,
Isaiah 44:23 - Sing, O heavens, for the LORD has done it! Shout, you lower parts of the earth; break forth into singing, you mountains, O forest, and every tree in it! For the LORD has redeemed Jacob, and glorified Himself in Israel.
Isaiah 49:13 - Sing, O heavens! Be joyful, O earth! And break out in singing, O mountains! For the LORD has comforted His people, and will have mercy on His afflicted.
Isaiah 55:12 - "For you shall go out with joy, and be led out with peace; the mountains and the hills shall break forth into singing before you, and all the trees of the field shall clap their hands.

How amazing! I can never look at the waves in the ocean, swaying trees in the wind, and rolling fields the same again, they have a song to sing to our Creator, Yahweh.

When Paul and Silas were thrown into prison after being stripped and beaten with wooden rods for casting a psychic demon out of a woman, they were thrown into the inner dungeon of the prison and shackled. Around midnight they began to pray and sing hymns to God, as the other prisoners listened. Acts 16:26 records, *"Suddenly there was a great earthquake, so that the foundations of the prison were shaken; and immediately all the doors were opened and everyone's chains were loosed."* **Paul and Silas's joy in their eternal hope in Christ surpassed the pain of their bloodied and bruised bodies. Their joy could not be taken away (John 16:22). It was a joy that was not based on their present circumstances but is a lasting Fruit of the Spirit, that causes prisoners to be set FREE!** It would have been easy for them to get discouraged, become too fearful to follow Yahweh, feel sorry for themselves and begin to complain and grumble, but they didn't, instead they rejoiced in their suffering.

It appears like more trouble, persecutions, and mockery come our way, when we choose to follow Christ. But know this; we are to **leap for joy when suffering for righteousness sake!** Hebrews 12:2 says, *"looking unto Jesus, the author and finisher of our faith, who for the joy that was set before Him endured the cross, despising the shame, and has sat down at the right hand of the throne of God."*

Luke 6:22-23 - Blessed are you when men hate you, and when they exclude you, and revile you, and cast out your name as evil, for the Son of Man's sake. 23 Rejoice in that day and leap for joy! For indeed your reward is great in heaven, for in like manner their fathers did to the prophets.

2 Corinthians 8:2 - that in a great trial of affliction the abundance of their joy and their deep poverty abounded in the riches of their liberality.

Hebrews 10:34 - for you had compassion on me in my chains, and joyfully accepted the plundering of your goods, knowing that you have a better and an enduring possession for yourselves in heaven.

James 1:2 - My brethren, count it all joy when you fall into various trials,

1 Peter 1:6 - In this you greatly rejoice, though now for a little while, if need be, you have been grieved by various trials,
1 Peter 4:13 - but rejoice to the extent that you partake of Christ's sufferings, that when His glory is revealed, you may also be glad with exceeding joy.
1 Thessalonians 1:6 - And you became followers of us and of the Lord, having received the word in much affliction, with joy of the Holy Spirit,
Colossians 1:11 - strengthened with all might according to His glorious power, for all patience and longsuffering with joy;

We are expected by Our Heavenly Father to be a source of joy in the lives of others. The only way that our lives will bring joy to others, is if the Fruit of Joy is developed on the tree of our soul. Isaiah 65:18 prophesied, *"But be glad and rejoice forever in what I create; for behold, I create Jerusalem as a rejoicing,* **and her people a joy***.*"

A smile on your face and a pep in your tone of voice, can bring joy to another.
Proverbs 15:30 – "The light of the eyes rejoices the heart, and a good report makes the bones healthy."

Leading others to Christ produces joy in us and in them.
John 4:36 - And he who reaps receives wages, and gathers fruit for eternal life, that both he who sows and he who reaps may rejoice together.

Teaching the Word of Yahweh, brings joy to others lives.
1 John 1:4 - And these things we write to you that your joy may be full.
2 Corinthians 1:24 - Not that we have dominion over your faith, but are fellow workers for your joy; for by faith you stand.

Acts 11:23 - When he came and had seen the grace of God, he was glad, and encouraged them all that with purpose of heart they should continue with the Lord.
Philippians 1:25 - And being confident of this, I know that I shall remain and continue with you all for your progress and joy of faith,

Praying for others brings joy to their lives.
Isaiah 56:7 - Even them I will bring to My holy mountain, and make them joyful in My house of prayer. Their burnt offerings and their sacrifices will be accepted on My altar; For My house shall be called a house of prayer for all nations."

Spending time with others produces joy in someone's life.
2 Timothy 1:4 - greatly desiring to see you, being mindful of your tears, that I may be filled with joy,

We bring joy by showing the love of God and lending a hand in another's area of need.
Psalm 41:1 - Blessed is he who considers the poor; the LORD will deliver him in time of trouble.
Job 29:13 - The blessing of a perishing man came upon me, and I caused the widow's heart to sing for joy.
2 Corinthians 9:12 - For the administration of this service not only supplies the needs of the saints, but also is abounding through many thanksgivings to God,
Philemon 1:7 - For we have great joy and consolation in your love, because the hearts of the saints have been refreshed by you, brother.
Acts 2:46 - So continuing daily with one accord in the temple, and breaking bread from house to house, they ate their food with gladness and simplicity of heart,

We bring joy to the lives of our leaders when we obey God.
Apostle Paul exhorts us in Philippians 2:12-18, *"Therefore, my beloved, as you have always obeyed, not*

as in my presence only, but now much more in my absence, work out your own salvation with fear and trembling; ¹³ *for it is God who works in you both to will and to do for His good pleasure.* ¹⁴ *Do all things without complaining and disputing,* ¹⁵ *that you may become blameless and harmless, children of God without fault in the midst of a crooked and perverse generation, among whom you shine as lights in the world,* ¹⁶ *holding fast the word of life,* **so that I may rejoice in the day of Christ that I have not run in vain or labored in vain.** ¹⁷ **Yes, and if I am being poured out as a drink offering on the sacrifice and service of your faith, I am glad and rejoice with you all.** ¹⁸ **For the same reason you also be glad and rejoice with me.**

2 Corinthians 2:3 - And I wrote this very thing to you, lest, when I came, I should have sorrow over those from whom I ought to have joy, having confidence in you all that my joy is the joy of you all.

Philippians 4:1 - Therefore, my beloved and longed-brethren, my joy and crown, so stand fast in the Lord, beloved.

Hebrews 13:17 - Remember those who rule over you, who have spoken the word of God to you, whose faith follow, considering the outcome of their conduct.

1 Thessalonians 2:19-20 - For what is our hope, or joy, or crown of rejoicing? Is it not even you in the presence of our Lord Jesus Christ at His coming? ²⁰ For you are our glory and joy.

1 Thessalonians 3:9 - For what thanks can we render to God for you, for all the joy with which we rejoice for your sake before our God,

Recognizing our faults and repenting produces joy in the lives of those we offend or hurt.

2 Corinthians 7:7 - and not only by his coming, but also by the consolation with which he was comforted in you, when he told us of your earnest desire, your mourning, your zeal for me, so that I rejoiced even more.

Godly children bring joy to their parents.
Proverbs 10:1 - The proverbs of Solomon: A wise son makes a glad father, but a foolish son is the grief of his mother.
Proverbs 15:20-21 - A wise son makes a father glad, but a foolish man despises his mother. 21 Folly is joy to him who is destitute of discernment, but a man of understanding walks uprightly.
Proverbs 23:24-25 - The father of the righteous will greatly rejoice, and he who begets a wise child will delight in him. 25 Let your father and your mother be glad, and let her who bore you rejoice.
Proverbs 29:3 - Whoever loves wisdom makes his father rejoice, but a companion of harlots wastes his wealth.
Proverbs 17:21 - He who begets a scoffer does so to his sorrow, and the father of a fool has no joy.
3 John 1:4 - I have no greater joy than to hear that my children walk in truth.

Scripture tells us in Matthew 3:17, 17:5, and Luke 3:22 that Jesus brought great joy to our Heavenly Father. If Christ's joy is in us, then we too can bring joy to our Heavenly Father. We should strive to BRING HIM JOY. I dare you to choose joy every second, every minute, and every hour of every day!

Rejoice always, 17 pray without ceasing, 18 in everything give thanks; for this is the will of God in Christ Jesus for you. - 1 Thessalonians 5:16-18

CHAPTER SEVEN
Developing: Peace

For I know the thoughts that I think toward you, says the LORD, thoughts of peace and not of evil, to give you a future and a hope. Jeremiah 29:11

If you were to imagine PEACE as a fruit that we eat, which fruit would you compare it to? When I think of peace, I think of relaxation, stress free living and a mind that is free from worry and anxiety. I've chosen the super fruit guava, which provides numerous health benefits. Two of its many gifts to the human body are magnesium and Vitamin C. Magnesium assists in fighting stress, aiding the relaxation of our muscles and nerves, and has also been used in treatment of depression. Did you know that Vitamin C fights the stress hormone cortisol? When consumed with its skin, guava provides three times more Vitamin C than the daily recommended intake, it contains more Vitamin C than an orange. The guava protects our physical hearts and minds, just as Yahweh's Peace guards our spiritual hearts and minds. Philippians 4:6-7, instructs us, *"Be anxious for nothing, but in everything by prayer and supplication, with thanksgiving, let your requests be made known to God; 7 and* **the peace of God, which**

surpasses all understanding, will guard your hearts and minds through Christ Jesus."

One of many Hebrew names for God is Yahweh Shalom, meaning Yahweh is Our Peace. Shalom is completeness, safety, soundness, welfare and peace, quiet, tranquility, and contentment. Because we live in the Kingdom of Yahweh, PEACE IS OUR INHERITANCE. According to Romans 14:17, *"for the kingdom of God is not eating and drinking, but righteousness and peace and joy in the Holy Spirit."*

THE LORD IS PEACE.
In Judges 6, at the sight of the Angel of the Lord, Gideon feared he would die. Immediately the Lord spoke Peace to Gideon. The angel conveyed that Yahweh would deliver the enemies of Israel into the hands of Gideon. Judges 6:22-24 records, *"now Gideon perceived that He was the Angel of the LORD. So Gideon said, "Alas, O Lord GOD! For I have seen the Angel of the LORD face to face." 23 Then the LORD said to him, "Peace be with you; do not fear, you shall not die." 24 So Gideon built an altar there to the LORD, and called it The-LORD-Is-Peace. To this day it is still in Ophrah of the Abiezrites."* Gideon's fear was replaced with an immeasurable outpouring of peace; he could have memorialized the altar with any other name about our Heavenly Father, but he chose PEACE.

Daniel 10 records Daniel's vision he had after fasting for three weeks. Verses 5- 6 describe, *"I lifted my eyes and looked, and behold, a certain man clothed in linen, whose waist was girded with gold of Uphaz! 6 His body was like beryl, his face like the appearance of lightning, his eyes like torches of fire, his arms and feet like burnished bronze in color, and the sound of his words like the voice of a multitude."* At the sight of this man, Daniel lost all strength in his body and fell into a deep sleep with his face to the ground. When this man clothed in linen touched Daniel, he trembled on his knees and palms, until he was able to stand while still trembling. As this man spoke with the voice of a multitude about the future, verse 15-17 continues, *"When he had spoken such words to me, I turned my face toward the ground and became speechless. ¹⁶ And suddenly, one having the likeness of the sons of men touched my lips; then I opened my mouth and spoke, saying to him who stood before me, "My lord, because of the vision my sorrows have overwhelmed me, and I have retained no strength. ¹⁷ For how can this servant of my lord talk with you, my lord? As for me, no strength remains in me now, nor is any breath left in me."* Pay very close attention to what this man says to cause Daniel to gain his strength back. We continue at verse 18-19, *"Then again, the one having the likeness of a man touched me and strengthened me. ¹⁹ And he said, "O man greatly beloved, fear not! Peace be to you; be strong, yes, be strong!" So when he spoke to me I was strengthened, and said, "Let my lord speak, for you have strengthened me.""* King David writes in Psalm 29:11, *"The LORD will give strength to His people; The LORD will bless His people with peace."*

To combat physical, mental, emotional and spiritual weakness, we must have LOVE, JOY and PEACE. Scripture teaches that the joy of the Lord is our strength and perfect love casts out all fear. Picture it this way. LOVE kicks fear out of our soul, leaving a clean room in our heart. Next, we invite Holy Spirit to fill this room with Yahweh's PEACE and JOY. As He exchanges our fear with His Peace and Joy, we are strengthened in every area of our lives.

After Yahshua resurrected, He would greet His disciples with a blessing of peace
Luke 24:36-39 - Now as they said these things, Jesus Himself stood in the midst of them, and said to them, "Peace to you." ³⁷ But they were terrified and

frightened, and supposed they had seen a spirit. *38* And He said to them, "Why are you troubled? And why do doubts arise in your hearts? *39* Behold My hands and My feet, that it is I Myself. Handle Me and see, for a spirit does not have flesh and bones as you see I have."
<u>John 20:19</u> - Then, the same day at evening, being the first day of the week, when the doors were shut where the disciples were assembled, for fear of the Jews, Jesus came and stood in the midst, and said to them, "Peace be with you."
<u>John 20:21</u> - So Jesus said to them again, "Peace to you! As the Father has sent Me, I also send you."
<u>John 20:26</u> - And after eight days His disciples were again inside, and Thomas with them. Jesus came, the doors being shut, and stood in the midst, and said, "Peace to you!"

Yahshua declares, "PEACE BE STILL!" to every storm of our lives. Mark 4:37-41 records, *"And a great windstorm arose, and the waves beat into the boat, so that it was already filling. 38 But He was in the stern, asleep on a pillow. And they awoke Him and said to Him,* <u>*"Teacher, do You not care that we are perishing?" 39 Then He arose and rebuked the wind, and said to the sea,*</u> **"Peace, be still!"** <u>*And the wind ceased and there was a great calm. 40 But He said to them, "Why are you so fearful? How is it that you have no faith?" 41 And they feared exceedingly, and said to one another, "Who can this be, that*</u> **even the wind and the sea obey Him!"**
How many times have you and I felt like Christ was asleep on the job. In the midst of horrible situations in our lives we often cry out to Him, "Do you not care that I am perishing?" We feel forgotten and ignored, but just as He spoke to those winds and that rain, He does the same in our lives today. He only asks that we have faith and not be afraid. **In Yahweh's peace there is no fear!**

Let's take a look at Yahweh's Covenant of Peace with us in Isaiah 54:9-17. *"For this is like the waters of Noah to*

Me; for as I have sworn that the waters of Noah would no longer cover the earth, so have I sworn that I would not be angry with you, nor rebuke you.* ¹⁰ ***For the mountains shall depart and the hills be removed, but My kindness shall not depart from you, nor shall My covenant of peace be removed," Says the LORD, who has mercy on you.*** *¹¹ "O you afflicted one, tossed with tempest, and not comforted, behold, I will lay your stones with colorful gems, and lay your foundations with sapphires. ¹² I will make your pinnacles of rubies, your gates of crystal, and all your walls of precious stones. ¹³* ***All your children shall be taught by the LORD, and great shall be the peace of your children.*** *¹⁴ In righteousness you shall be established; you shall be far from oppression, for you shall not fear; and from terror, for it shall not come near you. ¹⁵ Indeed they shall surely assemble, but not because of Me. Whoever assembles against you shall fall for your sake. ¹⁶ "Behold, I have created the blacksmith who blows the coals in the fire, who brings forth an instrument for his work; and I have created the spoiler to destroy. ¹⁷* ***No weapon formed against you shall prosper, and every tongue which rises against you in judgment you shall condemn. This is the heritage of the servants of the LORD, and their righteousness is from Me," Says the LORD.***

We must hold on to these promises and declare Yahweh's word over our lives and our families. When Yahweh makes a covenant, He seals it with the BLOOD OF YAHSHUA. As the reality becomes more sobering that we are living in the last days, we must hide HIS WORD in our hearts more than ever. He is telling us, although mountains and hills will be removed from their place, His covenant of peace is immovable. Yahshua says in John 16:33, *"These things I have spoken to you, that in Me you may have peace. In the world you will have tribulation; but be of good cheer, I have overcome the world."* Be encouraged because Christ lives in us and He has already overcome the world. Yes, we have an adversary, but his plan will not prosper against us in Yahshua's name! David writes in Psalm 55:18, *"He has redeemed my soul in peace from the battle that was against me, for there were many against me."*

Leviticus 26:6 - I will give **peace in the land**, and you shall lie down, and none will make you afraid; I will rid the land of evil beasts, and the sword will not go through your land.

Numbers 6:26 - The LORD lift up His countenance upon you, and **give you peace**.

Numbers 25:12 - Therefore say, 'Behold, I give to him **My covenant of peace**;

Job 25:2 - "Dominion and fear belong to Him; **He makes peace in His high places**.

Psalm 4:8 - I will both **lie down in peace, and sleep**; for You alone, O LORD, make me dwell in safety.

Psalm 147:14 - He **makes peace in your borders**, and fills you with the finest wheat.

Isaiah 26:12 - LORD, You will **establish peace for us**, for You have also done all our works in us.

Isaiah 45:7 - I form the light and create darkness, **I make peace** and create calamity; I, the LORD, do all these things.'

Isaiah 66:12 - For thus says the LORD: "Behold, I will **extend peace to her like a river**, and the glory of the Gentiles like a flowing stream. Then you shall feed; on *her* sides shall you be carried, And be dandled on *her* knees.

Isaiah 57:18-19 - I have seen his ways, and will heal him; I will also lead him, and restore comforts to him and to his mourners. ¹⁹ "I create the fruit of the lips: **Peace, peace to him who is far off and to him who is near**," Says the LORD, "And I will heal him."

Jeremiah 33:6 - Behold, I will bring it health and healing; I will heal them and **reveal to them the abundance of peace and truth**.

Ezekiel 34:25 - "I will make a **covenant of peace** with them, and cause wild beasts to cease from the land; and they will dwell safely in the wilderness and sleep in the woods.

Ezekiel 37:26 - Moreover I will make a **covenant of peace** with them, and it shall be an **everlasting covenant** with them; I will establish them and multiply them, and I will set My sanctuary in their midst forevermore.

Haggai 2:9 - The glory of this latter temple shall be greater than the former,' says the LORD of hosts. **'And in this place I will give peace**,' says the LORD of hosts."

Malachi 2:5-6 - "**My covenant was with him, one of life and peace**, And I gave them to him that he might fear Me; So he feared Me and was reverent before My name. ⁶ The law of truth was in his mouth, and injustice was not found on his lips. He **walked with Me in peace** and equity, and turned many away from iniquity.

Romans 15:33 - Now the **God of peace** be with you all. Amen.

2 Thessalonians 3:16 - Now may the **Lord of peace** Himself **give you peace** always in every way. The Lord be with you all.

In 2 Kings 4 we learn of a Shunammite woman who perceived the prophet Elisha as a holy man. She would prepare meals for him and his servant Gehazi, as often as they would pass by her home. She asked her husband and he agreed to build a small upper room for Elisha to rest when he would come by. Elisha was so moved by her kindness that he wanted to do something for her, but there was nothing that she wanted. When Gehazi told him that she was childless, Elisha prophesied to her that she would be embracing a son by the same time of the following year and it happened as he said. We are not told how old the child was, but we know he grew older, complained of a terrible headache and died some hours later in his mother's arms. Can you imagine yourself in her situation? Unable to have children, then Yahweh miraculously blesses you with a son, whom you love dearly, only to witness his final breath as you're left embracing his lifeless body. Would you be shaken? Angry? Grieved? What would you do? Although her soul was in *deep distress*, her response to it all was **"It is well"**, the Hebrew word used here is **shalom**. She laid her son down, went to find the prophet, and when she reached Elisha, he returned home with her, stretched himself over the child twice and prayed, then the child lived again!

What a Mighty God we serve! I know that not all of our stories end this way. Many have had to walk down the path of burying their children, who are now with the Lord. May I take this moment to encourage you? If you are grieving the loss of your loved one, I pray Yahweh's Shalom (Peace), over you now, in Yahshua's name. I pray that your hopes and dreams will not die with them, but that you will hold on to the peace that comes in knowing you will meet again. Until then, may the Lord's Peace guide you into your destiny and may you accomplish His perfect will for your life.

Yahshua understands that the trials and sorrows this world brings, easily cause us to live lives of stress, anxiety, and fear. In John 14:27 Yahshua says, *"Peace I leave with you, My peace I give to you; not as the world gives do I give to you. Let not your heart be troubled, neither let it be afraid."* The peace that the world offers does not compare to the peace we have through Christ. In Numbers 23:19 we are told that God is not a man that He should lie. Yahweh wants us to be confident in knowing that the peace the world gives is a lie, it disappoints, but we don't have to be afraid, because what He gives us is the real thing, not an imitation. Nero's (A Roman Emperor known for persecuting Christians) peace signs (also known as the cross of

Nero) have been used as a symbol for many generations to signify that the human race can accomplish peace if we love, accept and respect one another. This indeed is a beautiful notion, yet the truth is, there is only one way to true peace and it is through Christ. Nero's peace sign, which looks like an encircled upside down broken cross, used on banners, clothes, jewelry, etc., represents peace without Christianity. Christ mourns in Luke 19:42, *"saying, "If you had known, even you, especially in this your day, the things that make for your peace! But now they are hidden from your eyes."* Without Christ, there is just an appearance of peace and this type of peace last temporarily. Yahweh's peace defies all understanding and it is eternal.

Yahshua is our Prince of Peace and His peace will never end! The following passages (Isaiah 9:1-7, Zechariah 9:9-10, Micah 5:2-5) prophesied His coming and His Peace.

Isaiah 9:6-7 - For unto us a Child is born, unto us a Son is given; and the government will be upon His shoulder. And His name will be called Wonderful, Counselor, Mighty God, Everlasting Father, **Prince of Peace**.[7] Of the increase of His government and peace there will be no end, upon the throne of David and over His kingdom, to order it and establish it with judgment and justice from that time forward, even forever. The zeal of the LORD of hosts will perform this.

Zechariah 9:10 - I will cut off the chariot from Ephraim and the horse from Jerusalem; the battle bow shall be cut off. **He shall speak peace to the nations**; His dominion shall be 'from sea to sea, and from the River to the ends of the earth.'

Micah 5:5 - And this **One shall be peace**...

Yahshua became our peace offering.
Peace offerings were sacrificial offerings of thanksgiving, vows or voluntary offerings made by high priests on behalf of the people. They along with other types of

offerings, were used to get Yahweh's attention, acceptance, forgiveness and to solicit an answer or a sign from Him.
Ezekiel 45:15 - And **one lamb** shall be given from a flock of two hundred, from the rich pastures of Israel. These shall be for grain offerings, burnt offerings, and **peace offerings**, to make atonement for them," says the Lord GOD.
1 Chronicles 21:26 - And David built there an altar to the LORD, and offered burnt offerings and **peace offerings**, and called on the LORD; and **He answered him from heaven by fire** on the altar of burnt offering.
Ezekiel 43:27 - When these days are over it shall be, on the eighth day and thereafter, that the priests shall offer your burnt offerings and your **peace offerings on the altar; and I will accept you**,' says the Lord GOD."

Yahshua is the Lamb that was slain for us! John writes in Revelation 5:11-12, *"Then I looked, and I heard the voice of many angels around the throne, the living creatures, and the elders; and the number of them was ten thousand times ten thousand, and thousands of thousands, saying with a loud voice:* **"Worthy is the Lamb who was slain** *to receive power and riches and wisdom, and strength and honor and glory and blessing!"*

Christ's blood brought us peace, by reconciling us to Yahweh.
Isaiah 53:5 - But He was wounded for our transgressions, He was bruised for our iniquities; the chastisement for our peace was upon Him, and by
His stripes we are healed.
Colossians 1:20 - and by Him to reconcile all things to Himself, by Him, whether things on earth or things in heaven, having made peace through the blood of His cross.
Romans 5:1 - Therefore, having been justified by faith, we have peace with God through our Lord Jesus Christ,

Ephesians 2:14-15 - For He Himself is our peace, who has made both one, and has broken down the middle wall of separation, 15 having abolished in His flesh the enmity, that is, the law of commandments contained in ordinances, so as to create in Himself one new man from the two, thus making peace,

Yahweh sent His only begotten son, born of a virgin, to live a sinless life in the Earth for just over 33 years. Yahshua modeled the Father in all He said and did. We have a perfect example through Christ laying down His life, being beaten and bruised for our sins and diseases, dying on a cross; then 3 days later our Heavenly Father raised Him from the dead, so we could have everlasting life with Him. This message of peace is the Good News, the Gospel, we are called to share with others.

Nahum 1:15 - Behold, on the mountains the *feet of him who brings good tidings, who proclaims peace!* O Judah, keep your appointed feasts, perform your vows. For the wicked one shall no more pass through you; He is utterly cut off.

Isaiah 52:7 - How beautiful upon the mountains are the *feet of him who brings good news, who proclaims peace,* Who brings glad tidings of good *things,* Who proclaims salvation, Who says to Zion, "Your God reigns!" (The Apostle Paul quotes this in Romans 10:15)

Luke 2:14 - "Glory to God in highest, and on earth peace, goodwill toward men!"

Acts 10:36 - The word which *God* sent to the children of Israel, *preaching peace* through Jesus Christ—He is Lord of all—

Ephesians 2:17 - And He came and *preached peace to you* who were afar off and to those who were near.

Yahweh's message of peace and salvation being carried and delivered by us is beautiful to the Lord. As Believers in Christ we not only produce peace as a fruit, but we are to wear peace as our shoes. According to Ephesians 6:15, these shoes fully prepare us for spiritual battle, *"and having shod your feet with the preparation of the gospel of peace;"* Yahweh affirmed in Joshua 1:3, *"Every place that the sole of your foot will tread upon I have given you, as I said to Moses."* Our feet represent authority. **To walk in Yahweh's authority, we must be fully convinced that we are in Him and He is in us. In that place of assurance, we experience His peace that passes all understanding and are positioned strategically to take authority over the enemy of our souls.** Peace is an environment where we do not fear retaliation or abandonment by God; we don't question whether we are in the center of His will, even though the ground may be crumbling beneath us. We have the still confidence in our souls that Yahweh is for us and with us.

1 Corinthians 14:33 tells us, *"For God is not the author of confusion but of peace, as in all the churches of the saints."* We must be cautious of those who cunningly deceive the Body of Christ by twisting the Word of God for their own gain and our demise. Solomon warns in Proverbs 12:20, *"Deceit is in the heart of those who devise evil, But counselors of peace have joy."* Paul urges in Romans 16:17-20, *"Now I urge you, brethren, note those who cause divisions and offenses, contrary to the doctrine which you learned, and avoid them. [18] For those who are such do not serve our Lord Jesus Christ, but their own belly, and by smooth words and flattering speech deceive the hearts of the simple. [19] For your obedience has become known to all. Therefore I am glad on your behalf; but I want you to be wise in what is good, and simple concerning evil.* **[20] And the God of peace will crush Satan under your feet shortly**. *The grace of our Lord Jesus Christ be with you. Amen."* The enemy of our souls tries to rob us of our peace, but our God of Peace will crush him under our feet. We have the VICTORY! HALLELUAH!

In the natural, when pruning trees we remove dead, damaged and diseased branches in order to prevent insect and decay organisms from entering the tree. For us to have fewer "disease problems", we must prune the tree of our lives in order for the fruit of peace to be readily available to all those we come in contact with. Let's allow Yahweh to cut away some things.

CULTIVATING THE FRUIT OF PEACE

1. REMOVE HATRED FROM YOUR HEART
Genesis 37:4 - But when his brothers saw that their father loved him more than all his brothers, they hated him and could not speak peaceably to him.

2. ELIMINATE THE EVIL IN YOUR HEART
Psalm 28:3 - Do not take me away with the wicked and with the workers of iniquity, who speak peace to their neighbors, but evil is in their hearts.
Psalm 34:14 - Depart from evil and do good; Seek peace and pursue it.
Jeremiah 9:8 - Their tongue is an arrow shot out; it speaks deceit; one speaks peaceably to his neighbor with his mouth, but in his heart he lies in wait.
Deuteronomy 29:19 - and so it may not happen, when he hears the words of this curse, that he blesses himself in his heart, saying, 'I shall have peace, even though I follow the dictates of my heart' as though the drunkard could be included with the sober.
Isaiah 48:22 - "There is no peace," says the LORD, "for the wicked."
1 Peter 3:11 - Let him turn away from evil and do good; let him seek peace and pursue it.

3. DO NOT FOLLOW THOSE WHO HATE PEACE
Isaiah 59:8 - The way of peace they have not known, And there is no justice in their ways; they have made themselves crooked paths; whoever takes that way shall not know peace.

<u>Psalm 35:20</u> - For they do not speak peace, but they devise deceitful matters against the quiet ones in the land.

<u>Psalm 120:6-7</u> - My soul has dwelt too long with one who hates peace. ⁷ I am for peace; but when I speak, they are for war.

Yahweh offers, *"Or let him take hold of My strength, that he may make peace with Me; and he shall make peace with Me."* (Isaiah 27:5)

Let's pray.
Heavenly Father, I invite you to prune the branches in my life that bear bad fruit. Cultivate the soil of my soul. Like Joseph's brothers, there have been times that I have been envious and unable to speak peaceably with others because of the hatred in my heart. I repent and renounce to envy and hate and ask that you replace it with your love. I repent for the wickedness in my heart and for the deception on my tongue. I renounce to wickedness and deception and ask that you replace it with your righteousness and truth. I repent for anytime I have hated peace and for choosing friends who hate peace. Please fill me with Your Peace and surround me with those who love Your peace as I take hold of your strength, in Yahshua's name. Amen.

Peace is developed in our lives when we set our mind on the things of the Spirit.
What we think about and meditate on controls the direction and quality of our lives. Romans 8:6 teaches, *"For to be carnally minded is death, but to be spiritually minded is life and peace."* Isaiah 26:3 speaks of Yahweh, *"You will keep him in perfect peace, whose mind is stayed on You, because he trusts in You."* When a negative thought pops in your mind, do not meditate on it, expel it by replacing it with Yahweh's truth from His Word. Since we live in a society where information is at our fingertips, it is possible to get information on any

subject of interest within minutes. How we process the information is critical to our peace of mind. Every thought and teaching must align with and come under subjection to Yahshua. We are told about the use of our spiritual weapons in 2 Corinthians 10:5, *"casting down arguments and every high thing that exalts itself against the knowledge of God, bringing every thought into captivity to the obedience of Christ,"* Peter decreed a blessing over those who grow in the knowledge of God in 2 Peter 1:2, *"Grace and peace be multiplied to you in the knowledge of God and of Jesus our Lord,"*.

Paul writes in Romans 14:19, *"Therefore let us pursue the things which make for peace and the things by which one may edify another."* Hebrews 12:14 encourages us to, *"Pursue peace with all people, and holiness, without which no one will see the Lord:"* 2 Timothy 2:22 teaches, *"Flee also youthful lusts; but pursue righteousness, faith, love, peace with those who call on the Lord out of a pure heart."* We must have the courage to run away from the sinful desires of the flesh and pursue righteous living which produces a peaceful life.

<u>James 3:18</u> - Now the *fruit of righteousness is sown in peace* by those who make peace.

<u>Psalm 85:10</u> - Mercy and truth have met together; *righteousness and peace have kissed.*

<u>Isaiah 32:17-18</u> - The *work of righteousness will be peace*, and the effect of righteousness, quietness and assurance forever. My people will dwell in a peaceful habitation, in secure dwellings, and in quiet resting places,

<u>Hebrews 12:11</u> - Now no chastening seems to be joyful for the present, but painful; nevertheless, afterward it yields the *peaceable fruit of righteousness* to those who have been trained by it.

<u>Isaiah 38:17</u> - Indeed it was for my own peace that I had great bitterness; but You have lovingly delivered my soul from the pit of corruption, for You have cast all my sins behind Your back.

When we obey Yahweh and walk righteously before Him, He speaks His peace over our lives.
Philippians 4:9 - The things which you learned and received and heard and saw in me, these do, and the God of peace will be with you.
Psalm 37:37 - Mark the blameless man, and observe the upright; for the future of that man is peace.
Psalm 85:8 - will hear what God the LORD will speak, for He will speak peace to His people and to His saints; but let them not turn back to folly.
Psalm 119:165 - Great peace have those who love Your law, and nothing causes them to stumble.
Proverbs 3:1-2 - My son, do not forget my law, but let your heart keep my commands; for length of days and long life and peace they will add to you.
Proverbs 16:7 - When a man's ways please the LORD, He makes even his enemies to be at peace with him.
Mark 5:34 - And He said to her, "Daughter, your faith has made you well. Go in peace, and be healed of your affliction."

What do you think peace tastes like to those who eat of this fruit that is produced by the Spirit of Yahweh?

Our acts of kindness extends peace to others.
In James' discussion on faith and works he writes in James 2:16, *"-and one of you says to them, "Depart in peace, be warmed and filled," but you do not give them the things which are needed for the body, what does it profit?"* We offer peace to an individual when we allow our Heavenly Father to use us to meet their needs. It is not enough for us to wish someone well, when we have the ability to assist them. As that need is met, that momentary stress, anxiety and fear disappears and peace of mind returns.

Our prayers extend peace to others.
The scripture instructs us to pray for the peace of Jerusalem (Psalm 122:6-7), peace for our cities

(Jeremiah 29:7), and to pray for all people and leaders so we can live peaceful lives (1 Timothy 2:2).

Therefore I exhort first of all that supplications, prayers, intercessions, and giving of thanks be made for all men, 2 for kings and all who are in authority, **that we may lead a quiet and peaceable life in all godliness and reverence.** *3 For this is good and acceptable in the sight of God our Savior, 4 who desires all men to be saved and to come to the knowledge of the truth. 5 For there is one God and one Mediator between God and men, the Man Christ Jesus, 6 who gave Himself a ransom for all, to be testified in due time, 7 for which I was appointed a preacher and an apostle—I am speaking the truth in Christ and not lying—a teacher of the Gentiles in faith and truth. 8 I desire therefore that the men pray everywhere, lifting up holy hands,* **without wrath and doubting***;* (1 Timothy 2:1-8)

Living a life of peace, extends peace to others.
By living lives free of fear, confusion and controversy we are setting an example to others and bringing peace to our territories. Romans 12:18 instructs, *"If it is possible, as much as depends on you, live peaceably with all men."*
Proverbs 11:12 - He who is devoid of wisdom despises his neighbor, but a man of understanding holds his peace.
Matthew 5:9 -Blessed are the peacemakers, for they shall be called sons of God.
2 Peter 3:14 - Therefore, beloved, looking forward to these things, be diligent to be found by Him in peace, without spot and blameless;
Joshua 9:15 - So Joshua made peace with them, and made a covenant with them to let them live; and the rulers of the congregation swore to them.
Mark 9:50 - Salt is good, but if the salt loses its flavor, how will you season it? Have salt in yourselves, and have peace with one another."

Luke 1:79 - To give light to those who sit in darkness and the shadow of death, to guide our feet into the way of peace."
Luke 10:5-6 - But whatever house you enter, first say, 'Peace to this house.' 6 And if a son of peace is there, your peace will rest on it; if not, it will return to you.
2 Corinthians 13:11 - Finally, brethren, farewell. Become complete. Be of good comfort, be of one mind, live in peace; and the God of love and peace will be with you.
Colossians 3:15 - And let the peace of God rule in your hearts, to which also you were called in one body; and be thankful.
1 Thessalonians 5:13 - and to esteem them very highly in love for their work's sake. Be at peace among yourselves.
Ephesians 4:3 - endeavoring to keep the unity of the Spirit in the bond of peace.

Peace is the glue that causes us to stick together and be one in Christ.

The road that allows for edification and improvement to occur in each of our lives will lead to the elimination of argument and strife with each other. Solomon explains it this way in Proverbs 27:17, *"As iron sharpens iron, so a man sharpens the countenance of his friend."* To sharpen the countenance of those around us, we need wisdom! Often times in our quest to prove our points of view we push people away from God because we always want to have the last word. Ask Yahweh for His wisdom. In His wisdom we know when to speak and when to be silent. Yahshua modeled this perfectly, from the time of His arrest to the time of His death. Yahweh's wisdom produces peace.
Proverbs 3:17 - Her ways are ways of pleasantness, and all her paths are peace.
Proverbs 17:28 - Even a fool is counted wise when he holds his peace; when he shuts his lips, he is considered

perceptive.

Proverbs 29:9 - If a wise man contends with a foolish man, whether the fool rages or laughs, there is no peace.

James 3:17 - But the wisdom that is from above is first pure, then peaceable, gentle, willing to yield, full of mercy and good fruits, without partiality and without hypocrisy.

Let us ask our Heavenly Father to give us His love for peace. Zechariah 8:19 records, "Thus says the LORD of hosts: The fast of the fourth month, the fast of the fifth, the fast of the seventh, and the fast of the tenth, shall be joy and gladness and cheerful feasts for the house of Judah. Therefore love truth and peace.'

Yahweh's peace is available 100% of the time. His Peace brings us victory in and through every trial. His peace equips us to obey Him and produces every good thing in our lives through Yahshua, our Lord.

Now may the **God of peace who brought up our Lord Jesus from the dead**, *that great Shepherd of the sheep, through the blood of the everlasting covenant,* ²¹ **make you complete in every good work to do His will**, *working in you what is well pleasing in His sight, through Jesus Christ, to whom be glory forever and ever. Amen.*
Hebrews 13:20-21

Now may the **God of peace Himself sanctify you completely**; *and may your whole spirit, soul, and body be preserved blameless at the coming of our Lord Jesus Christ.* ²⁴ *He who calls you is faithful, who also will do it. 1 Thessalonians 5:23-24*

CHAPTER EIGHT
Developing: Longsuffering/Patience
Therefore, as the elect of God, holy and beloved, put on tender mercies, kindness, humility, meekness, longsuffering;
Colossians 3:12

This next fruit we will discuss is *Makrothymia*. In Galatians 5:22, this Greek word is translated as longsuffering or patience, depending on your preferred translation of the Bible. In other scripture passages it is translated as endurance, constancy, steadfastness, perseverance, forbearance, and slowness in avenging wrongs. The sufferings and challenges that produce patience are the sour times in our lives. I sought out a fruit that by its very name, created a clear picture of the journey the development of this fruit takes on. I chose the delicious Soursop. Like longsuffering, the outside of the Soursop's bitter skin is covered in prickles that soften once ripened. Although longsuffering can be a bitter process, it should not make you a bitter person. As you cut pass the bitter skin, inside this tropical fruit you'll enjoy a creamy, white, sweet somewhat tangy pulp, filled with multiple medicinal properties. It is believed by many, although not yet proven medically, to aid in the cure of cancer.

To avoid the Soursop from becoming badly bruised, this fruit is usually harvested while still green. Once it ripens, if it falls from the tree it will become damaged. Our falls, failures, tribulations and hardships can leave us badly bruised and damaged. Yahshua still carried the scars of his crucifixion after He was resurrected. John 20:27 records, *"Then He said to Thomas, "Reach your finger here, and look at My hands; and reach your hand here, and put it into My side. Do not be unbelieving, but believing."*

Our desire for patience seems to unleash numerous trials that expose how short tempered, hasty and anxious we truly are. This is because, the fruit of patience is only evidenced in our lives during times of waiting on Yahweh to rescue, provide for or answer us; during times of great trials, challenging circumstances and when we are tempted to handle situations on our own, without His guidance. We must not succumb to our flesh's impatience, but to the Spirit of Yahweh. Each time we choose to bear provocation, annoyance, hardship, or pain, **without complaint, loss of temper, irritation, or the like**, the fruit called patience, continues to grow into a luscious sweet nutritional meal for those around us.

As with each fruit, we look to our Heavenly Father as our example on how to live patient lives. As we read through several Biblical accounts, we will see the frequency that Yahweh's patience was tested by the rebellious doubtful hearts of His children. **When was the last time you tested His patience?**
Psalm 78:41 - Yes, again and again they tempted God, and limited the Holy One of Israel.
Psalm 95:9 - When your fathers tested Me; they tried Me, though they saw My work.
Psalm 106:14 -But lusted exceedingly in the wilderness, and tested God in the desert.

Isaiah 7:13 - Then he said, "Hear now, O house of David! Is it a small thing for you to weary men, but will you weary my God also?
Hebrews 3:9 - Where your fathers tested Me, tried Me, and saw My works forty years.

Peter reminds us in 2 Peter 3:15, *"and consider that the longsuffering of our Lord is salvation—as also our beloved brother Paul, according to the wisdom given to him, has written to you,"*. It is Yahweh's patience that gives us time to repent and leads us to His salvation.
Numbers 14:18 - The LORD is longsuffering and abundant in mercy, forgiving iniquity and transgression; but He by no means clears the guilty, visiting the iniquity of the fathers on the children to the third and fourth generation.'
Psalm 86:15 - But You, O Lord, are a God full of compassion, and gracious, longsuffering and abundant in mercy and truth.
2 Peter 3:9 - The Lord is not slack concerning His promise, as some count slackness, but is longsuffering toward us, not willing that any should perish but that all should come to repentance.
Romans 2:4 - Or do you despise the riches of His goodness, forbearance, and longsuffering, not knowing that the goodness of God leads you to repentance?
Hebrews 2:9-18 - But we see Jesus, who was made a little lower than the angels, for the *suffering of death crowned with glory and honor*, that He, by the grace of God, might taste death for everyone. 10 For it was fitting for Him, for whom are all things and by whom are all things, in bringing many sons to glory, *to make the captain of their salvation perfect through sufferings.* 11 For both He who sanctifies and those who are being sanctified are all of one, for which reason He is not ashamed to call them brethren, 12 saying: "I will declare Your name to My brethren; In the midst of the assembly I will sing praise to You." 13 And again: "I will put My trust in Him." And again: "Here am I and the children

whom God has given Me." ¹⁴ Inasmuch then as the children have partaken of flesh and blood, He Himself likewise shared in the same, that through death He might destroy him who had the power of death, that is, the devil, ¹⁵ and release those who through fear of death were all their lifetime subject to bondage. ¹⁶ For indeed He does not give aid to angels, but He does give aid to the seed of Abraham. ¹⁷ Therefore, in all things He had to be made like His brethren, that He might be a merciful and faithful High Priest in things *pertaining* to God, to make propitiation for the sins of the people.¹⁸ *For in that He Himself has suffered, being tempted, He is able to aid those who are tempted.*

As our Savior, Yahshua was dying on a cross, he prayed Psalm 22:1. As we meditate on the entire Psalm, let us allow Holy Spirit to prepare our hearts to embrace longsuffering.
My God, My God, why have You forsaken Me? Why are You so far from helping Me, and from the words of My groaning? ² *O My God, I cry in the daytime, but You do not hear; and in the night season, and am not silent.* ³ *But You are holy, Enthroned in the praises of Israel.* ⁴ *Our fathers trusted in You; they trusted, and You delivered them.* ⁵ *They cried to You, and were delivered; they trusted in You, and were not ashamed.* ⁶ *But I am a worm, and no man; A reproach of men, and despised by the people.* ⁷ *All those who see Me ridicule Me; They shoot out the lip, they shake the head, saying,* ⁸ *"He trusted in the* LORD, *let Him rescue Him; let Him deliver Him, since He delights in Him!"* ⁹ *But You are He who took Me out of the womb; You made Me trust while on My mother's breasts.* ¹⁰ *I was cast upon You from birth. From My mother's womb You have been My God.* ¹¹ *Be not far from Me, for trouble is near; for there is none to help.* ¹² *Many bulls have surrounded Me; Strong bulls of Bashan have encircled Me.* ¹³ *They gape at Me with their mouths, like a raging and roaring lion.* ¹⁴ *I am poured out like water, and all My bones are out of joint; My heart is like wax; It has*

melted within Me. ⁱ⁵ My strength is dried up like a potsherd, And My tongue clings to My jaws; You have brought Me to the dust of death. ¹⁶ For dogs have surrounded Me; The congregation of the wicked has enclosed Me. They pierced My hands and My feet; ¹⁷ I can count all My bones. They look and stare at Me. ¹⁸ They divide My garments among them, And for My clothing they cast lots. ¹⁹ But You, O LORD, do not be far from Me; O My Strength, hasten to help Me! ²⁰ Deliver Me from the sword, My precious life from the power of the dog. ²¹ Save Me from the lion's mouth and from the horns of the wild oxen! You have answered Me. **²² I will declare Your name to My brethren; In the midst of the assembly I will praise You. ²³ You who fear the LORD, praise Him! All you descendants of Jacob, glorify Him, and fear Him, all you offspring of Israel! ²⁴ For He has not despised nor abhorred the affliction of the afflicted; nor has He hidden His face from Him; But when He cried to Him, He heard. ²⁵ My praise shall be of You in the great assembly; I will pay My vows before those who fear Him.** ²⁶ The poor shall eat and be satisfied; those who seek Him will praise the LORD. Let your heart live forever! ²⁷ All the ends of the world shall remember and turn to the LORD, and all the families of the nations shall worship before You. ²⁸ For the kingdom is the LORD's, and He rules over the nations. ²⁹ All the prosperous of the earth shall eat and worship; all those who go down to the dust shall bow before Him, even he who cannot keep himself alive. ³⁰ A posterity shall serve Him. It will be recounted of the Lord to the next generation, ³¹ they will come and declare His righteousness to a people who will be born, that He has done this.

Because Christ suffered, we will suffer for doing what is right in the eyes of Yahweh and strange in the eyes of unbelievers. We need the mind of Christ to endure the process of the development of this fruit. Our flesh does not want to die to its sinful nature, yet nothing crucifies the flesh more effectively than suffering. Be encouraged by the wonderful results of Yahshua's suffering, as you read 1 Peter 3:13-22.

And who is he who will harm you if you become followers of what is good? **14 But even if you should suffer for righteousness' sake, you are blessed. "And do not be afraid of their threats, nor be troubled."** *15 But sanctify the Lord God in your hearts, and always be ready to give a defense to everyone who asks you a reason for the hope that is in you, with meekness and fear;* **16 having a good conscience, that when they defame you as evildoers, those who revile your good conduct in Christ may be ashamed. 17 For it is better, if it is the will of God, to suffer for doing good than for doing evil. 18 For Christ also suffered once for sins, the just for the unjust, that He might bring us to God, being put to death in the flesh but made alive by the Spirit,** *19 by whom also He went and preached to the spirits in prison, 20 who formerly were disobedient, when once the Divine longsuffering waited in the days of Noah, while the ark was being prepared, in which a few, that is, eight souls, were saved through water.21 There is also an antitype which now saves us—baptism (not the removal of the filth of the flesh, but the answer of a good conscience toward God), through the resurrection of Jesus Christ, 22 who has gone into heaven and is at the right hand of God, angels and authorities and powers having been made subject to Him.*

Paul writes in 1 Timothy 1:16, *"However, for this reason I obtained mercy, that in me first Jesus Christ might show all longsuffering, as a pattern to those who are going to believe on Him for everlasting life."* Paul described his suffering for Christ as a pattern that would be modeled for future believers. He explains that Yahweh gave him MERCY to endure the journey of longsuffering. In 2 Corinthians 12:7-10 Paul informs us that Yahweh's GRACE was also given, *"And lest I should be exalted above measure by the abundance of the revelations, a thorn in the flesh was given to me, a messenger of Satan to buffet me, lest I be exalted above measure. 8 Concerning this thing I pleaded with the Lord three times that it might depart from me. 9 And He said to me, "My grace is sufficient for you, for My strength is made perfect in weakness." Therefore most gladly I will rather boast in my infirmities, that the power of Christ may rest upon me. 10 Therefore I take pleasure in infirmities, in reproaches, in needs, in persecutions, in distresses, for Christ's sake. For when I am weak, then I am strong."*

We note from Paul that the thorn was given to keep him humble. In Ecclesiastes 7:8 , Solomon teaches us that patience is better than pride, *"The end of a thing is better than its beginning; the patient in spirit is better than the proud in spirit."* The Hebrew word used here is *arek*, meaning patient, slow to anger. I had never thought to compare a patient spirit to a proud spirit, it implies that a patient person is humble and slow to anger, while an impatient person is a *gabah* (in Hebrew), one who is high or proud, showing arrogant superiority to and disdain of those one views as unworthy. 1 Peter 5:5-11 instructs us that Yahweh gives grace to the humble and resist the proud, therefore we must clothe ourselves in humility.

Likewise you younger people, submit yourselves to your elders. Yes, all of you be submissive to one another, and be clothed with humility, for "God resists the proud, but gives grace to the humble." 6 Therefore humble yourselves under the mighty hand of God, that He may exalt you in due time, 7 casting all your care upon Him, for He cares for you. 8 **Be sober, be vigilant; because your adversary the devil walks about like a roaring lion, seeking whom he may devour. 9 Resist him, steadfast in the faith, knowing that the same sufferings are experienced by your brotherhood in the world. 10 But may the God of all grace, who called us to His eternal glory by Christ**

Jesus, after you have suffered a while, perfect, establish, strengthen, and settle you. ¹¹ *To Him be the glory and the dominion forever and ever. Amen.*

I love that our Heavenly Father wastes absolutely nothing. After we have suffered a while, He in His grace PERFECTS US, ESTABLISHES US, STRENGTHENS US and SETTLES US! We must hold onto this promise when we go through trials and tribulations. Please join me in prayer.

Heavenly Father,
As I look to you and your Son, as my example of longsuffering, I ask you for Your MERCY and GRACE needed for this fruit to be developed in my life. I repent for giving pride and impatience a seat of honor in my heart, today I dethrone and renounce pride and impatience, and invite you to replace it with your patience and humility. Thank you for giving me the courage and joy to submit to your will in the mighty name of Yahshua, Amen.

In chapter six we spoke about rejoicing while suffering for the sake of righteousness; we are further challenged to be patient during these times. Paul instructs us on being a Living Sacrifice to God in Romans 12:12 he writes, *"-rejoicing in hope, patient in tribulation, continuing steadfastly in prayer;"* 1 Peter 2:18-25 instructs, *"Servants, be submissive to your masters with all fear, not only to the good and gentle, but also to the harsh.* ¹⁹ *For this is commendable, if because of conscience toward God one endures grief, suffering wrongfully.* ²⁰ *For what credit is it if, when you are beaten for your faults, you take it patiently?* ***But when you do good and suffer, if you take it patiently, this is commendable before God.*** ²¹ ***For to this you were called, because Christ also suffered for us, leaving us an example, that you should follow His steps:*** ²² *"Who committed no sin, nor was deceit found in His* mouth"; ²³ *who, when He was reviled, did not revile in return;* **when He suffered, He did not threaten, but committed Himself to Him who judges righteously;** ²⁴ *who Himself bore our sins in His own body on the tree, that we, having died to sins, might live for righteousness —by whose stripes you were healed.* ²⁵ *For you were like sheep going astray, but have now returned to the Shepherd and Overseer of your souls."*

Our Lord Yahshua, teaches us in Matthew 5:10-12, *"Blessed are those who are persecuted for righteousness sake, for theirs is the kingdom of heaven.* ¹¹ *"Blessed are you when they revile and persecute you, and say all kinds of evil against you falsely for My sake.* ¹² *Rejoice and be exceedingly glad, for great is your reward in heaven, for so they persecuted the prophets who were before you."* It is a blessing to be persecuted for the sake of Christ, our reward is the Kingdom of Heaven. In so many ways we are challenged to elevate our mindsets by humbling ourselves to receive this teaching. It is more comfortable to hear a Gospel that only promises you good things now, with no hardships to endure. Yes, Christ promises abundant life in Him now and eternal life, but our death to our flesh is required of us. In Philippians 1:29-30, Paul tells us, *"For to you it has been granted on behalf of Christ, not only to believe in Him, but also to suffer for His sake,* ³⁰ *having the same conflict which you saw in me and now hear is in me."*

Peter further explains in 1 Peter 4:1-6; 12-19.
Therefore, **since Christ suffered for us in the flesh, arm yourselves also with the same mind, for he who has suffered in the flesh has ceased from sin,** ² **that he no longer should live the rest of his time in the flesh for the lusts of men, but for the will of God.** ³ *For we have spent enough of our past lifetime in doing the will of the Gentiles—when we walked in lewdness, lusts, drunkenness, revelries, drinking parties, and abominable idolatries.* ⁴ *In regard*

to these, they think it strange that you do not run with them in the same flood of dissipation, speaking evil of you. ⁵ They will give an account to Him who is ready to judge the living and the dead. ⁶ For this reason the gospel was preached also to those who are dead, that they might be judged according to men in the flesh, but live according to God in the spirit. **¹² Beloved, do not think it strange concerning the fiery trial which is to try you, as though some strange thing happened to you; ¹³ but rejoice to the extent that you partake of Christ's sufferings, that when His glory is revealed, you may also be glad with exceeding joy.** ¹⁴ If you are reproached for the name of Christ, blessed are you, for the Spirit of glory and of God rests upon you. On their part He is blasphemed, but on your part He is glorified. **¹⁵ But let none of you suffer as a murderer, a thief, an evildoer, or as a busybody in other people's matters. ¹⁶ Yet if anyone suffers as a Christian, let him not be ashamed, but let him glorify God in this matter.** ¹⁷ For the time has come for judgment to begin at the house of God; and if it begins with us first, what will be the end of those who do not obey the gospel of God? ¹⁸ Now "If the righteous one is scarcely saved, where will the ungodly and the sinner appear?" **¹⁹ Therefore let those who suffer according to the will of God commit their souls to Him in doing good, as to a faithful Creator.**

Paul declared in Philippians 3:7-8, "But what things were gain to me, these I have counted loss for Christ. ⁸ Yet indeed I also count all things loss for the excellence of the knowledge of Christ Jesus my Lord, for whom I have suffered the loss of all things, and count them as rubbish, that I may gain Christ". Heavenly Father please give us the endurance spoken of in Hebrews 10:32-37, "But recall the former days in which, after you were illuminated, you endured a great struggle with sufferings: ³³ partly while you were made a spectacle both by reproaches and tribulations, and partly while *you became companions of those who were so treated; ³⁴ for you had compassion on me in my chains, and joyfully accepted the plundering of your goods, knowing that you have a better and an enduring possession for yourselves in heaven. ³⁵ Therefore do not cast away your confidence, which has great reward. ³⁶For you have need of endurance, so that after you have done the will of God, you may receive the promise:"*

In Chapter 5, I began to share a very special dream with you. Here is its continuation.

In the dream, it was hidden from me what I saw and heard when I felt my spirit separate from my body and go up with Yahshua, from where I saw Him first appear. The next thing I remember is seeing my lifeless body hanging over the chair that faced the window, when suddenly my spirit was placed back into it. I could feel the weight of the flesh. It took all of my strength to lift my body from the chair. There were three things I repeated several times in this dream.
1st- I just had an Encounter with Jesus!
2nd- Jesus put something inside of me!
3rd- Jesus is Coming Soon!

Later that day, I asked the Lord, why He allowed me to have this encounter with Him. He took me to Acts 7, where Stephen is martyred for sharing His faith in Yahshua. Acts 7:54-60 records,
*When they heard these things they were cut to the heart, and they gnashed at him with their teeth. ⁵⁵ But **he, being full of the Holy Spirit, gazed into heaven and saw the glory of God, and Jesus standing at the right hand of God,** ⁵⁶ and said, "Look! I see the heavens opened and the Son of Man standing at the right hand of God!" ⁵⁷ Then they cried out with a loud voice, stopped their ears, and ran at him with one accord; ⁵⁸ and they cast him out of the city and stoned him. And the witnesses laid down their clothes at the feet of a young*

man named Saul. ⁵⁹ And they stoned Stephen as he was calling on God and saying, "Lord Jesus, receive my spirit." **⁶⁰ Then he knelt down and cried out with a loud voice, "Lord, do not charge them with this sin." And when he had said this, he fell asleep.**

The Lord explained to me, that many stones are going to be thrown at the body of Christ in the United States of America and there are two things that we must do.
1. We must keep our eyes fixed on Yahshua.
2. We must maintain hearts of forgiveness, or else we will become like the ones who are throwing the stones.

Are you ready for the stones to be thrown?
We must hold on to Romans 5:3-5, *"And not only that, but we also glory in tribulations, knowing that tribulation produces perseverance; and perseverance, character; and character, hope. ⁵ Now hope does not disappoint, because the love of God has been poured out in our hearts by the Holy Spirit who was given to us."*

The Apostle Paul, whose former name was Saul, was the same young man who witnessed and approved the stoning of Stephen, before Paul himself had an encounter with Christ. He writes in Romans 8:18-25, **¹⁸ For I consider that the sufferings of this present time are not worthy to be compared with the glory which shall be revealed in us.** *¹⁹ For the earnest expectation of the creation eagerly waits for the revealing of the sons of God. ²⁰ For the creation was subjected to futility, not willingly, but because of Him who subjected it in hope; ²¹ because the creation itself also will be delivered from the bondage of corruption into the glorious liberty of the children of God. ²² For we know that the whole creation groans and labors with birth pangs together until now. ²³ Not only that, but we also who have the first fruits of the Spirit, even we ourselves groan within ourselves, eagerly waiting for the adoption, the* *redemption of our body.* **²⁴ For we were saved in this hope, but hope that is seen is not hope; for why does one still hope for what he sees? ²⁵ But if we hope for what we do not see, we eagerly wait for it with perseverance.**

The minor suffering I have endured for Christ does not compare to those whose current suffering is on a much greater scale in the persecuted church across the globe. Paul describes his suffering and those ministering alongside him in 2 Corinthians 6:4-10, *"But in all things we commend ourselves as ministers of God: in much patience, in tribulations, in needs, in distresses,⁵ in stripes, in imprisonments, in tumults, in labors, in sleeplessness, in fastings; ⁶ by purity, by knowledge, by longsuffering, by kindness, by the Holy Spirit, by sincere love, ⁷ by the word of truth, by the power of God, by the armor of righteousness on the right hand and on the left, ⁸ by honor and dishonor, by evil report and good report; as deceivers, and yet true; ⁹ as unknown, and yet well known; as dying, and behold we live; as chastened, and yet not killed; ¹⁰ as sorrowful, yet always rejoicing; as poor, yet making many rich; as having nothing, and yet possessing all things."* He continues about himself in 2 Corinthians 11:23-28, *"Are they ministers of Christ?—I speak as a fool—I am more: in labors more abundant, in stripes above measure, in prisons more frequently, in deaths often. ²⁴ From the Jews five times I received forty stripes minus one.²⁵ Three times I was beaten with rods; once I was stoned; three times I was shipwrecked; a night and a day I have been in the deep; ²⁶ in journeys often, in perils of waters, in perils of robbers, in perils of my own countrymen, in perils of the Gentiles, in perils in the city, in perils in the wilderness, in perils in the sea, in perils among false brethren; ²⁷ in weariness and toil, in sleeplessness often, in hunger and thirst, in fastings often, in cold and nakedness ²⁸ besides the other things, what comes upon me daily: my deep concern for all the churches."*

As believers and followers of Christ, we are instructed to live lives with longsuffering and patience.

Ephesians 4:1-2 - I, therefore, the prisoner of the Lord, beseech you to walk worthy of the calling with which you were called, 2 with all lowliness and gentleness, with longsuffering, bearing with one another in love,

Titus 2:1-2 - But as for you, speak the things which are proper for sound doctrine: 2 that the older men be sober, reverent, temperate, sound in faith, in love, in patience;

2 Timothy 3:10 - But you have carefully followed my doctrine, manner of life, purpose, faith, longsuffering, love, perseverance,

2 Timothy 4:2 - Preach the word! Be ready in season and out of season. Convince, rebuke, exhort, with all longsuffering and teaching.

1 Thessalonians 5:14 - Now we exhort you, brethren, warn those who are unruly, comfort the fainthearted, uphold the weak, be patient with all.

Colossians 1:9-11 - For this reason we also, since the day we heard it, do not cease to pray for you, and to ask that you may be filled with the knowledge of His will in all wisdom and spiritual understanding; 10 that you may walk worthy of the Lord, fully pleasing Him, being fruitful in every good work and increasing in the knowledge of God; 11 strengthened with all might, according to His glorious power, for all patience and longsuffering with joy;

WAIT PATIENTLY ON GOD

We are all familiar with Abraham and how he waited for many years for God to fulfill His promise of a son. Abraham and Sarah did not give birth to Isaac until Abraham was 100 years old and Sarah was 90. Imagine how difficult it must have been for them to believe that Yahweh would fulfill His promise after Sarah was beyond child bearing years. Paul writes of Abraham in Hebrews 6:15, *"And so, after he had patiently endured, he obtained the promise."*

Psalm 37:7 - Rest in the LORD, and wait patiently for Him; do not fret because of him who prospers in his way, Because of the man who brings wicked schemes to pass.

Psalm 40:1 - "I waited patiently for the LORD; and He inclined to me, and heard my cry.

Romans 2:7 - eternal life to those who by patient continuance in doing good seek for glory, honor, and immortality;

James 5:7-12 - Therefore be patient, brethren, until the coming of the Lord. See how the farmer waits for the precious fruit of the earth, waiting patiently for it until it receives the early and latter rain. 8 You also be patient. Establish your hearts, for the coming of the Lord is at hand. 9 Do not grumble against one another, brethren, lest you be condemned. Behold, the Judge is standing at the door! 10 My brethren, take the prophets, who spoke in the name of the Lord, as an example of suffering and patience. 11 Indeed we count them blessed who endure. You have heard of the perseverance of Job and seen the end intended by the Lord—that the Lord is very compassionate and merciful. 12 But above all, my brethren, do not swear, either by heaven or by earth or with any other oath. But let your "Yes" be "Yes," and your "No," "No," lest you fall into judgment.

James speaks of Yahweh's kindness to Job after Job endured so much. Other prophets who suffered were: Moses with his murmuring followers, Hosea with his prostitute wife, Ezekiel as he mirrored the Israelites coming judgments, Jeremiah, known as the weeping prophet, and the list goes on. Yahweh used them so mightily in history through their suffering.

Think about all of the complaining you and I do when things don't turn out the way we plan. We get irritated when we are pulled from our comfort zones and thrown into a place of relying on Christ to truly be our daily bread, in the most literal sense. We must be careful not to become impatient with the promises of God on our lives. In 1 Samuel 13:8-14, we learn of how Saul's impatience cost him and his children the throne. *"Then he waited seven days, according to the time set by Samuel. But Samuel did not come to Gilgal; and the people were scattered from him. ⁹ So Saul said, "Bring a burnt offering and peace offerings here to me." And he offered the burnt offering. ¹⁰ Now it happened, as soon as he had finished presenting the burnt offering, that Samuel came; and Saul went out to meet him, that he might greet him. ¹¹ And Samuel said, "What have you done?" Saul said, "When I saw that the people were scattered from me, and that you did not come within the days appointed, and that the Philistines gathered together at Michmash, ¹² then I said, 'The Philistines will now come down on me at Gilgal, and I have not made supplication to the LORD.' Therefore I felt compelled, and offered a burnt offering."¹³ And Samuel said to Saul, "You have done foolishly. You have not kept the commandment of the LORD your God, which He commanded you. For now the LORD would have established your kingdom over Israel forever. ¹⁴ But now your kingdom shall not continue. The LORD has sought for Himself a man after His own heart, and the LORD has commanded him to be commander over His people, because you have not kept what the LORD commanded you."*

How often do you and I feel compelled to do something out of fear, worry or concern of what people think, say or do, instead of just resting patiently while waiting on God to fulfill His promises in our lives? Can you imagine the negative consequences and delays we have brought about in our own lives because of disobedience and impatience? When our hearts are truly after God we will obey even in times where it seems He's late in coming to our rescue. Remember the story of Lazarus? It really appeared that Christ came late. Usually I'll hear people say, "He comes on time, He'll show up at 11:59pm!" I always want to reply, "It feels like He shows up at 12:01am". In the case of Lazarus, He was four days late. I don't think Lazarus nor his sisters were expecting him to die, he was expecting his Friend and his Lord to heal him. Amazingly enough, Lazarus was healed, not the way he and his family thought it would happen, but the way Yahweh saw it fit to happen. He was raised from the dead!

WARNING! Our impatience with Yahweh will lead us to idolatry, it provokes us to find answers from sources outside of our Heavenly Father, which is seen in Exodus 32. *"Now when the people saw that Moses delayed coming down from the mountain, the people gathered together to Aaron, and said to him, "Come, make us gods that shall go before us; for as for this Moses, the man who brought us up out of the land of Egypt, we do not know what has become of him." 2 And Aaron said to them, "Break off the golden earrings which are in the ears of your wives, your sons, and your daughters, and bring them to me." 3 So all the people broke off the golden earrings which were in their ears, and brought them to Aaron. 4 And he received the gold from their hand, and he fashioned it with an engraving tool, and made a molded calf. Then they said, "This is your god, O Israel, that brought you out of the land of Egypt!" 5 So when Aaron saw it, he built an altar before it. And Aaron made a proclamation and said, "Tomorrow is a feast to the* LORD.*" 6 Then they rose early on the next day, offered burnt offerings, and brought peace offerings; and the people sat down to eat and drink, and rose up to play.* **7 And the** LORD **said to Moses, "Go, get down! For your people whom you brought out of the land of Egypt have corrupted themselves. 8 They have turned aside quickly out of the way which I commanded them. They have made themselves a molded calf, and worshiped it and sacrificed to it, and said, 'This is your god, O Israel, that brought you out of the land of Egypt!'"**

Although you and I may not be melting our jewelry and forming it into images we call god, we must examine ourselves and see if there is idolatry in our hearts. When Yahweh doesn't show up on your time frame, what measures do you take, to make something happen? Who do you call? Where do you go? Is Yahweh pleased when you plow forward without His presence? Our idols are anyone or anything we put before Yahweh. It's important to continue to trust God even when our hearts grow discouraged in times of waiting. Proverbs 16:9 explains, *"A man's heart plans his way, But the LORD directs his steps"* It's easier for patience to grow when we realize that God is in control!

Have you ever had a cashier tell you, "thank you for your patience"? He/ She is fully aware that something hindered you from getting your items paid for in a timelier manner, and it was his/her fault or the customer in front of you. You had a choice to act out inconsiderably, and behave as a tyrant, or to quietly stand, wait and pray for the peace of those around you. I realize that we all lead busy lives, we're always in a hurry and probably consider ourselves more important than we ought to; but the fruit of patience is a refreshing gift to those around us. Our afflictions, while they are there to mold us into the likeness of Christ, also help us to become compassionate for others. Through our own journeys we are able to comfort others in their times of tribulation. Paul tells us in Romans 15:4-6, *"For whatever things were written before were written for our learning, that we through the patience and comfort of the Scriptures might have hope. 5 Now may the God of patience and comfort grant you to be like-minded toward one another, according to Christ Jesus, 6 that you may with one mind and one mouth glorify the God and Father of our Lord Jesus Christ."*

As we meditate on 2 Corinthians 1:3-10, may the Lord give us the desire to comfort others in their time of trouble.

"Blessed be the God and Father of our Lord Jesus Christ, the Father of mercies and God of all comfort, ⁴ who comforts us in all our tribulation, that we may be able to comfort those who are in any trouble, with the comfort with which we ourselves are comforted by God. ⁵ For as the sufferings of Christ abound in us, so our consolation also abounds through Christ. ⁶ Now if we are afflicted, it is for your consolation and salvation, which is effective for enduring the same sufferings which we also suffer. Or if we are comforted, it is for your consolation and salvation. ⁷ And our hope for you is steadfast, because we know that as you are partakers of the sufferings, so also you will partake of the consolation. ⁸ For we do not want you to be ignorant, brethren, of our trouble which came to us in Asia: that we were burdened beyond measure, above strength, so that we despaired even of life. ⁹ Yes, we had the sentence of death in ourselves, that we should not trust in ourselves but in God who raises the dead, ¹⁰ who delivered us from so great a death, and does deliver us; in whom we trust that He will still deliver us"

Keep in my mind, our faith will be tested, and it is in these times of testing that the fruit of Patience is developed. James 1:2-4 explains, *"My brethren, count it all joy when you fall into various trials, ³ knowing that the testing of your faith produces patience.* **⁴ But let patience have its perfect work, that you may be perfect and complete, lacking nothing**.*"* Do not run in fear from the process, allow the Lord to complete the work He started in you.

Love suffers long and is kind...
1 Corinthians 13:4

CHAPTER NINE
Developing: Kindness
And be kind to one another, tenderhearted, forgiving one another, even as God in Christ forgave you.
Ephesians 4:32

The lovely papaya will be our representation of the spiritual fruit of Kindness. Our acts of kindness towards others should be as abundant as the hundreds of seeds contained in this mouthwatering fruit. Papaya is known to prevent cholesterol build up in our arteries, improve our digestion, and its' low sugar content makes it the perfect fruit for diabetics. While boosting our immunity, it keeps our eyes, bones, skin and hair healthy. Yahweh's kindness provokes us to want to experience more of Him and in that place of digesting His Word, we grow into the full experience of salvation. It is important to realize that when the Fruit of Kindness is developed in our lives, people begin to taste of the Lord through their experiences with us, and see that He is KIND! Psalm 117:2 proclaims, *"For His merciful kindness is great toward us, and the truth of the LORD endures forever. Praise the LORD!"*

Kindness is the quality of being friendly, generous, considerate, sympathetic and compassionate. Solomon tells us in Proverbs 19:22, *"What is desired in a man is kindness, and a poor man is better than a liar."* When I'm driving and indicate that I need to move over into the next lane, I always say a prayer for the person who lets me in. He/she would never know that prayers of salvation, protection and blessings were be spoken over their lives for their simple act of slowing down and letting me in. We all desire kindness from one another. It can be the simplest of gestures to the greatest, but each act of kindness allows us to believe in the potential that Yahweh has placed in humanity.

There are so many ways we can show kindness to one another. Scripture gives us many examples of how to exercise kindness. Read these with me;

SPEAK KINDLY TO OTHERS.
Genesis 50:21 - Now therefore, do not be afraid; I will provide for you and your little ones." And he comforted them and spoke kindly to them.
Ruth 2:13 - Then she said, "Let me find favor in your sight, my lord; for you have comforted me, and have spoken kindly to your maidservant, though I am not like one of your maidservants."
2 Kings 25:28 and Jeremiah 52:32 - He spoke kindly to him, and gave him a more prominent seat than those of the kings who were with him in Babylon.
Proverbs 31:26 - She opens her mouth with wisdom, and on her tongue is the law of kindness.

DISCIPLINE IS A KINDNESS.
Psalm 141:5 - Let the righteous strike me; it shall be a kindness. And let him rebuke me; it shall be as excellent oil; Let my head not refuse it. For still my prayer is against the deeds of the wicked.

KEEPING YOUR WORD IS A KINDNESS.
Genesis 47:29 - When the time drew near that Israel must die, he called his son Joseph and said to him, "Now if I have found favor in your sight, please put your hand under my thigh, and deal kindly and truly with me. Please do not bury me in Egypt,"

Have you said, or heard someone say, "It's nice to know there are still good people in the world." People long for a friendly smile, or an unexpected pass to cut you in line because they have two items and you have twenty. The person on crutches or in a wheel chair is grateful, that someone instinctively opens a door, without them having to ask. Just as papaya is the perfect balance of sweet, so a diabetic can consume it, and the avid sugar lover like myself can enjoy every bite; kindness adds the perfect amount of sweet to our days and someone else's. Our Heavenly Father's cup of undeserved kindness continually runs over into our lives, in turn we should pour it out and share it with others.

Genesis 24:12 -Then he said, "O LORD God of my master Abraham, please give me success this day, and show kindness to my master Abraham.

Genesis 24:14 - Now let it be that the young woman to whom I say, 'Please let down your pitcher that I may drink,' and she says, 'Drink, and I will also give your camels a drink'—let her be the one You have appointed for Your servant Isaac. And by this I will know that You have shown kindness to my master."

1 Kings 3:5-6 - At Gibeon the LORD appeared to Solomon in a dream by night; and God said, "Ask! What shall I give you?" 6 And Solomon said: "You have shown great mercy to Your servant David my father, because he walked before You in truth, in righteousness, and in uprightness of heart with You; You have continued this great kindness for him, and You have given him a son to sit on his throne, as it is this day.

Psalm 31:21 - Blessed be the LORD, for He has shown me His marvelous kindness in a strong city!

Isaiah 54:8 - With a little wrath I hid My face from you for a moment; but with everlasting kindness I will have mercy on you," says the LORD, your Redeemer.

Isaiah 54:10 - For the mountains shall depart and the hills be removed, but My kindness shall not depart from you, nor shall My covenant of peace be removed," says the LORD, who has mercy on you.

Joel 2:13 - So rend your heart, and not your garments; return to the LORD your God, for He is gracious and merciful, slow to anger, and of great kindness; and He relents from doing harm.

Ephesians 2:7 - that in the ages to come He might show the exceeding riches of His grace in His kindness toward us in Christ Jesus.

Nehemiah 9:17 - They refused to obey, and they were not mindful of Your wonders that You did among them. But they hardened their necks, and in their rebellion they appointed a leader to return to their bondage. But You are God, ready to pardon, gracious and merciful, slow to anger, abundant in kindness, and did not forsake them.

Titus 3:4-7 - But when the kindness and the love of God our Savior toward man appeared, 5 not by works of righteousness which we have done, but according to His mercy He saved us, through the washing of regeneration and renewing of the Holy Spirit, 6 whom He poured out on us abundantly through Jesus Christ our Savior, 7 that having been justified by His grace we should become heirs according to the hope of eternal life.

Thank you Father for Your great kindness and love! Even when I do not deserve it, you see fit to bless me anyway! Luke 6:35 speaks of Yahweh, *"...For He is kind to the unthankful and evil".* Job 6:14 tells, *"To him who is afflicted, kindness should be shown by his friend, even though he forsakes the fear of the Almighty."* The kindness that we show others should not be contingent on how they treat us, but on how Yahweh treats us. Paul instructs us in Romans 12:10 to, *"Be kindly affectionate to one another with brotherly love, in honor giving preference to one another;"* 2 Peter 1:7 urges, *"to godliness brotherly kindness, and to brotherly kindness love."*

Yahweh's Kindness is a comfort to us, and our kindness is a comfort to others. The psalmist prays in Psalm

119:76, *"Let, I pray, Your merciful kindness be for my comfort, according to Your word to Your servant.* In Acts 27 and 28 we read of the Apostle Paul's journey to Rome as a prisoner. Julius, the centurion who Paul and other prisoners had been delivered to, is spoken about in Acts 27:3, *"And the next day we landed at Sidon. And Julius treated Paul kindly and gave him liberty to go to his friends and receive care."* Later, Paul warned Julius and the others to stay docked and not sail through a storm, or they would have loss of lives and cargo. Julius chose to listen to the helmsman and owner of the ship. Many days later after much loss of cargo and days without eating, Paul stood among them, and said, *"and now I urge you to take heart, for there will be no loss of life among you, but only of the ship. 23 For there stood by me this night an angel of the God to whom I belong and whom I serve, 24 saying, 'Do not be afraid, Paul; you must be brought before Caesar; and indeed God has granted you all those who sail with you.' 25 Therefore take heart, men, for I believe God that it will be just as it was told me. 26 However, we must run aground on a certain island."* (Acts 27:22-26).

Acts 27:42-43 exposes, *"and the soldiers' plan was to kill the prisoners, lest any of them should swim away and escape. 43 But the centurion, wanting to save Paul, kept them from their purpose, and commanded that those who could swim should jump overboard first and get to land,"* All 276 persons arrived safely on the island of Malta. Acts 28:2 continues, *"And the natives showed us unusual kindness; for they kindled a fire and made us all welcome, because of the rain that was falling and because of the cold."* Paul in turn showed kindness, Acts 28:7-10 records, *"In that region there was an estate of the leading citizen of the island, whose name was Publius, who received us and entertained us courteously for three days. 8 And it happened that the father of Publius lay sick of a fever and dysentery. Paul went in to him and prayed, and he laid his hands on him and healed him.* ⁹ *So when this was done, the rest of those on the island who had diseases also came and were healed.* ¹⁰*They also honored us in many ways; and when we departed, they provided such things as were necessary."* It is important that we do not repay someone's kindness with evil. Paul repaid Julius's kindness by being the voice of Yahweh, and bringing hope when all hope was gone. All of the passengers on the ship benefited by Paul repaying the kindness shown by the natives, through his prayers of healing. In return when they left the island, they had everything they needed.

When King Rehoboam consulted with the elders of how to rule his father, King Solomon's kingdom, they advised him in 2 Chronicles 10:7, *"And they spoke to him, saying, "If you are kind to these people, and please them, and speak good words to them, they will be your servants forever."* He chose not take the advice and Israel rebelled against his leadership.
<u>Judges 8:35</u> - nor did they show kindness to the house of Jerubbaal (Gideon) in accordance with the good he had done for Israel.
<u>2 Chronicles 24:22</u> - Thus Joash the king did not remember the kindness which Jehoiada his father had done to him, but killed his son; and as he died, he said, "The LORD look on it, and repay!"

Is there anyone in your life who has repaid your kindness with ungratefulness, injustice, indifference and unkindness? We have all opened the door for a stranger, without their acknowledgment with a thank you. How about your spouse? Are you the one always going out of your way to do kind and thoughtful things, with absolutely no recognition or reciprocated actions? How about a child who seems to never be satisfied with what has been provided, one who constantly complains, is disrespectful and unruly? As a parent you wonder, how can I be so kind to my child, and I am repaid with such evil? How about your close group of friends, is there one who is always taking your advice, resources, and your time, but when you are in need, he/she is unable to assist you? This is a real problem for all of us, why we choose to stop being kind, we've been bitten while being kind to others. We do not want to be taken advantage of nor be taken for granted. The reality is, we cannot control another's response to our kindness, so when we walk in kindness we have to check our motives. If you are doing something kind to get something out of the other person, our motives have already failed us. Let's ask Yahweh to give us pure motives as we trust in Him to provide the rewards for our kindness.

Heavenly Father, our hearts are hesitant to love, to trust and to help others with kind acts. We do not want to be taken advantage of and treated as fools. We are asking you today for your help. Uproot everything in the soil of our lives that would prevent the fruit of Kindness to be developed. We give you permission to uproot the pain, disappointments, and anger as we forgive our offenders. Purify our motives, that we would show kindness without expectations of being repaid, that our only motive would be to please you by allowing others to experience your kindness through our lives. In Yahshua's name, Amen.

BENEFITS OF KINDNESS
<u>OTHERS WILL ASK GOD TO BLESS YOU FOR YOUR KINDNESS.</u>
<u>Ruth 1:8</u> - And Naomi said to her two daughters-in-law, "Go, return each to her mother's house. The LORD deal kindly with you, as you have dealt with the dead and with me.
<u>Ruth 2:20</u> - Then Naomi said to her daughter-in-law, "Blessed be he of the LORD, who has not forsaken His kindness to the living and the dead!" And Naomi said to

her, "This man is a relation of ours, one of our close relatives."

Ruth 3:10 - Then he said, "Blessed are you of the LORD, my daughter! For you have shown more
kindness at the end than at the beginning, in that you did not go after young men, whether poor or rich.

2 Samuel 2:4-7 - Then the men of Judah came, and there they anointed David king over the house of Judah. And they told David, saying, "The men of Jabesh Gilead were the ones who buried Saul." 5 So David sent messengers to the men of Jabesh Gilead, and said to them, "You are blessed of the LORD, for you have shown this kindness to your lord, to Saul, and have buried him. 6 And now may the LORD show kindness and truth to you. I also will repay you this kindness, because you have done this thing. 7Now therefore, let your hands be strengthened, and be valiant; for your master Saul is dead, and also the house of Judah has anointed me king over them."

SHOWING KINDNESS WILL GIVE YOU FAVOR IN TIMES OF TROUBLE.

Genesis 40:14 - But remember me when it is well with you, and please show kindness to me; make mention of me to Pharaoh, and get me out of this house.

1 Samuel 15:6 - Then Saul said to the Kenites, "Go, depart, get down from among the Amalekites, lest I destroy you with them. For you showed kindness to all the children of Israel when they came up out of Egypt." So the Kenites departed from among the Amalekites.

Joshua 2:14 - So the men answered her, "Our lives for yours, if none of you tell this business of ours. And it shall be, when the LORD has given us the land, that we will deal kindly and truly with you."

YOUR CHILDREN WILL BE BLESSED FOR YOUR KINDNESS.

Genesis 21:23 - Now therefore, swear to me by God that you will not deal falsely with me, with my offspring, or with my posterity; but that according to the kindness that I have done to you, you will do to me and to the land in which you have dwelt."
Joshua 2:12 - Now therefore, I beg you, swear to me by the Lord, since I have shown you kindness, that you also will show kindness to my father's house, and give me a true token,
1 Samuel 20:14-15 - And you shall not only show me the kindness of the Lord while I still live, that I may not die; but you shall not cut off your kindness from my house forever, no, not when the Lord has cut off every one of the enemies of David from the face of the earth."
2 Samuel 9:3 - Then the king said, "Is there not still someone of the house of Saul, to whom I may show the kindness of God?" And Ziba said to the king, "There is still a son of Jonathan who is lame in his feet."
2 Samuel 9:7 - So David said to him, "Do not fear, for I will surely show you kindness for Jonathan your father's sake, and will restore to you all the land of Saul your grandfather; and you shall eat bread at my table continually."
2 Samuel 10:2 and 1 Chronicles 19:2 - Then David said, "I will show kindness to Hanun the son of Nahash, as his father showed kindness to me." So David sent by the hand of his servants to comfort him concerning his father. And David's servants came into the land of the people of Ammon.
1 Kings 2:7 - "But show kindness to the sons of Barzillai the Gileadite, and let them be among those who eat at your table, for so they came to me when I fled from Absalom your brother.

Thank Yahweh for all of the benefits we experience through the kindness of others and our kindness shown in their lives.

CHAPTER TEN
Developing: Goodness
*Depart from evil, and do good; seek peace, and pursue it.
Psalm 34:14*

In the introduction, I shared a portion of my journal from 2008. I spoke about my excitement of having a *Naseberry* (Sapodilla) Tree, yet disappointment when the fruit stayed the same size, seemingly forever. A few days after that journal entry, I wrote the following...

Friday, February 22, 2008 10:20AM (A page from my journal)

So I tried to pick it, you know the largest Naseberry on the tree. I took the big long stick with the hook and pulled as hard as I could at this tree three times my size. I GOT IT! It fell, tumbled, split in half, and had the milky sap coming out of all parts of it, all because it wasn't ripe. As I threw it away, I thought, "another one wasted, why, didn't I just wait, patiently"?

I've wasted others by attempting to consume them before they were fully ripen; to my dismay, the milky sticky latex, coming from the unripen fruit left an unforgettable bitter taste in my mouth. Once ripen, the Naseberry, softens, and releases sweet delights that make my taste buds sing. This high calorie fruit, has an abundance of minerals, Vitamin A and Vitamin C aiding our health in numerous ways, while preventing unwanted ailments. Being high in fiber, it assists in digestion and works great as a laxative. A high fiber spiritual diet, cleanses and prepares us for every good work, 2 Timothy 2:21 teaches, *"Therefore if anyone **cleanses himself** from the latter, he will be a vessel for honor, sanctified and useful for the Master, **prepared for every good work**."*

Yahweh gives us a clear definition of what He defines as good in Micah 6:8, *"He has shown you, O man, what is good; and what does the LORD require of you but to do justly, to love mercy, and to walk humbly with your God?"* We must understand that doing good is something we learn, which also means it is something that must be taught. Isaiah 1:17 tells us, *"**Learn to do good**; Seek justice, Rebuke the oppressor; Defend the fatherless, Plead for the widow."* Titus 3:14 encourages, *"And let our people also **learn to maintain good works**, to meet urgent needs, that they may not be unfruitful."*

As we touch on justice, mercy and humility in this chapter, please note we will discuss in greater detail about humility in Chapter 12, living justly in Chapter Fifteen, and loving mercy in Chapter Sixteen.

LEARN TO DO WHAT IS GOOD

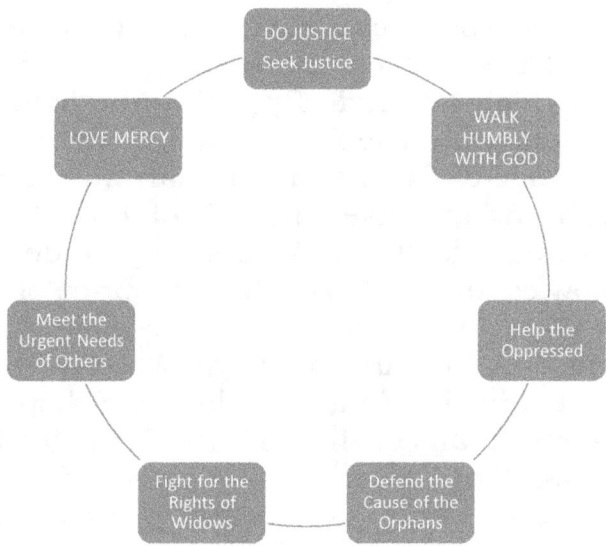

On our quest to develop the fruit of goodness, we will focus on doing what is right for others. We will look at good as a verb and not as an adjective in describing ourselves. We are not to view ourselves or others as good, for only Yahweh is good. Mark 10:17-18 records, *"Now as He was going out on the road, one came running, knelt before Him, and asked Him, "Good Teacher, what shall I do that I may inherit eternal life?" 18 So Jesus said to him, "Why do you call Me good? No one is good but One, That is, God."*

Ecclesiastes 7:20 - For there is not a just man on earth who does good and does not sin.

Romans 4:2 - For if Abraham was justified by works, he has something to boast about, but not before God.

Romans 7:18 - For I know that in me (that is, in my flesh) nothing good dwells; for to will is present with me, but how to perform what is good I do not find.

Romans 7:19 - For the good that I will to do, I do not do; but the evil I will not to do, that I practice.

As we read the creation account in Genesis 1, we understand that everything that Yahweh created, He declared it to be good, including man. In Genesis 2, we are introduced to the Tree of Life and the Tree of the Knowledge of Good and Evil. By eating the fruit of the Tree of Life man could live forever and by eating of the Tree of Knowledge of Good and Evil man was cursed to die. Although, Adam, Eve and all of creation were experiencing God's goodness, as humans we desired to have the knowledge of evil accepting its' price of death. If only Yahweh is truly good, how do we have a chance of developing this fruit in our lives? We have become new in Christ, and by Yahshua alone we display His goodness. Paul speaks of Him in Titus 2:14, *"who gave Himself for us, that He might redeem us from every lawless deed and purify for Himself His own special people, zealous for good works."*

Psalm 16:2 - "O my soul, you have said to the LORD, "You are my Lord, My goodness is nothing apart from You."

Ephesians 2:9-10 - not of works, lest anyone should boast. [10] For we are His workmanship, created in Christ Jesus for good works, which God prepared beforehand that we should walk in them.

Philippians 1:6 - being confident of this very thing, that He who has begun a good work in you will complete it until the day of Jesus Christ;

2 Timothy 3:16-17 - All Scripture is given by inspiration of God, and is profitable for doctrine, for reproof, for correction, for instruction in righteousness, [17] that the man of God may be complete, thoroughly equipped for every good work.

2 Thessalonians 1:11 - Therefore we also pray always for you that our God would count you worthy of this calling, and fulfill all the good pleasure of His goodness and the work of faith with power,

We are instructed to prove we have changed by the good things we do. Therefore we must turn from evil and do what is pleasing to the Lord.

Proverbs 2:20 - So you may walk in the way of goodness, and keep to the paths of righteousness.

Proverbs 14:22 - Do they not go astray who devise evil? But mercy and truth belong to those who devise good.

Psalm 37:3 - Trust in the LORD, and do good; dwell in the land, and feed on His faithfulness.

Psalm 37:27 - Depart from evil, and do good; and dwell forevermore.

Acts 26:20 - but declared first to those in Damascus and in Jerusalem, and throughout all the region of Judea, and then to the Gentiles, that they should repent, turn to God, and do works befitting repentance.

Ephesians 4:28 - Let him who stole steal no longer, but rather let him labor, working with his hands what is good, that he may have something to give him who has need.

Romans 12:9 - Let love be without hypocrisy. Abhor what is evil. Cling to what is good.

3 John 1:11 - Beloved, do not imitate what is evil, but what is good. He who does good is of God, but he who does evil has not seen God.

In Exodus 33, Moses and the Lord were having an intense conversation. Yahweh in His frustration was sending His people, led by Moses, to the promise land without His Presence lest he destroy them on the way. Moses pleaded with the Lord not to let them go without Him, so our Lord being moved with compassion agreed to go with them. Then Moses asked the Lord to show him His Glory and He responds in Exodus 33:19, *"Then He said, "I will make all My goodness pass before you, and I will proclaim the name of the LORD before you. I will be gracious to whom I will be gracious, and I will have compassion on whom I will have compassion."* Our Heavenly Father could of showed him any attribute, but He chose for Moses to experience what Adam and Eve experienced in the Garden before they ate of the forbidden tree. David writes in Psalm 23:6, *"Surely goodness and mercy shall follow me all the days of my life; and I will dwell in the house of the LORD Forever."* In Psalm 27:13, David sings, *"I would have lost heart, unless I had believed that I would see the goodness of the LORD In the land of the living."*

For centuries many have said, if God is so good, then why do bad things happen? It is the 3 year old child in all of us, that no matter how much we age, we limit ourselves to reason as a child, yet even a child can understand that bad things happen because bad people do bad things. It is not a reflection of Yahweh's goodness or in another's opinion, his lack thereof. Unlike us, Yahweh is GOOD because, like LOVE, He is the definition of what GOOD is. Yahshua tells us in John 10:11, *"I am the good shepherd. The good shepherd gives His life for the sheep."* He continues in John 10:14, *"I am the good shepherd; and I know My sheep, and am known by My own."* What makes Him good? He is our good Shepherd that gave His life for us. He always does what is right, while teaching and directing our paths. Yahweh blesses us with life, children, and provision. He is compassionate and keeps His promises; He is forgiving, full of unfailing love and mercy. Our Heavenly Father is good because He is our strong refuge, who delivers us from our enemies and our chains.

<u>Deuteronomy 30:9</u> - The LORD your God will make you abound in all the work of your hand, in the fruit of your body, in the increase of your livestock, and in the produce of your land for good. For the LORD
will again rejoice over you for good as He rejoiced over your fathers,

<u>2 Chronicles 6:41</u> - "Now therefore, Arise, O LORD God, to Your resting place, You and the ark of Your strength. Let Your priests, O LORD God, be clothed with salvation, and let Your saints rejoice in goodness.

<u>2 Chronicles 7:3</u> - When all the children of Israel saw how the fire came down, and the glory of the Lord on the temple, they bowed their faces to the ground on the pavement, and worshiped and praised the Lord, saying: "For He is good, for His mercy endures forever."
<u>Psalm 25:8</u> - Good and upright is the Lord; therefore He teaches sinners in the way.
<u>Psalm 33:5</u> - He loves righteousness and justice; the earth is full of the goodness of the Lord.
<u>Psalm 34:8</u> - Oh, taste and see that the Lord is good; blessed is the man who trusts in Him!
<u>Psalm 52:9</u> - I will praise You forever, because You have done it; and in the presence of Your saints I will wait on Your name, for it is good.
<u>Psalm 54:6</u> - I will freely sacrifice to You; I will praise Your name, O Lord, for it is good.
<u>Psalm 73:1</u> - Truly God is good to Israel, to such as are pure in heart.
<u>Psalm 86:5</u> - For You, Lord, are good, and ready to forgive, and abundant in mercy to all those who call upon You.
<u>Psalm 119:68</u> - You are good, and do good; teach me Your statutes.
<u>Psalm 145:9</u> - The Lord is good to all, and His tender mercies are over all His works.
<u>Nahum 1:7</u> - The Lord is good, a stronghold in the day of trouble; and He knows those who trust in Him.
<u>Nehemiah 9:20</u> - You also gave Your good Spirit to instruct them, and did not withhold Your manna from their mouth, and gave them water for their thirst.
<u>Acts 14:17</u> - Nevertheless He did not leave Himself without witness, in that He did good, gave us rain from heaven and fruitful seasons, filling our hearts with food and gladness."

Yahweh is our good father who gives His children good and perfect gifts. James 1:17 declares, *"Every good gift and every perfect gift is from above, and comes down from the Father of lights, with whom there is no variation or shadow of turning."*

Luke 11:13 - If you then, being evil, know how to give good gifts to your children, how much more will your heavenly Father give the Holy Spirit to those who ask Him!"

Deuteronomy 26:11 - So you shall rejoice in every good thing which the LORD your God has given to you and your house, you and the Levite and the stranger who is among you.

Psalm 103:5 - Who satisfies your mouth with good things, So that your youth is renewed like the eagle's.

Jeremiah 31:12 - Therefore they shall come and sing in the height of Zion, streaming to the goodness of the LORD. For wheat and new wine and oil, for the young of the flock and the herd; their souls shall be like a well-watered garden, and they shall sorrow no more at all.

Jeremiah 31:14 - I will satiate the soul of the priests with abundance, and My people shall be satisfied with My goodness, says the LORD."

Nehemiah 9:35 - For they have not served You in their kingdom, or in the many good things that You gave them, or in the large and rich land which You set before them; nor did they turn from their wicked works.

All that Yahweh does is good. Even at the times when He sends or allows times of calamity and suffering and when He disciplines us. He is still good.

GOD WORKS OUT ALL THINGS FOR OUR GOOD.
Genesis 50:20 - But as for you, you meant evil against me; but God meant it for good, in order to bring it about as it is this day, to save many people alive.

Romans 8:28 - And we know that all things work together for good to those who love God, to those who are the called according to His purpose.

GOD HUMBLES AND TEST US FOR OUR OWN GOOD.
Deuteronomy 8:16 - who fed you in the wilderness with manna, which your fathers did not know, that He might humble you and that He might test you, to do you good in the end.
Psalm 73:28 - But it is good for me to draw near to God; I have put my trust in the Lord GOD, that I may declare all Your works.

SING OF YAHWEH'S GOODNESS!
1 Chronicles 16:34 - Oh, give thanks to the LORD, for He is good! For His mercy endures forever.
2 Chronicles 5:13 - indeed it came to pass, when the trumpeters and singers were as one, to make one sound to be heard in praising and thanking the LORD, and when they lifted up their voice with the trumpets and cymbals and instruments of music, and praised the LORD, saying: "For He is good, for His mercy endures forever," that the house, the house of the LORD, was filled with a cloud,
Isaiah 63:7 - I will mention the loving kindnesses of the LORD and the praises of the LORD, According to all that the LORD has bestowed on us, and the great goodness toward the house of Israel, Which He has bestowed on them according to His mercies, according to the multitude of His loving kindnesses.
Ezra 3:11 - And they sang responsively, praising and giving thanks to the LORD: "For He is good, for His mercy endures forever toward Israel." Then all the people shouted with a great shout, when they praised the LORD, because the foundation of the house of the LORD was laid.
Psalm 135:3 - Praise the LORD, for the LORD is good; Sing praises to His name, for it is pleasant.
Psalm 145:7 - They shall utter the memory of Your great goodness, and shall sing of Your righteousness.
Psalm 147:1 - Praise the LORD! For it is good to sing praises to our God; for it is pleasant, and praise is beautiful.

Because of Yahweh's goodness to us, there is a depth of reverence that we should have for Him. His goodness is an amazing wonder. Psalm 31:19 declares, *"Oh, how great is Your goodness, which You have laid up for those who fear You, which You have prepared for those who trust in You In the presence of the sons of men!"*

Hosea 3:5 - Afterward the children of Israel shall return and seek the LORD their God and David their king. They shall fear the LORD and His goodness in the latter days.

Jeremiah 33:9 - Then it shall be to Me a name of joy, a praise, and an honor before all nations of the earth, who shall hear all the good that I do to them; they shall fear and tremble for all the goodness and all the prosperity that I provide for it.'

Romans 11:22 - Therefore consider the goodness and severity of God: on those who fell, severity; but toward you, goodness, if you continue in His goodness. Otherwise you also will be cut off.

Out of our fear, love and appreciation of God, we are urged to live a life of goodness. It can be very challenging to do good to those who seem not to deserve it, nevertheless we are called to a higher way of living, and we are called to do good to everyone.

Proverbs 17:13 - Whoever rewards evil for good, evil will not depart from his house.

Proverbs 28:21 - To show partiality is not good, because for a piece of bread a man will transgress.

1 Samuel 24:17 - Then he said to David: "You are more righteous than I; for you have rewarded me with good, whereas I have rewarded you with evil.

1 Samuel 24:19 - For if a man finds his enemy, will he let him get away safely? Therefore may the LORD reward you with good for what you have done to me this day.

Luke 6:27 - "But I say to you who hear: Love your enemies, do good to those who hate you,

Luke 6:33 - And if you do good to those who do good to you, what credit is that to you? For even sinners do the same.

Luke 6:35 - But love your enemies, do good, and lend, hoping for nothing in return; and your reward will be great, and you will be sons of the Most High. For He is kind to the unthankful and evil.
Romans 12:21 - Do not be overcome by evil, but overcome evil with good.
1 Thessalonians 5:15 - See that no one renders evil for evil to anyone, but always pursue what is good both for yourselves and for all.

Solomon tells us that by seeking to do good we will find favor from the Lord. *"He who earnestly seeks good finds favor, but trouble will come to him who seeks evil."* (Proverbs 11:27) *"A good man obtains favor from the LORD, but a man of wicked intentions He will condemn."* (Proverbs 12:2) Yahweh rewards for doing good.
Deuteronomy 6:18 - And you shall do what is right and good in the sight of the LORD, that it may be well with you, and that you may go in and possess the good land of which the LORD swore to your fathers,
Psalm 84:11 - For the LORD God is a sun and shield; the LORD will give grace and glory; No good thing will He withhold from those who walk uprightly.
Proverbs 14:14 - The backslider in heart will be filled with his own ways, but a good man will be satisfied from above.
Proverbs 28:10 - Whoever causes the upright to go astray in an evil way, he himself will fall into his own pit; but the blameless will inherit good.
Lamentations 3:25-27 - The LORD is good to those who wait for Him, to the soul who seeks Him. ²⁶ It is good that one should hope and wait quietly for the salvation of the LORD. ²⁷ It is good for a man to bear the yoke in his youth.
John 5:29 - and come forth—those who have done good, to the resurrection of life, and those who have done evil, to the resurrection of condemnation.

Romans 2:7 - eternal life to those who by patient continuance in doing good seek for glory, honor, and immortality;

Romans 2:10 - but glory, honor, and peace to everyone who works what is good, to the Jew first and also to the Greek.

2 Corinthians 5:10 - For we must all appear before the judgment seat of Christ, that each one may receive the things done in the body, according to what he has done, whether good or bad.

Ephesians 6:8 - knowing that whatever good anyone does, he will receive the same from the Lord, whether he is a slave or free.

Galatians 6:9 - And let us not grow weary while doing good, for in due season we shall reap if we do not lose heart.

Let us review, God is good and everything He does is good. Without Christ it is impossible to develop the fruit of goodness because only God is truly good. We are directed to turn from evil and to rise above the temptation to repay evil with evil. And we know that our Heavenly Father rewards His children for doing good.

We will now explore the ways we can show goodness to others. Hebrews 13:21 states, *"make you complete in every good work to do His will, working in you what is well pleasing in His sight, through Jesus Christ, to whom be glory forever and ever. Amen."*

Every good thing we do must be done with pure motives for Yahweh's glory. Matthew 6:1 warns, *"Take heed that you do not do your charitable deeds before men, to be seen by them. Otherwise you have no reward from your Father in heaven."* Solomon wrote in Proverbs 25:27, *"It is not good to eat much honey; so to seek one's own glory is not glory."*

Esther 10:3 - For Mordecai the Jew was second to King Ahasuerus, and was great among the Jews and well received by the multitude of his brethren, seeking the good of his people and speaking peace to all his countrymen.

Proverbs 3:27 - Do not withhold good from those to whom it is due, when it is in the power of your hand to do so.

Matthew 5:16 - Let your light so shine before men, that they may see your good works and glorify your Father in heaven.

Acts 10:38 - how God anointed Jesus of Nazareth with the Holy Spirit and with power, who went about doing good and healing all who were oppressed by the devil, for God was with Him.

1 Corinthians 10:24 - Let no one seek his own, but each one the other's well-being.

1 Timothy 5:25 - Likewise, the good works of some are clearly evident, and those that are otherwise cannot be hidden.

1 Timothy 6:18-19 - Let them do good, that they be rich in good works, ready to give, willing to share, [19] storing up for themselves a good foundation for the time to come, that they may lay hold on eternal life.

Titus 3:1 - Remind them to be subject to rulers and authorities, to obey, to be ready for every good work,

Titus 3:8 - This is a faithful saying, and these things I want you to affirm constantly, that those who have believed in God should be careful to maintain good works. These things are good and profitable to men.

Galatians 6:6 - Let him who is taught the word share in all good things with him who teaches.

Galatians 6:10 - Therefore, as we have opportunity, let us do good to all, especially to those who are of the household of faith.

Hebrews 10:24 - And let us consider one another in order to stir up love and good works,

Hebrews 13:16 - But do not forget to do good and to share, for with such sacrifices God is well pleased.

The Lord encourages us to follow good examples and to lead by good example. We are all leaders, either in our home, jobs, ministry and community. For people to trust us, it is vital to have a good reputation. Solomon, the wealthiest man, in his day, wrote in Proverbs 22:1, *"A good name is to be chosen rather than great riches, loving favor rather than silver and gold."* Have you valued your reputation more than your net worth? If you have not been, then it is time to reprioritize. He goes on to tell us in Ecclesiastes 7:1, *"A good name is better than precious ointment, and the day of death than the day of one's birth;"* We must ask our Heavenly Father to teach us good judgment, knowledge and understanding as we live our lives privately and publicly. We need His wisdom!

<u>Psalm 119:66</u> - Teach me good judgment and knowledge, for I believe Your commandments.

<u>Proverbs 4:1-2</u> - Hear, my children, the instruction of a father, and give attention to know understanding; 2 For I give you good doctrine: Do not forsake my law.

<u>Proverbs 13:15</u> - Good understanding gains favor, But the way of the unfaithful is hard.

People form their opinions about us based on the words we speak. It is very important that we are speaking words that edify others. In Ephesians 4:29 we are instructed to, *"Let no corrupt word proceed out of your mouth, but what is good for necessary edification, that it may impart grace to the hearers."* There is a debate about the use of language and whether there is such a thing as a good or bad word. For this reason, we will use a meter, for our words. If the words you speak include gossiping, hurting another's feelings or tearing down someone's character, don't use them. Rather use words that speak life over each person's purpose in Christ. Proverbs 15:30, enlightens us, *"The light of the eyes rejoices the heart, and a good report makes the bones healthy."* Learn to give good reports when speaking to others. The best report we can give is the Good News (GOSPEL) of Salvation.

<u>1 Chronicles 16:23</u> - Sing to the LORD, all the earth; proclaim the good news of His salvation from day to day.

<u>Psalm 96:2</u> - Sing to the LORD, bless His name; proclaim the good news of His salvation from day to day.

<u>Isaiah 40:9</u> - O Zion, You who bring good tidings, Get up into the high mountain; O Jerusalem, You who bring good tidings, lift up your voice with strength, lift it up, be not afraid; say to the cities of Judah, "Behold your God!"

<u>Mark 16:15</u> - And He said to them, "Go into all the world and preach the gospel to every creature.

<u>Luke 4:18</u> - "The Spirit of the LORD is upon Me, because He has anointed Me to preach the gospel to the poor; He has sent Me to heal the brokenhearted, to proclaim liberty to the captives and recovery of sight to the blind, to set at liberty those who are oppressed;

While most times scripture speaks to all of us as children of Yahweh, there are times men, women, and children are individually addressed. As we focus on becoming good examples, I would like to speak to the men reading this book first. Paul gives an outline to Titus of the qualities of a healthy church. He speaks of the men in Titus 2:1-2, *"But as for you, speak the things which are proper for sound doctrine: 2 that the older men be sober, reverent, temperate, sound in faith, in love, in patience;"* He continues in verses 6-8, *"Likewise, exhort the young men to be sober-minded, <u>7 in all things showing yourself to be a pattern of good works</u>; in doctrine showing integrity, reverence, incorruptibility, sound speech that cannot be condemned, that one who is an opponent may be ashamed, having nothing evil to say of you."* As it concerns elders in the church, Paul writes in Titus 1:6-9, *"if a man is blameless, the husband of one wife, having faithful children not accused of dissipation or insubordination. 7 For a bishop must be blameless, as a steward of God, not self-willed, not* *quick-tempered, not given to wine, not violent, not greedy for money, ⁸ but hospitable,* ***a lover of what is good****, sober-minded, just, holy, self-controlled, ⁹ holding fast the faithful word as he has been taught, that he may be able, by sound doctrine, both to exhort and convict those who contradict."* Paul instructs Timothy in 1 Timothy 3:2, *"A bishop then must be blameless, the husband of one wife, temperate, sober-minded, of* ***good behavior****, hospitable, able to teach;"* Men, you set the example for our families, ask Yahweh for the strength and desire to live honorable lives.

Now, to all of the ladies, Yahweh's word invites us to be virtuous women, who represent Him in every area of our lives. King Lemuel's mother gave him great advice in choosing a wife. It is this lesson that we know as the Proverbs 31 woman. She is trust worthy, a hard working business woman, land owner and an investor, she assists the poor, she is well dressed and she makes sure her family is well dressed. She is strong and honorable, wise and kind. Her husband and children bless her for she is a woman who fears the Lord! As wives we are advised to do good to our husbands in Proverbs 31:12, *"She does him good and not evil all the days of her life."* Titus 2:3-5 tells us, *"the older women likewise, that they be reverent in behavior, not slanderers, not given to much wine, teachers of good things — ⁴ that they admonish the young women to love their husbands, to love their children, ⁵ to be discreet, chaste, homemakers, good, obedient to their own husbands, that the word of God may not be blasphemed."* We are called to do good works in 1 Timothy 2:10, *"but, which is proper for women professing godliness, with good works."* When speaking of a widow's good works, Paul identifies the following in 1 Timothy 5:10, *"well reported for good works: if she has brought up children, if she has lodged strangers, if she has washed the saints' feet, if she has relieved the afflicted, if she has diligently followed every good work."*

Ladies we carry a huge responsibility to be teachers of good things, not only by word but by our deeds.

While Yahweh's goodness being lived through our lives is a blessing to many, for others it is upsetting. Solomon writes in Proverbs 17:26, *"Also, to punish the righteous is not good, nor to strike princes for their uprightness."* As we have already learned, our good works may cause suffering in our lives. It is important to remember that Yahweh is pleased when you continue in goodness even if it causes you to suffer.
Psalm 119:71 - It is good for me that I have been afflicted, that I may learn Your statutes.
John 10:32-33 - Jesus answered them, "Many good works I have shown you from My Father. For which of those works do you stone Me?" ³³ The Jews answered Him, saying, "For a good work we do not stone You, but for blasphemy, and because You, being a Man, make Yourself God."
1 Peter 2:20 - For what credit is it if, when you are beaten for your faults, you take it patiently? But when you do good and suffer, if you take it patiently, this is commendable before God.
1 Peter 3:16-17 - having a good conscience, that when they defame you as evildoers, those who revile your good conduct in Christ may be ashamed. ¹⁷ For it is better, if it is the will of God, to suffer for doing good than for doing evil.
2 Timothy 2:3 - You therefore must endure hardship as a good soldier of Jesus Christ.

"Now may our Lord Jesus Christ Himself, and our God and Father, who has loved us and given us everlasting consolation and good hope by grace, ¹⁷ comfort your hearts and establish you in every good word and work." 2 Thessalonians 2:16-17

Decide today, that nothing and no one will stop you from bearing the fruit our Lord has required of us. In the words of Apostle Paul, in 2 Thessalonians 3:13, *"But as for you, brethren, do not grow weary in doing good."*

CHAPTER ELEVEN
Developing: Faith/Faithfulness
Now faith is the substance of things hoped for, the evidence of things not seen. Hebrews 11:1

In Galatians 5:22 the Greek word *pistos*, is translated as faithfulness or faith. In this chapter we will discuss our level of belief in Yahweh as it connects to our level of commitment to Him. The first fruit I thought of as it relates to faith is the fig. There are more than 150 types of figs, this peculiar bulb shaped fruit is one of the oldest fruits known to man. When sliced open it appears to me like an explosion of tiny flowers. This very sweet, antioxidant and fiber-rich fruit, is high in potassium, which is the mineral that assists in lowering blood pressure. We find a fascinating occurrence recorded in Mark 11:20-24, as it relates to faith and the fig tree.

Now in the morning, as they passed by, they saw the fig tree dried up from the roots. 21 And Peter, remembering, said to Him, "Rabbi, look! The fig tree which You cursed has withered away." 22 So Jesus answered and said to them, **"Have faith in God.** *23 For assuredly, I say to you, whoever says to this mountain, 'Be removed and be cast into the sea,' and* **does not doubt in his heart, but believes that those things he says will be done, he**

will have whatever he says. [24] ***Therefore I say to you, whatever things you ask when you pray, believe that you receive them, and you will have them.***

This is the same fruitless fig tree we discussed in Chapter 4. The disciples were amazed that the fig tree had withered away at the command of Yahshua. We understand that faith is exercised in a heart that is free from doubt and overflowing with belief, knowing that what we declare and ask for in Yahshua's name will be done. I often ask our Heavenly Father, *how do I know if I am asking for something that is not in your will? Will you do it anyway? Where is the dividing line between the power of my faith and the power of your will?* I am asking Holy Spirit to give each of us, His revelation of FAITH as we walk through the scriptures together.

Faith is defined in Hebrews 11:1-3, *"Now faith is the substance of things hoped for, the evidence of things not seen. ² For by it the elders obtained a good testimony. ³ By faith we understand that the worlds were framed by the word of God, so that the things which are seen were not made of things which are visible."* Everything Yahweh created in the universe was created by His invisible yet audible words. Those who obtained a good testimony by it are those who heard His instructions and His promises and believed. They did not lose faith, although the manifestation of the promise often times took many years. Paul teaches us in Romans 10:17 that faith comes by hearing the word of God, in Hebrews 4:2 we are told, *"For indeed the gospel was preached to us as well as to them; but the word which they heard did not profit them, not being mixed with faith in those who heard it."* Therefore, those who hear the Word must respond in faith (BELIEF) to the Word. Romans 4:17-21 speaks of Abraham, *"(as it is written, "I have made you a father of many nations") in the presence of Him whom he believed—God, who gives life to the dead and calls those things which do not exist as though they did;* ¹⁸ *who, contrary to hope, in hope believed, so that he became the father of many nations, according to what was spoken, "So shall your descendants be."* ¹⁹ *And not being weak in faith, he did not consider his own body, already dead (since he was about a hundred years old), and the deadness of Sarah's womb.* ²⁰ *He did not waver at the promise of God through unbelief, but was strengthened in faith, giving glory to God,* ²¹ *and being fully convinced that what He had promised He was also able to perform."*

Ephesians 6:16 tells us that our faith is a shield, *"above all, taking the shield of faith with which you will be able to quench all the fiery darts of the wicked one."* 1 Thessalonians 5:8 tells us our faith is also a breastplate, *"But let us, who are of the day, be sober, putting on the breastplate of faith and love; and for a helmet, the hope of salvation."* By faith, the invisible is made visible, by faith, we put out the fiery darts of the enemy. Faith, love and righteousness make up our breastplate, which covers our hearts from doubt, sin and fear. It is amazing that our evidence of Yahweh's existence and greatness, is an invisible substance! When we do not see any proof in the natural that Yahweh will fulfill His promises in our lives, we should not lose heart. Yahweh doesn't need anything seen to make things happen. Paul tells us in 2 Corinthians 5:7, *"For we walk by faith, not by sight."*

According to Hebrews 11:6, it is impossible to please God without faith, *"But without faith it is impossible to please Him, for he who comes to God **must believe** that **He is**, and that **He is a rewarder of those who diligently seek Him**."* Our lack of faith is connected to our lack of knowledge of who Yahweh truly is. How much do you believe in who Yahweh is? Faith is a conviction that is unshakeable.

When teaching that men should always pray without losing heart, Yahshua asks in Luke 18:7-8, *"And shall*

God not avenge His own elect who cry out day and night to Him, though He bears long with them? ⁸ I tell you that He will avenge them speedily. **Nevertheless, when the Son of Man comes, <u>will He really find faith on the earth</u>?**" Ouch! That verse hits me in the gut. How much worst are things going to get in the body of Christ, that Yahshua would ask us, if He will find any faith on the Earth when He returns? Brothers and Sisters, we must check our faith meter. Will we be able to say, *"I have fought the good fight, I have finished the race, I have kept the faith. (2 Timothy 4:7)"*? Paul warns in 1 Timothy 4:1-2, *"Now the Spirit expressly says that in latter times some will depart from the faith, giving heed to deceiving spirits and doctrines of demons, ² speaking lies in hypocrisy, having their own conscience seared with a hot iron,".* I began Chapter 4 with this verse, *"Examine yourselves as to whether you are in the faith. Test yourselves. Do you not know yourselves, that Jesus Christ is in you? unless indeed you are disqualified."* (2 Corinthians 13:5)

Does Yahshua offend you to the point of disbelief? Mark 6:1-13 records a city whose unbelief prevented them from receiving all that Yahweh had for them.
Then He went out from there and came to His own country, and His disciples followed Him. ² And when the Sabbath had come, He began to teach in the synagogue. And many hearing Him were astonished, saying, "Where did this Man get these things? And what wisdom is this which is given to Him, that such mighty works are performed by His hands! ³ Is this not the carpenter, the Son of Mary, and brother of James, Joses, Judas, and Simon? And are not His sisters here with us?" **So they were offended at Him**. *⁴ But Jesus said to them, "A prophet is not without honor except in his own country, among his own relatives, and in his own house." ⁵* **Now He could do <u>no mighty work</u> there, <u>except</u> that He laid His hands on a few sick people and healed them. ⁶ <u>And He marveled because of</u>**

their unbelief. *Then He went about the villages in a circuit, teaching. And He called the twelve to Himself, and began to send them out two by two, and* <u>*gave them power over unclean spirits.*</u> *⁸ He commanded them to take nothing for the journey except a staff, no bag, no bread, no copper in their money belts ⁹ but to wear sandals, and not to put on two tunics. ¹⁰ Also He said to them, "In whatever place you enter a house, stay there till you depart from that place. ¹¹ And whoever will not receive you nor hear you, when you depart from there, shake off the dust under your feet as a testimony against them. Assuredly, I say to you, it will be more tolerable for Sodom and Gomorrah in the day of judgment than for that city!" ¹²* <u>**So they went out and preached that people should repent. ¹³ And they cast out many demons, and anointed with oil many who were sick, and healed them.**</u>

Yahshua was amazed at their unbelief, he went there to do mighty works, the only ones who received there healing and deliverance, were those who believed. Do you believe? We get a glimpse at Yahshua's frustration, in Matthew 17:14-21 and Mark 9:14-29, with the lack of faith also exemplified in His disciples when they were unable to heal an epileptic boy. Yahshua responds in Matthew 17:17-21, *"Then Jesus answered and said, "O faithless and perverse generation, how long shall I be with you? How long shall I bear with you? Bring him here to Me." ¹⁸ And Jesus rebuked the demon, and it came out of him; and the child was cured from that very hour." ¹⁹ Then the disciples came to Jesus privately and said, "Why could we not cast it out?" ²⁰ So Jesus said to them,* **"Because of your unbelief; for assuredly, I say to you, if you have faith as a mustard seed, you will say to this mountain, 'Move from here to there,' and it will move; and** <u>**nothing will be impossible for you.**</u> *²¹ However, this kind does not go out except by prayer and fasting."* Mark records Yahshua's words to the boy's father in Mark 9:23-24, *"Jesus said to him,* **"If** *you can believe, **all things are possible** to him who believes."* ²⁴ *Immediately the father of the child cried out and said with tears,* **"Lord, I believe; help my unbelief!"**

The disciples also asked for help with their unbelief in Luke 17:5-6, *"And the apostles said to the Lord, **"Increase our faith."** ⁶ So the Lord said, **"If you have faith as a mustard seed, you can say to this mulberry tree, 'Be pulled up by the roots and be planted in the sea,' and it would obey you**."* Our Lord explains that faith the size of a mustard seed not only moves mountains but it uproots and replants.

At times we may become like the disciple Thomas, who needed to see the Resurrected Christ and touch Him, before he could truly believe that Yahshua had risen from the dead. In John 20:27-29 Yahshua responds, *"Then He said to Thomas, "Reach your finger here, and look at My hands; and reach your hand here, and put it into My side. Do not be unbelieving, but believing. ²⁸ And Thomas answered and said to Him, "My Lord and my God!" ²⁹ Jesus said to him, "Thomas,* **because you have seen Me, you have believed. Blessed are those who have not seen and yet have believed**.*"*

One day while in prayer with a few friends, the Lord spoke to me, **"Daughter, you don't even have mustard seed faith."** At that moment I understood. We all think that we have at least the faith the size of a mustard seed, but many of us do not. If we did, **we would be walking in the work of faith with power**. Paul writes in 1 Corinthians 2:4-5, *"And my speech and my preaching were not with persuasive words of human wisdom, but in demonstration of the Spirit and of power, ⁵ that your faith should not be in the wisdom of men but in the power of God."* Our faith must be grounded in the power of Yahweh, not in the wisdom of men. 2 Thessalonians 1:3-4;11-12 states, *"We are *bound to thank God always for you, brethren, as it is fitting, because <u>your faith grows exceedingly</u>, and the love of every one of you all abounds toward each other, ⁴ so that we ourselves boast of you among the churches of God for your patience and faith in all your persecutions and tribulations that you endure, ¹¹ Therefore we also pray always for you that our God would count you worthy of this calling, and fulfill all the good pleasure of His goodness and <u>the work of faith with power</u>, ¹² that the name of our Lord Jesus Christ may be glorified in you, and you in Him, according to the grace of our God and the Lord Jesus Christ."*

Perhaps my faith is the size of an orchid seed, which is the size of dust, therefore smaller than the mustard seed. It does not take much faith to see great things happen, which tells me, just how small the fruit of faith is on my tree. My faith must grow, how about yours? Jude 1:20 instructs, *"But you, beloved, building yourselves up on your most holy faith, praying in the Holy Spirit,"* We need our belief in Yahweh to increase daily. 1 Corinthians 10:15-16 says, *"not boasting of things beyond measure, that is, in other men's labors, but having hope, that **as your faith is increased**, we shall be greatly enlarged by you in our sphere, ¹⁶ to preach the gospel in the regions beyond you, and not to boast in another man's sphere of accomplishment."*

We understand in Romans 12:3-8 that we are each given a measure of faith, *"For I say, through the grace given to me, to everyone who is among you, not to think of himself more highly than he ought to think, but to think*

soberly, **as God has dealt to each one a measure of faith.** ⁴ *For as we have many members in one body, but all the members do not have the same function,* ⁵ *so we, being many, are one body in Christ, and individually members of one another.* ⁶ *Having then gifts differing according to the grace that is given to us, let us use them: if prophecy,* **let us prophesy in proportion to our faith;** ⁷ *or ministry, let us use it in our ministering; he who teaches, in teaching;* ⁸ *he who exhorts, in exhortation; he who gives, with liberality; he who leads, with diligence; he who shows mercy, with cheerfulness."*

Ephesians 4:11-16 tells us, *"And He Himself gave some to be apostles, some prophets, some evangelists and some pastors and teachers,* ¹² *for the equipping of the saints for the work of ministry, for the edifying of the body of Christ,* ¹³ **till we all come to the unity of the faith and of the knowledge of the Son of God, to a perfect man, to the measure of the stature of the fullness of Christ;** ¹⁴ *that we should no longer be children, tossed to and fro and carried about with every wind of doctrine, by the trickery of men, in the cunning craftiness of deceitful plotting,* ¹⁵ *but, speaking the truth in love, may grow up in all things into Him who is the head-Christ* ¹⁶ *from whom the whole body, joined and knit together by what every joint supplies, according to the effective working by which every part does its share, causes growth of the body for the edifying of itself in love.*

1 Corinthians 12:7-11 continues, *"But the manifestation of the Spirit is given to each one for the profit of all:* ⁸ *for to one is given the word of wisdom through the Spirit, to another the word of knowledge through the same Spirit,* ⁹ **to another faith by the same Spirit**, *to another gifts of healings by the same Spirit,* ¹⁰ *to another the working of miracles, to another prophecy, to another discerning of spirits, to another different kinds of tongues, to another the interpretation of tongues.* ¹¹ *But*

one and the same Spirit works all these things, distributing to each one individually as He wills.

We are expected to do something with the measure of faith we have been given. James 2:14-26 expounds, *"What does it profit, my brethren, <u>if someone says he has faith but does not have works</u>? Can faith save him? 15 If a brother or sister is naked and destitute of daily food, 16 and one of you says to them, "Depart in peace, be warmed and filled," but you do not give them the things which are needed for the body, what does it profit? 17 Thus also **faith by itself, if it does not have works, is dead.** 18 But someone will say, "You have faith, and I have works." Show me your faith without your works, and **I will show you my faith by my works**. 19 You believe that there is one God. You do well. Even the demons believe—and tremble! 20 But do you want to know, O foolish man, that faith without works is dead? 21 Was not Abraham our father justified by works when he offered Isaac his son on the altar? 22 Do you see that faith was working together with his works, and **by works faith was made perfect**? 23 And the Scripture was fulfilled which says, "Abraham believed God, and it was accounted to him for righteousness." And he was called the friend of God. 24 You see then that a man is justified by works, and not by faith only. 25 Likewise, was not Rahab the harlot also justified by works when she received the messengers and sent them out another way? 26 **For as the body without the spirit is dead, so faith without works is dead also.**"*

What have you done with the gifts our Heavenly Father has given you by His Spirit? Do you function in them according to the measure of faith He has given you? Let's ask Him to increase your faith. When we are faithful with the little, He trusts us with more.

Yahshua shares a parable in Matthew 25:14-30 likening the Kingdom of Heaven to a man who traveled to a distant country and entrusted his goods to three of his servants. According to each one's ability he gave one five talents, the other two and the other one. A long time goes by and the master returns to settle the accounts. Matthew 25:20-30 continues, *"So he who had received five talents came and brought five other talents, saying, 'Lord, you delivered to me five talents; look, I have gained five more talents besides them.'* 21 *His lord said to him,* **'Well done, good and faithful servant; you were faithful over a few things, I will make you ruler over many things. Enter into the joy of your lord.'** 22 *He also who had received two talents came and said, 'Lord, you delivered to me two talents; look, I have gained two more talents besides them.'* 23 *His lord said to him,* **'Well done, good and faithful servant; you have been faithful over a few things, I will make you ruler over many things. Enter into the joy of your lord.'** 24 *"Then he who had received the one talent came and said, 'Lord, I knew you to be a hard man, reaping where you have not sown, and gathering where you have not scattered seed.* 25 *And I was afraid, and went and hid your talent in the ground. Look, there you have what is yours.'* 26 *"But his lord answered and said to him,* **'You wicked and lazy servant**, *you knew that I reap where I have not sown, and gather where I have not scattered seed.* 27 *So you ought to have deposited my money with the bankers, and at my coming I would have received back my own with interest.* 28 *Therefore* **take the talent from him, and give it to him who has ten talents.** 29 **'For to everyone who has, more will be given, and he will have abundance; but from him who does not have, even what he has will be taken away**. 30 *And cast the unprofitable servant into the outer darkness. There will be weeping and gnashing of teeth."*

Yahweh is a God of multiplication. When He created Adam and Eve, He told them to be fruitful and multiply. When He saved Noah and his family, He sent the animals, both male and female, so they could be fruitful and multiply. He expects us to be fruitful and multiply in our journey with Him. Be an energetic believer, as you honor our Creator and King, being faithful with everything He entrusts to you. Yahshua tells another parable in Luke 12, we'll pick up at verses 42-48, *"And the Lord said, "Who then is that faithful and wise steward, whom his master will make ruler over his household, to give them their portion of food in due season? ⁴³ Blessed is that servant whom his master will find so doing when he comes. ⁴⁴ Truly, I say to you that he will make him ruler over all that he has. ⁴⁵ But if that servant says in his heart, 'My master is delaying his coming,' and begins to beat the male and female servants, and to eat and drink and be drunk, ⁴⁶ the master of that servant will come on a day when he is not looking for him, and at an hour when he is not aware, and will cut him in two and appoint him his portion with the unbelievers. ⁴⁷ And that servant who knew his master's will, and did not prepare himself or do according to his will, shall be beaten with many stripes. ⁴⁸ But he who did not know, yet committed things deserving of stripes, shall be beaten with few. For everyone to whom much is given, from him much will be required; and to whom much has been committed, of him they will ask the more."*

It is easier to have faith, when things are going great in our lives; we have the security of our five senses. When trouble comes and you cannot depend on what you see, feel, hear, taste and smell, it is another story. In Matthew 8:23-26, we read the account of a storm that rocked the faith of the disciples, *"Now when He got into a boat, His disciples followed Him. ²⁴ And suddenly a great tempest arose on the sea, so that the boat was covered with the waves. But He was asleep. ²⁵ Then His disciples came to Him and awoke Him, saying, "Lord, save us! We are perishing!" ²⁶ But He said to them, "Why are you fearful, O you of little faith?" Then He arose and rebuked the winds and the sea, and there was a great* *calm."* They focused on the waves overtaking the boat, the strong sound of the wind, the taste and feel of the cold water on their skin and clothes, the smell of the Sea of Galilee. When we focus our eyes on Christ rather than our troubles, faith will rise up in us like a faithful friend in Yahshua's ability to save us. Fear will creep steadily out of our hearts. Do you remember when Peter asked Yahshua to invite him to walk on the water with Him? *"So He said, "Come." And when Peter had come down out of the boat, he walked on the water to go to Jesus. 30 But when he saw that the wind was boisterous, he was afraid; and beginning to sink he cried out, saying, "Lord, save me!" 31 And immediately Jesus stretched out His hand and caught him, and said to him, "<u>O you of little faith, why did you doubt</u>?" 32 And when they got into the boat, the wind ceased." (Matthew 14:29-32)*

In Matthew 16:5-12 the disciples' faith is questioned again, *"Now when His disciples had come to the other side, they had forgotten to take bread. 6 Then Jesus said to them, "Take heed and beware of the leaven of the Pharisees and the Sadducees." 7 And they reasoned among themselves, saying, "It is because we have taken no bread." 8 But Jesus, being aware of it, said to them, "<u>O you of little faith</u>, why do you reason among yourselves because you have brought no bread? 9 Do you not yet understand, or remember the five loaves of the five thousand and how many baskets you took up? 10 Nor the seven loaves of the four thousand and how many large baskets you took up? 11 <u>How is it you do not understand</u> that I did not speak to you concerning bread? — but to beware of the leaven of the Pharisees and Sadducees." 12 Then they understood that He did not tell them to beware of the leaven of bread, but of the doctrine of the Pharisees and Sadducees.*

Indulge me as I put this in my own words. Yahshua must be thinking;

Why on earth would you think I am concerned that you forgot to take bread?
Haven't you seen my provision?
Seriously, where is your faith, don't you know who I am? Where is your belief and trust in me?
I'm using an analogy to teach you about protecting yourselves from doctrine that is sinful, and you're thinking about food?

When Yahshua makes the statement, *"oh you of little faith."* What does He really mean? Remember, He had given the disciples power to cast out demons and heal the sick. I perceive, they still were not all fully convinced of who He was, is and will always be. If they knew who He was, they would have feared nothing, there would be no hesitation in obeying His words, there would be no denying or betraying Him, there would be absolute conviction as His mother had, when she told the men at the wedding in Cana of Galilee, *"Whatever He says to you, do it"* (John 2:5). Mary, knew who her son was.

Yet, Yahshua prayed for their faith and He prays for ours, he told Peter, *"And the Lord said, "Simon, Simon! Indeed, Satan has asked for you, that he may sift you as wheat. ³² But **I have prayed for you, that your faith should not fail; and when you have returned to Me, strengthen your brethren**." ³³ But he said to Him, "Lord, I am ready to go with You, both to prison and to death." ³⁴ Then He said, "I tell you, Peter, the rooster shall not crow this day before you will deny three times that you know Me."* (Luke 22:31-34)

We must be prepared for our faith to be tested and be faithful in persecution. The level and stability of our faith is often revealed by fiery trials.
<u>1 Peter 1:6-9; 20-21</u> - In this you greatly rejoice, though now for a little while, if need be, you have been grieved by various trials, **7 that the genuineness of your faith, being much more precious than gold that perishes,**

though it is tested by fire, may be found to praise, honor, and glory at the revelation of Jesus Christ, **8 whom having not seen you love.** Though now you do not see Him, yet believing, you rejoice with joy inexpressible and full of glory, **9 receiving the end of your faith—the salvation of your souls**. 20 He indeed was foreordained before the foundation of the world, but was manifest in these last times for you21 **who through Him believe in God, who raised Him from the dead and gave Him glory, so that your faith and hope are in God.**

James 1:2-8 - My brethren, count it all joy when you fall into various trials, 3 knowing that **the testing of your faith produces patience**. 4 But let patience have its perfect work, that you may be perfect and complete, lacking nothing. 5 If any of you lacks wisdom, let him ask of God, who gives to all liberally and without reproach, and it will be given to him. 6 But **let him ask in faith, with no doubting, for he who doubts is like a wave of the sea driven and tossed by the wind. 7 For let not that man suppose that he will receive anything from the Lord; 8 he is a double-minded man, unstable in all his ways**.

Revelation 2:10-11 - Do not fear any of those things which you are about to suffer. Indeed, the devil is about to throw some of you into prison, that you may be tested, and you will have tribulation ten days. **Be faithful until death, and I will give you the crown of life**. 11 "He who has an ear, let him hear what the Spirit says to the churches. He who overcomes shall not be hurt by the second death."'

Revelation 13:9-10 - If anyone has an ear, let him hear. 10 He who leads into captivity shall go into captivity; he who kills with the sword must be killed with the sword. Here is the patience and the faith of the saints.

In 2004 as a woman prayed for me she kept repeating, *"You must be convinced."* At the time, I truly did not understand; I would ask the Lord, *"Convinced of what?"*

Hebrews 11 gives an overview of the men and women who were convinced that what Yahweh had spoken to them, would come to pass in their lives. I encourage you to make time to meditate on how their faith caused them to obey Yahweh and as Hebrews 11:32-40 recalls, *"And what more shall I say? For the time would fail me to tell of Gideon and Barak and Samson and Jephthah, also of David and Samuel and the prophets: 33 who* ***through faith subdued kingdoms, worked righteousness, obtained promises, stopped the mouths of lions, 34 quenched the violence of fire, escaped the edge of the sword, out of weakness were made strong, became valiant in battle, turned to fight the armies of the aliens. 35 Women received their dead raised to life again.*** *Others were tortured, not accepting deliverance, that they might obtain a better resurrection. 36 Still others had trial of mockings and scourgings, yes, and of chains and imprisonment. 37 They were stoned, they were sawn in two, were tempted, were slain with the sword. They wandered about in sheepskins and goatskins, being destitute, afflicted, tormented 38 of whom the world was not worthy. They wandered in deserts and mountains, in dens and caves of the earth. 39* ***And all these, having obtained a good testimony through faith, did not receive the promise****, 40 God having provided something better for us, that they should not be made perfect apart from us."*

Like these men and women, we must be established and steadfast in our faith.

<u>Colossians 1:21-23</u> - And you, who once were alienated and enemies in your mind by wicked works, yet now He has reconciled 22 in the body of His flesh through death, to present you holy, and blameless, and above reproach in His sight 23 if indeed you **continue in the faith, grounded and steadfast, and are not moved away from the hope of the gospel which you heard**, which was preached to every creature under heaven, of which I, Paul, became a minister.

Colossians 2:6-7 - As you therefore have received Christ Jesus the Lord, so walk in Him,**7 rooted and built up in Him and established in the faith**, as you have been taught, abounding in it with thanksgiving.

Hebrews 10:22-23 - let us draw near with **a true heart in full assurance of faith**, having our hearts sprinkled from an evil conscience and our bodies washed with pure water. **23 Let us hold fast the confession of our hope without wavering, for He who promised is faithful.**

It is by our faith in Yahshua that we are purified and justified and not by our deeds of the law. In Acts 15, a meeting is recorded amongst the Apostles. There was an in depth discussion as to whether or not the Gentiles who converted to faith in Yahshua had to be circumcised and keep the law of Moses. It was decided that since the Lord poured out His Spirit on the Gentile believers as a sign of their salvation, that it would not be right to place the burden of the law on them, Peter said, *"And God, which knoweth the hearts, bare them witness, giving them the Holy Ghost, even as he did unto us; 9 And put no difference between us and them,* ***purifying their hearts by faith.*** *10 Now therefore why tempt ye God, to put a yoke upon the neck of the disciples, which neither our fathers nor we were able to bear? 11 But we believe that through the grace of the* L<small>ORD</small> *Jesus Christ we shall be saved, even as they."* (Acts 15:8-11) Colossians 2:11-15 tells us, *"In Him you were also circumcised with the circumcision made without hands, by putting off the body of the sins of the flesh, by the circumcision of Christ, 12 buried with Him in baptism, in which you also were* ***raised with Him through faith in the working of God****, who raised Him from the dead. 13 And you, being dead in your trespasses and the uncircumcision of your flesh, He has made alive together with Him, having forgiven you all trespasses, 14 having wiped out the handwriting of requirements that was against us, which was contrary* to us. And He has taken it out of the way, having nailed it to the cross. *15 Having disarmed principalities and powers, He made a public spectacle of them, triumphing over them in it.* Paul teaches us in Romans 3:28-31, **"Therefore we conclude that a man is justified by faith without the deeds of the law.** *29 Is he the God of the Jews only? Is he not also of the Gentiles? Yes, of the Gentiles also:* **seeing it is one God, which shall justify the circumcision by faith, and uncircumcision through faith.** *31 Do we then make void the law through faith? God forbid: yea, we establish the law."* Paul tells us that it is the law that points us to Christ, *"But before faith came, we were kept under guard by the law, kept for the faith which would afterward be revealed. 24 Therefore the law was our tutor to bring us to Christ, that we might be justified by faith. 25 But after faith has come, we are no longer under a tutor. 26 For you are all sons of God through faith in Christ Jesus."* (Galatians 3:23-26)

To prepare our hearts to become more faithful (committed) and faith filled, let us meditate on all the ways our Heavenly Father continues to be faithful in our lives, despite our faults and failures. Isaiah 25:1 tells us, *"O LORD, You are my God. I will exalt You, I will praise Your name, for You have done wonderful things; Your counsels of old are faithfulness and truth."* Moses tells us in Deuteronomy 7:9 *"Therefore know that the LORD your God, He is God, the faithful God who keeps covenant and mercy for a thousand generations with those who love Him and keep His commandments;"* The psalmist rejoices in Psalm 119:89-90, *"Forever, O LORD, Your word is settled in heaven. Your faithfulness endures to all generations; You established the earth, and it abides."* The writer of Lamentations 3:22-24, encouraged himself as he prayed to the Lord in the midst of sorrow, *"Through the LORD's mercies we are not consumed, because His compassions fail not. 23 They are new every morning; great is Your faithfulness. 24 "The*

LORD *is my portion," says my soul, "Therefore I hope in Him!"* Paul declares in 1 Corinthians 1:9, *"God is faithful, by whom you were called into the fellowship of His Son, Jesus Christ our Lord."* Our Heavenly Father is faithful to keep His promises to us, for a thousand generations, who love and obey him. We can put our hope in the Lord!

Yahshua had to become flesh and blood, enduring what it is to be human, overcoming sin and death, to give aid to his brethren. He is our MERCIFUL and FAITHFUL HIGH PRIEST.

<u>1 Samuel 2:35</u> - Then I will raise up for Myself a faithful priest who shall do according to what is in My heart and in My mind. I will build him a sure house, and he shall walk before My anointed forever.

<u>Hebrews 3:1-2</u> - Therefore, holy brethren, partakers of the heavenly calling, consider the Apostle and High Priest of our confession, Christ Jesus, 2 who was faithful to Him who appointed Him, as Moses also was faithful in all His house.

<u>Hebrews 2:14-18</u> - Inasmuch then as the children have partaken of flesh and blood, He Himself likewise shared in the same, that through death He might destroy him who had the power of death, that is, the devil, 15 and release those who through fear of death were all their lifetime subject to bondage. 16 For indeed He does not give aid to angels, but He does give aid to the seed of Abraham. 17 Therefore, in all things He had to be made like His brethren, that He might be a merciful and **faithful High Priest** in things pertaining to God, to make propitiation for the sins of the people. 18 For in that He Himself has suffered, being tempted, He is able to aid those who are tempted.

Did you catch that? Temptation is described as suffering. He aids us when we are tempted because He has suffered being tempted. Apostle Paul explains in 1 Corinthians 10:13, *"No temptation has overtaken you except such as is common to man;* **but God is faithful, who will not allow you to be tempted beyond what you are able***, but with the temptation will also make the way of escape, that you may be able to bear it."* As a teenager growing into my early twenties, I spent a lot of time asking Yahweh to remove temptations, not understanding that He was allowing them to come. Often times it felt like more than what I was able to resist and I surrendered to temptations repeatedly, I rarely took His ways of escape. I needed to be delivered from the bondage of sin. I had unclean spirits that needed to be cast out. If you find yourself in a cycle of sin that you are struggling to break free from, do not be afraid to seek those you trust in the faith to assist in your deliverance.

How often have we not trusted Yahweh's faithfulness to make a way of escape for us in the midst of temptation? Or should I ask, how often have we refused that way? No wonder Yahshua teaches us to pray, in Matthew 6:13, **"And do not lead us into temptation, but <u>deliver us</u> from the evil one. For Yours is the kingdom and the power and the glory forever. Amen"**. Yahweh is **faithful to protect us,** 2 Thessalonians 3:3 says, *"But the <u>Lord is faithful</u>, who will establish you and guard you from the evil one."* 1 Thessalonians 5:23-24 tells us that Yahweh is **faithful to preserve us** as blameless, *"Now may the God of peace Himself sanctify you completely; and may your whole spirit, soul, and body be preserved blameless at the coming of our Lord Jesus Christ. ²⁴ <u>He who calls you is faithful</u>, who also will do it."*

Yahweh is **faithful to forgive**. 1 John 1:9 says, *"If we confess our sins, <u>He is faithful</u> and just to forgive us our sins and to cleanse us from all unrighteousness."* Do you have the faith to receive forgiveness? Often times we live our lives thinking that our sins are too great for Yahweh to forgive. We say, "He could never forgive me for_____

_____"; you fill in the blank. In Matthew 9:2-8 we read an account of a paralytic that encountered Yahshua, *"Then behold, they brought to Him a paralytic lying on a bed.* **When Jesus saw their faith, He said to the paralytic, "Son, be of good cheer; your sins are forgiven you.**" *³ And at once some of the scribes said within themselves, "This Man blasphemes!" ⁴ But Jesus, knowing their thoughts, said, "Why do you think evil in your hearts? ⁵ For which is easier, to say, 'Your sins are forgiven you,' or to say, 'Arise and walk'? ⁶ But that you may know that the Son of Man has power on earth to forgive sins"—then He said to the paralytic, "Arise, take up your bed, and go to your house." ⁷ And he arose and departed to his house. ⁸ Now when the multitudes saw it, they marveled and glorified God, who had given such power to men.* Yahshua told this man to be of good cheer because his sins were forgiven. The greater miracle was the forgiveness of his sins. No one knows the depth of how dark our individual sins are, except Yahweh, and he tells us to change our frowns to smiles, because He made the way for us to be forgiven of all of our sins.

Let's pray.

Heavenly Father, thank you for Yahshua! Thank you for making a way for my sins to be forgiven and for my deliverance and healing. I repent for every displeasing thought, word and action. Thank you for forgiving me. You responded to the faith of the paralytic and His friends, so increase my faith. Help and forgive my unbelief. I want to know and trust you more. Help me to multiply the talents you have placed in me by your precious Holy Spirit. I long to hear you say, well done, good and faithful servant. In Yahshua's name, Amen.

We are so loved and cared for by our Heavenly Father! In His presence our faith is strengthened and renewed. Will you take a moment, put this book down, clap your hands, shout Hallelujah and tell Him thank you for how faithful He has been to you and your family. *"It is good to give thanks to the* L̲o̲r̲d̲*, and to sing praises to Your name, O Most High; ² To declare Your loving kindness in the morning, and Your faithfulness every night, ³ On an instrument of ten strings, on the lute, and on the harp, with harmonious sound. ⁴ For You,* L̲o̲r̲d̲*, have made me glad through Your work; I will triumph in the works of Your hands."* (Psalm 92:1-4)

Allow Yahweh's Word to stir up a praise inside of you. His faithfulness will continue to a thousand of your generations, His mercies are new every morning, He is our Provider, our Protector and the one who rescues us in time of trouble. Are you in trouble today? Do you have an unpaid bill that you are worried about? Are you struggling with sadness, feelings of insecurity and rejection? Do you have a family member trapped in their mess and it looks like there is no way out? Let's call on Yahshua, right now. He is faithful to hear and answer your call!

Ethan the Ezrahite says it like this in Psalm 89:1-13, *"***I will sing of the mercies of the** L̲o̲r̲d̲ **forever; with my mouth will I make known Your faithfulness to all generations. ² For I have said, "Mercy shall be built up forever; Your faithfulness You shall establish in the very heavens."** ³ *"I have made a covenant with My chosen, I have sworn to My servant David: ⁴ 'Your seed I will establish forever, and build up your throne to all generations.'" Selah* ⁵ **And the heavens will praise Your wonders, O** L̲o̲r̲d̲**; Your faithfulness also in the assembly of the saints.** ⁶ *For who in the heavens can be compared to the* L̲o̲r̲d̲*? Who among the sons of the mighty can be likened to the* L̲o̲r̲d̲*? ⁷ God is greatly to be feared in the assembly of the saints, and to be held in reverence by all those around Him.* ⁸ **O** L̲o̲r̲d̲ **God of hosts, who is mighty like You, O** L̲o̲r̲d̲**? Your faithfulness also surrounds You.** ⁹ <u>You rule the raging of the sea; when its waves rise, You still them.</u> ¹⁰ <u>You</u>

have broken Rahab in pieces, as one who is slain; You have scattered Your enemies with Your mighty arm. ¹¹ The heavens are Yours, the earth also is Yours; The world and all its fullness, You have founded them. ¹² The north and the south, You have created them; Tabor and Hermon rejoice in Your name. ¹³ You have a mighty arm; strong is Your hand, and high is Your right hand."

Yahshua is **faithful to heal us**. Isaiah 53:5 declares the prophecy, *"But He was wounded for our transgressions, He was bruised for our iniquities; the chastisement for our peace was upon Him, and by His stripes we are healed."* Throughout the gospels we read of many healings and deliverances that took place at the command of Yahshua. 1 Peter 2:24 tells us, *"who Himself bore our sins in His own body on the tree, that we, having died to sins, might live for righteousness—by whose stripes you were healed."* When Peter and John healed a lame man at the temple in the name of Yahshua the Christ, the people marveled. Peter clarified that it was not by their own power or godliness that the man was healed, Acts 3:16 records, *"And His name, <u>through faith in His name</u>, has made this man strong, whom you see and know. Yes, <u>the faith</u> which comes through Him <u>has given him this perfect soundness</u> in the presence of you all."* James 5:13-18 tells us, *"Is anyone among you suffering? Let him pray. Is anyone cheerful? Let him sing psalms. ¹⁴ Is anyone among you sick? Let him call for the elders of the church, and let them pray over him, anointing him with oil in the name of the Lord.* **¹⁵ And the prayer of faith will save the sick, and the Lord will raise him up. And if he has committed sins, he will be forgiven.** *¹⁶ Confess your trespasses to one another, and pray for one another, that you may be healed. The effective, fervent prayer of a righteous man avails much. ¹⁷ Elijah was a man with a nature like ours, and he prayed earnestly that it would not rain; and it did not rain on the land for three years* and six months. ¹⁸ *And he prayed again, and the heaven gave rain, and the earth produced its fruit."*

The many stories of the mighty works done by Yahshua, are written as a testimony of who He is and to help to fertilize our faith. Here are a few more that Yahshua healed according to their faith:

Two blind men- Matthew 9:29 - *Then he touched their eyes, saying, "According to your faith let it be to you."*

The woman from Canaan with a demon possessed daughter- Matthew 15:28 - *Then Jesus answered and said to her, "O woman, great is your faith! Let it be to you as you desire." And her daughter was healed from that very hour.*

The woman with the issue of blood for twelve years. Mark 5:34 - *And He said to her, "Daughter, your faith has made you well. Go in peace, and be healed of your affliction."*

The centurion that came on behalf of his servant - Luke 7:9 - *When Jesus heard these things, He marveled at him, and turned around and said to the crowd that followed Him, "I say to you, I have not found such great faith, not even in Israel!"*

The woman who anointed His feet- Luke 7:50 - *Then He said to the woman, "Your faith has saved you. Go in peace."*

The one Samaritan leper, out of the ten, who came back to say thanks - Luke 17:19 - *And He said to him, "Arise, go your way. Your faith has made you well."*

The blind beggar, Bartimaeus, who the people tried to silence- Luke 18:42 - *Then Jesus said to him, "Receive your sight; your faith has made you well."*

I am so excited about the fact that Yahweh is our healer, and I know you are!

Yahshua is also called the **faithful witness**. John identifies Him in Revelation 1:5-6, *"and from Jesus Christ, **the faithful witness**, the firstborn from the* *dead, and the ruler over the kings of the earth. To Him who loved us and washed us from our sins in His own blood, ⁶ and has made us kings and priests to His God and Father, to Him be glory and dominion forever and ever. Amen."*

Revelation 3:14 - And to the angel of the church of the Laodiceans write, 'These things says the Amen, **the Faithful and True Witness**, the Beginning of the creation of God:

Revelation 19:11-14 - Now I saw heaven opened, and behold, a white horse. **And He who sat on him was called Faithful and True**, and in righteousness He judges and makes war. ¹² His eyes were like a flame of fire, and on His head were many crowns. He had **a name written that no one knew except Himself.** ¹³ He was clothed with a robe dipped in blood, and **His name is called The Word of God**.

Revelation 21:5-8 - Then He who sat on the throne said, "Behold, I make all things new." And He said to me, **"Write, for these words are true and faithful**." ⁶ And He said to me, "It is done! I am the Alpha and the Omega, the Beginning and the End. I will give of the fountain of the water of life freely to him who thirsts. ⁷ He who overcomes shall inherit all things, and I will be his God and he shall be My son. ⁸ But the cowardly, unbelieving, abominable, murderers, sexually immoral, sorcerers, idolaters, and all liars shall have their part in the lake which burns with fire and brimstone, which is the second death."

Revelation 22:6-7 - Then he said to me, "**These words are faithful and true**." And the Lord God of the holy prophets sent His angel to show His servants the things which must shortly take place. ⁷ "Behold, I am coming quickly! Blessed is he who keeps the words of the prophecy of this book."

Yahweh is **faithful to provide**. The obstacle course around this truth, is, do we really believe He will provide for all of our needs? Yahshua tells us to pray in Matthew

6:11, *"Give us this day our daily bread."* Tell me, is His daily bread enough for you? Exodus 16:4 records, *"Then the LORD said to Moses, "Behold, I will rain bread from heaven for you. And the people shall go out and gather a certain quota every day, that I may test them, whether they will walk in My law or not."* The children of Yahweh were not happy with His provision and they continually wanted more. We wrestle with that same spirit of unsatisfaction in Christ. Here's the key, Yahweh not only looks at our hearts but He pays attention to our fruit. He explained to Moses that He was testing them as to whether they would obey Him or not. Are you willing to obey our Heavenly Father, even if He does not give you everything you want?

Yahshua tells us, *"Therefore I say to you, do not worry about your life, what you will eat or what you will drink; nor about your body, what you will put on. Is not life more than food and the body more than clothing? 26 Look at the birds of the air, for they neither sow nor reap nor gather into barns; yet your heavenly Father feeds them. Are you not of more value than they? 27 Which of you by worrying can add one cubit to his stature? 28 "So why do you worry about clothing? Consider the lilies of the field, how they grow: they neither toil nor spin; 29 and yet I say to you that even Solomon in all his glory was not arrayed like one of these. 30 Now if God so clothes the grass of the field, which today is, and tomorrow is thrown into the oven, will He not much more clothe you,* **O you of little faith***? 31 "Therefore do not worry, saying, 'What shall we eat?' or 'What shall we drink?' or 'What shall we wear?' 32 For after all these things the Gentiles seek. For your heavenly Father knows that you need all these things.* **33 But seek first the kingdom of God and His righteousness, and all these things shall be added to you.** - Matthew 6:25-33

Apostle Paul teaches us in 1 Timothy 6:6-12, *"Now godliness with contentment is great gain. 7 For we* *brought nothing into this world, and it is certain we can carry nothing out.⁸ And having food and clothing, with these we shall be content. ⁹ But those who desire to be rich fall into temptation and a snare, and into many foolish and harmful lusts which drown men in destruction and perdition. ¹⁰ For the love of money is a root of all kinds of evil, for which <u>some have strayed from the faith in their greediness</u>, and pierced themselves through with many sorrows. ¹¹ But you, O man of God, flee these things <u>and pursue righteousness, godliness, faith, love, patience, gentleness</u>. ¹² Fight the good fight of faith, lay hold on eternal life, to which you were also called and have confessed the good confession in the presence of many witnesses.* Solomon warns in Proverbs 28:20, *"A faithful man will abound with blessings, but he who hastens to be rich will not go unpunished."* James 2:5 gives us perspective, *"Listen, my beloved brethren: Has God not chosen the poor of this world to be rich in faith and heirs of the kingdom which He promised to those who love Him?"* Faith grows when we need it the most!

Will you obey our Heavenly Father and seek His kingdom before your kingdom (personal life) and His righteousness? Everything we need is added to us when we are in position to receive, this location on a map is called OBEDIENCE.

Yahweh wants us to become faithful just as He is faithful. Let's take an honest inventory of our lives.

Are You...	Always	Almost Always	Sometimes	Not Often	Never
A Faithful spouse, friend, employee?					
Dedicated to complete tasks you committed to?					
Consistent, can others rely on you?					
Easily Waiver in Your Belief in Christ?					

It is not an easy task to live a faith filled life nor a faithful one. Yet, we expect those nearest to us to be the most loyal; unfortunately, some become to us like Judas was to Christ, or perhaps we become Judas in someone else's life. In developing the fruit of faithfulness, we must choose not to betray each other. Malachi 2:10 asks, *"Are we not all children of the same Father? Are we not all created by the same God? Then why do we betray each other, violating the covenant of our ancestors"* We fall short in so many areas in our relationship with Yahweh and with others. We can talk a great talk, but our words in the end, make us out to be liars. We've all made promises we genuinely intended to keep, but unfortunately, did not. In Proverbs 20:6, we learn, *"Most men will proclaim each his own goodness: But who can find a faithful man?"*

In Proverbs 27:6 we're told, *"Faithful are the wounds of a friend; but the kisses of an enemy are deceitful."* We can count on our friends to hurt us whether unintentionally or purposefully at some point in our journey. Yet an enemy, the one who says they're your friend, but really isn't, will kiss you as Judas kissed Christ. I'm certain that the kiss of betrayal was not the first kiss Judas had given Christ. When Christ chose Judas, He knew he was His betrayer. Thankfully,

Yahweh has invited us to allow Holy Spirit to root out unbelief and unfaithfulness in the soil of our souls and plant seeds of faith, loyalty and hope.

Faithfulness is the quality we all long for in our spouse, children, family and friends. It magnifies the integrity of the positive individuals in our lives, the loyalty we strive to show others and the hope that it will be reciprocated. 2 Chronicles 19:9 tells us, *"And he commanded them, saying, "Thus you shall act in the fear of the LORD, faithfully and with a loyal heart:"* In Revelation 17:14, we see those who are with Christ are called faithful, *"These will make war with the Lamb, and the Lamb will overcome them: for He is Lord of lords, and King of kings; and those who are with him are called, chosen, and faithful."*

Proverbs 11:13 - A talebearer reveals secrets, but he who is of a faithful spirit conceals a matter.

Proverbs 13:17 - A wicked messenger falls into trouble, but a faithful ambassador brings health.

Proverbs 14:5 - A faithful witness does not lie, but a false witness will utter lies.

Proverbs 25:13 - Like the cold of snow in time of harvest is a faithful messenger to those who send him, for he refreshes the soul of his masters.

The following verses clearly lay out Yahweh's desire for His children to walk faithfully in every area and every season of our lives.

Let us take a moment and speak about doing business and handling finances and properties entrusted to us, by the Lord, with integrity. In 2 Kings 12 we read the account of a righteous king of Jerusalem, who reigned there for forty years (835-796 BC), named Jehoash. His desire was to repair the damages of the temple, so he instructed the priests how all the money that was brought in to the house of the Lord should be handled. Twenty-three years pass and the priests had not made any effort in repairing the temple, the King instructed that they take no more money from their constituency, and make the needed repairs with monies they had been collecting over the 23 years. We read that the priests agree to take no more money, yet refuse to repair temple damages. Some accountability measures are put in place and only the king's scribe and the high priest bagged and counted the monies given to the Lord, then they paid those hired to repair the temple damages. 2 Kings 12:15 records, *"Moreover they did not require an account from the men into whose hand they delivered the money to be paid to workmen, for they dealt faithfully."*

Approximately 155 years later we read in 2 Kings 22 about these same types of workers, perhaps they were the grandchildren and great-grandchildren of those mentioned before. During the reign of King Josiah (641-609BC), it is recorded in verse 5-7, *"And let them deliver it into the hand of those doing the work, who are the overseers in the house of the LORD; let them give it to those who are in the house of the LORD doing the work, to repair the damages of the house ⁶ to carpenters and builders and masons and to buy timber and hewn stone to repair the house. ⁷ However* **there need be no accounting made with them of the money delivered into their hand, because they deal faithfully**.*"* These skilled carpenters, builders, masons and stonecutters were considered so faithful that they did not need to implement any accountability measures to ensure their prices for materials and wages paid were honest, they had a great reputation. That should be you and I.

In 2 Corinthians 4:2 Paul tells us, *"Moreover it is required in stewards that one be found faithful."* Whether we are managing money, our families, our homes, our careers, everything that we have been given by Yahweh to supervise, we are required to be faithful. Yahshua tells us in Luke 16:10-13, *"He who is faithful in what is least is faithful also in much; and he who is* unjust in what is least is unjust also in much. ¹¹ Therefore if you have not been faithful in the unrighteous mammon, who will commit to your trust the true riches? ¹² And if you have not been faithful in what is another man's, who will give you what is your own? ¹³ "No servant can serve two masters; for either he will hate the one and love the other, or else he will be loyal to the one and despise the other. You cannot serve God and mammon."

Let's pause here and whisper this prayer together:

Heavenly Father, please help me to be faithful in all I say and do. I repent for the times I have served money instead of you. Please forgive me for every unfaithful act. Thank you, in Yahshua's name, Amen.

Let this be our motto, "*I have been crucified with Christ; it is no longer I who live, but Christ lives in me; and the life which I now live in the flesh* **I live by faith in the Son of God**, *who loved me and gave Himself for me. (Galatians 2:20)*" Our faith in Yahshua gives us VICTORY to overcome the world! He is the author and finisher of our faith (Hebrews 12:2). I John 5:3-5 tells us, "*For this is the love of God, that we keep His commandments. And His commandments are not burdensome.* ⁴ *For whatever is born of God overcomes the world.* **And this is the victory that has overcome the world - our faith.** ⁵ *Who is he who overcomes the world, but he who believes that Jesus is the Son of God?*"

"*Oh, love the LORD, all you His saints!*
For the LORD preserves the faithful, and fully repays the proud person." *Psalm 31:23*

CHAPTER TWELVE
Developing: Gentleness/Meekness
Let your gentleness be known to all men. The Lord is at hand. Philippians 4:5

In Galatians 5:23, the Greek word, *praotēs,* is translated as gentleness, mildness, and meekness. In Hebrew, the word *anva,* is translated as humility and meekness. As we develop the fruit of Gentleness, we will look at three aspects, likening it unto a KIWI, because we are able to consume its' fuzzy brown skin (which has more fiber than its pulp), tiny black seeds (an excellent source of omega-3 fatty acids) and sweet green pulp. This super fruit is a powerful antioxidant that supports our immune system, with vital nutrients such as Vitamins C and B6, while providing high amounts of Vitamin K to our diets. Kiwi continues to be researched for its preventative and medicinal benefits to our bodies.

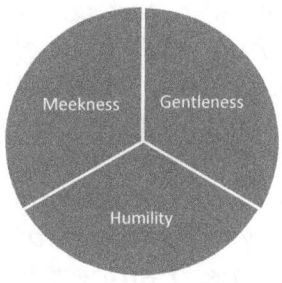

Throughout scripture, depending on your preferred translation, meekness, gentleness and humility, seem to be used interchangeably. In Titus 3:2 we are instructed, *"to speak evil of no one, to be peaceable, gentle, showing all humility to all men."* Paul writes in Ephesians 4:1-3, *"I, therefore, the prisoner of the Lord, beseech you to walk worthy of the calling with which you were called, <u>with all lowliness and gentleness</u> (KJV translates as meekness), with longsuffering, bearing with one another in love, endeavoring to keep the unity of the Spirit in the bond of peace."*

James 1:21 says, *"Therefore lay aside all filthiness and overflow of wickedness, and <u>receive with meekness the implanted word</u>, which is able to save your souls."* It takes meekness to receive Yahweh's word as it is planted in the soil of our souls. A meek person is one who is continually growing because he/she remains teachable. Once you view yourself as complete, not needing to grow in the ways of Yahshua, then you are unable to receive. You will hear the Word, but will be unable to apply the word, because you have deceived yourself into thinking you have reached your highest height of holiness.

Our Lord Yahshua shares a parable in Luke 18:9-14 about a self-righteous religious leader and a humble sinner. *"Also He spoke this parable <u>to some who trusted in themselves that they were righteous, and despised others</u>:* [10] *"Two men went up to the temple to pray, one a Pharisee and the other a tax collector.* [11] *The Pharisee stood and prayed thus with himself, 'God, I thank You that I am not like other men—extortioners, unjust, adulterers, or even as this tax collector.* [12] *I fast twice a week; I give tithes of all that I possess.'* [13] *And the tax collector, standing afar off, would not so much as raise his eyes to heaven, but beat his breast, saying, 'God, be merciful to me a sinner!'*[14] *I tell you, this man went down to his house justified rather than the other;*

for everyone who exalts himself will be humbled, and he who humbles himself will be exalted." Notice the Pharisee came boldly before Yahweh, giving praises for his own "righteousness", whereas the tax collector came humbly acknowledging his sin and pleading for mercy. It is he that the Lord justified. James 4:6 says, *"But He gives more grace. Therefore, He says: "God resists the proud, but gives grace to the humble."*

We must guard our hearts from the temptation of thinking more highly of ourselves than we ought to, so as not to allow pride to gain a foothold in our lives. Yahshua honors pure motives. Many times pride is falsified as humility. Pray that your motives are pure and that pride is not falsified as humility in your life. Do not allow others to praise and worship you as if you are Christ incarnate in the Earth. In Acts 10:25-26, we see Cornelius falling down at Peter's feet to worship him, but Peter lifts him from the floor and says, *"Stand up; I myself am also a man."* Let us not forget that we ourselves are still men and women, no matter how many lives our Heavenly Father allows us to impact.

<u>Colossians 2:18</u> - Let no one cheat you of your reward, taking delight in false humility and worship of angels, intruding into those things which he has not seen, vainly puffed up by his fleshly mind,

<u>Colossians 2:23</u> - These things indeed have an appearance of wisdom in self-imposed religion, false humility, and neglect of the body, but are of no value against the indulgence of the flesh.

Yahweh speaks through Zephaniah in 3:11-13, *"In that day you shall not be shamed for any of your deeds in which you transgress against Me; <u>for then I will take away from your midst those who rejoice in your pride, and you shall no longer be haughty in My holy mountain.</u> ¹² <u>I will leave in your midst a meek and humble people, and they shall trust in the name of the</u> LORD. ¹³ The remnant of Israel shall do no unrighteousness and speak* no lies, nor shall a deceitful tongue be found in their mouth; for they shall feed their flocks and lie down, and no one shall make them afraid."* A day is coming, when Yahweh will remove the proud and haughty and leave a meek and humble people, who trust in the name of the Lord, do no unrighteousness, speak no lies and live without fear. Psalm 37:11 states, *"But the meek shall inherit the earth, and shall delight themselves in the abundance of peace"* Yahshua reiterates this in Matthew 5:5, *"Blessed are the meek, for they shall inherit the earth."* What a blessing for those of us who chose to allow Holy Spirit to cultivate this fruit in our lives!

Gentleness is likened to a nursing mother cherishing her children. It is an affection that is acted out selflessly. Paul writes in 1 Thessalonians 2:4-9, *"But as we have been approved by God to be entrusted with the gospel, even so we speak, not as pleasing men, but God who tests our hearts. ⁵ For neither at any time did we use flattering words, as you know, nor a cloak for covetousness—God is witness. ⁶ Nor did we seek glory from men, either from you or from others, when we might have made demands as apostles of Christ. ⁷ <u>But we were gentle among you, just as a nursing mother cherishes her own children. ⁸ So, affectionately longing for you, we were well pleased to impart to you not only the gospel of God, but also our own lives, because you had become dear to us.</u> ⁹ For you remember, brethren, our labor and toil; for laboring night and day, that we might not be a burden to any of you, we preached to you the gospel of God."* When I think of a mother's gentleness, I have a clearer and deeper understanding of this fruit the Lord is requiring from us. It does not matter how old my children get, I always see them as the fragile baby that I once held in one arm. As a parent, you become very protective, not wanting anyone or anything to harm your child. This is how we are to treat people, as fragile, not wanting to break them with our words or actions, but tenderly caring for them with the love of Yahweh. Paul and those with him, labored on behalf of the Thessalonians, asking for nothing in return. You'll know this fruit is growing when you expect nothing in return for your labor of love in others' lives, except the fruit of salvation.

When those you are laboring for fall into sin, should you still deal with them gently? Paul asked in 1Corinthians 4:21, *"What do you want? Shall I come to you with a rod, or in love and a spirit of gentleness?"* He writes in 2 Corinthians 10:1, *"Now I, Paul, myself am <u>pleading with you by the meekness and gentleness of Christ—who in presence am lowly among you</u>, but being absent am bold toward you."*

When one of us is found in fault, we are told in Galatians 6:1, *"Brethren, if a man is overtaken in any trespass, you who are spiritual restore such a one in a <u>spirit of gentleness</u>, considering yourself lest you also be tempted."* We can do more harm than good to others, when correction is brought, if not done in the right spirit. We are warned not to forget that we ourselves can be tempted, that's why the wisest position is the gentle and humble one, never thinking you are untouchable, unbreakable and unshameable. Solomon teaches in Proverbs 11:2, *"When pride comes, then comes shame; but with the humble is wisdom."*

We are called to share Yahweh's truth in meekness. *"But sanctify the Lord God in your hearts, and always <u>be ready to give a defense</u> to everyone who asks you a reason for the hope that is in you, <u>with meekness and fear</u>;"* (1 Peter 3:15) Peter tells us we must always be ready to speak about Yahshua, from a heart of humility and reverence for Yahweh. Gentleness is a pleasant non-quarrelling demeanor as well as a lowly position we take, for the sake of peace and drawing others to Yahshua. Paul tells Timothy, *"But avoid foolish and* *ignorant disputes, knowing that they generate strife. ²⁴ And a servant of the Lord <u>must not quarrel but be gentle to all</u>, able to teach, patient, ²⁵ <u>in humility correcting those who are in opposition</u>, if God perhaps will grant them repentance, so that they may know the truth, ²⁶ and that they may come to their senses and escape the snare of the devil, having been taken captive by him to do his will."* (2 Timothy 2:23-26) Oh man, I have gotten this wrong on too many occasions. My passion for Christ at times may have come out like a volcanic explosion unintentionally burning everyone in my path. In these times of my life, I probably pushed more people away from Christ than drawing them to Him. Our gentle delivery can bring someone to their senses, thereby freeing them from the enemy's grip. But if you and I are more concerned about getting our points across and always being right, then we have lost sight of the soul that stands before us.

James teaches that our works should be done in the **meekness of wisdom**. He discusses the differences between Yahweh's Wisdom and Earthly Wisdom. *"Who is wise and understanding among you? Let him show by good conduct that his works are done in the <u>meekness of wisdom</u>. ¹⁴ But if you have bitter envy and self-seeking in your hearts, do not boast and lie against the truth. ¹⁵ This wisdom does not descend from above, but is earthly, sensual, demonic. ¹⁶ For where envy and self-seeking exist, confusion and every evil thing are there. ¹⁷ <u>But the wisdom that is from above is first pure, then peaceable, gentle, willing to yield, full of mercy and good fruits, without partiality and without hypocrisy.</u>"* (James 3:13-17)

YAHWEH'S WISDOM	EARTHLY WISDOM
Meekness	Bitterness
Purity	Envy
Peaceable	Self-Seeking
Gentle	Sensual
Willing to Yield	Demonic
Merciful	Confusion
Full of Good Fruits	Every Evil Thing
Impartiality	Partiality
Sincerity	Hypocrisy

We need Yahweh's wisdom in everything we do and say. Let's take a few minutes and search our hearts. If you identify with any of the characteristics of earthly wisdom, repent, ask for forgiveness and invite Holy Spirit to uproot everything not like Him and replace it with everything that is Him. In Matthew 10:16 Yahshua instructs, *"Behold, I send you out as sheep in the midst of wolves. Therefore, be wise as serpents and harmless as doves."* We must be a wise and harmless people. Romans 12:16 instructs, *"Be of the same mind toward one another. Do not set your mind on high things, but associate with the humble. Do not be wise in your own opinion."*

Yahweh uses longsuffering as a tool to humble us. Often times we don't understand His timing or His will for our lives. It is important that we consider just how important the development of humility is to Him. This is seen more clearly in His handling of the Israelites in the wilderness. Yahweh considered Moses to be the most humble man on the face of the earth at this time. Numbers 12:3 describes, *"(Now the man Moses was very humble, more than all men who were on the face of the earth.)"* Although Moses led from a heart of humility, those entrusted to his care had some pride and disobedience issues. Remember, we cannot grow without meekness. The Lord's desire is for us all to grow, even if it takes forty years.

Deuteronomy 8:2 - And you shall remember that the Lord your God led you all the way these forty years in the wilderness, to humble you and test you, to know what was in your heart, whether you would keep His commandments or not.
Deuteronomy 8:3 - So He humbled you, allowed you to hunger, and fed you with manna which you did not know nor did your fathers know, that He might make you know that man shall not live by bread alone; but man lives by every word that proceeds from the mouth of the Lord.
Deuteronomy 8:16 - who fed you in the wilderness with manna, which your fathers did not know, that He might humble you and that He might test you, to do you good in the end

Choosing humility daily can prove to be challenging, but our Heavenly Father promises to revive us and increase our joy in Him.
Isaiah 29:19 - The humble also shall increase their joy in the Lord, and the poor among men shall rejoice In the Holy One of Israel.
Isaiah 57:15 - For thus says the High and Lofty One Who inhabits eternity, whose name is Holy: "I dwell in the high and holy place, with him who has a contrite and humble spirit, to revive the spirit of the humble, and to revive the heart of the contrite ones.

At times we may feel that, being humble, meek and gentle is equivalent to us being weak; allowing others to take advantage of us. We might even say, "Don't confuse my kindness for weakness!" But this is not what God is asking of us when he invites us to allow Him to develop this fruit in our lives. We are made in Yahweh's image and He invites us to be just like Him. He is gentle, meek and humble and His gentleness makes us great. *"You have also given me the shield of Your salvation; Your gentleness has made me great." (2 Samuel 22:36).* King David sang, *"You have also given me the shield of Your salvation; Your right hand has held me up, Your gentleness has made me great." (Psalm 18:35)*

Psalm 45:4 - And in Your majesty ride prosperously because of truth and humility (KJV translates as meekness) and righteousness; and Your right hand shall teach You awesome things.

Psalm 113:5-6 - Who is like the LORD our God, Who dwells on high, ⁶ who humbles Himself to behold the things that are in the heavens and in the earth?

Hosea 11:4 - I drew them with gentle cords, with bands of love, and I was to them as those who take the yoke from their neck. I stooped and fed them.

Matthew 11:29 - Take My yoke upon you and learn from Me, for I am gentle and lowly in heart, and you will find rest for your souls.

Philippians 2:3-11 - Let nothing be done through selfish ambition or conceit, but in lowliness of mind let each esteem others better than himself. ⁴ Let each of you look out not only for his own interests, but also for the interests of others. ⁵ Let this mind be in you which was also in Christ Jesus, ⁶ who, being in the form of God, did not consider it robbery to be equal with God, ⁷ but made Himself of no reputation, taking the form of a bondservant, and coming in the likeness of men. ⁸ And being found in appearance as a man, He humbled Himself and became obedient to the point of death, even the death of the cross. ⁹ Therefore God also has highly exalted Him and given Him the name which is above every name, ¹⁰ that at the name of Jesus every knee should bow, of those in heaven, and of those on earth, and of those under the earth, ¹¹ and that every tongue should confess that Jesus Christ is Lord, to the glory of God the Father.

Just as our Heavenly Father exalted Yahshua because He humbled himself, Yahshua tells us in Matthew 18:4, *"Therefore whoever humbles himself as this little child is the greatest in the kingdom of heaven."* The humble will be exalted.

Psalm 147:6 - The Lord lifts up the humble; He casts the wicked down to the ground.
Proverbs 16:19 - Better to be of a humble spirit with the lowly, than to divide the spoil with the proud.
Proverbs 22:4 - By humility and the fear of the Lord are riches and honor and life.
Proverbs 29:23 - A man's pride will bring him low, but the humble in spirit will retain honor.
Proverbs 15:33 - The fear of the LORD is the instruction of wisdom, and before honor is humility.
Proverbs 18:12 - Before destruction the heart of a man is haughty, and before honor is humility.
Isaiah 10:33 - Behold, the Lord, The Lord of hosts, Will lop off the bough with terror; those of high stature will be hewn down, and the haughty will be humbled.
Matthew 23:12 - And whoever exalts himself will be humbled, and he who humbles himself will be exalted.
James 4:10 - Humble yourselves in the sight of the Lord, and He will lift you up.
1 Peter 5:5-6 - Likewise you younger people, submit yourselves to your elders. Yes, all of you be submissive to one another, and be clothed with humility, for "God resists the proud, but gives grace to the humble." [6] Therefore humble yourselves under the mighty hand of God, that He may exalt you in due time,

Yahweh gives many promises to the humble, let's meditate on them. Just as Kiwi is used as a meat tenderizer, when our hearts become tender we are then able to humble ourselves. *"because your heart was tender, and you humbled yourself before the Lord when you heard what I spoke against this place and against its inhabitants, that they would become a desolation and a curse, and you tore your clothes and wept before Me, I also have heard you,"* says the Lord." (2 Kings 22:19). Our Heavenly Father promises to answer the prayers of the humble and repentant.
2 Chronicles 7:14 - if My people who are called by My name will humble themselves, and pray and seek My

face, and turn from their wicked ways, then I will hear from heaven, and will forgive their sin and heal their land.

2 Chronicles 32:26 - Then Hezekiah humbled himself for the pride of his heart, he and the inhabitants of Jerusalem, so that the wrath of the Lord did not come upon them in the days of Hezekiah.

Psalm 10:17 - Lord, You have heard the desire of the humble; You will prepare their heart; You will cause Your ear to hear,

Daniel 10:12 - Then he said to me, "Do not fear, Daniel, for from the first day that you set your heart to understand, and to humble yourself before your God, your words were heard; and I have come because of your words."

Zephaniah 2:3 implores, *"Seek the LORD, all you meek of the earth, who have upheld His justice. Seek righteousness, seek humility* (KJV translates as meekness). *It may be that you will be hidden in the day of the LORD's anger."* Zephaniah describes the characteristics of those who are meek as those who **uphold justice. He implores them to seek the Lord, seek righteousness and seek humility, that they may be hidden in the day of the Lord's anger.** David says in Psalm 25:9, *"The humble He guides in justice, and the humble He teaches His way."* What a benefit! I need justice displayed in my life and more than anything I desire to be taught by our Lord and Savior. Yahweh promises to save those who are humble.

Psalm 18:27 - For You will save the humble people, But will bring down haughty looks.

Psalm 149:4 - For the Lord takes pleasure in His people; He will beautify the humble with salvation.

Proverbs 3:34 - Surely He scorns the scornful, but gives grace to the humble.

2 Samuel 22:28 - You will save the humble people; but Your eyes are on the haughty, that You may bring them down.

<u>Isaiah 11:4</u> - But with righteousness He shall judge the poor, and <u>decide with equity for the meek of the earth</u>; He shall strike the earth with the rod of His mouth, and with the breath of His lips He shall slay the wicked.

Heavenly Father, please help me to be gentle, meek and humble for your glory and the salvation and healing of others. I repent and renounce the spirit of haughtiness and exchange it for a gentle, meek and humble spirit. In Yahshua's name, Amen.

CHAPTER THIRTEEN
Developing: Self-Control/Temperance
"to knowledge self-control, to self-control perseverance, to perseverance godliness," 2 Peter 1:6

When my eldest child took a trip to the Emergency Room, his potassium levels came back slightly lower than they should be, the doctor told him to eat a banana. I found out that an avocado contains more potassium than a banana. The avocado, which grows in abundance in my yard, claims its' fame, for being high in healthy fats and fiber, which makes losing weight fun without sacrificing that delicious creamy taste. Used as a side dish, in salads, shakes, dips and more, avocado is packed with nutrients that benefit our entire health.

Imagine this...

Your favorite junk food is calling your name. Its midnight and you know you shouldn't eat it. Do you exercise self-control by choosing a healthy snack or give into the craving?

You are courting your very attractive future spouse. Your bodies entice you to engage in acts that should be saved for marriage. Do you give into the raw cravings, or exercise self-control by quickly leaving the environment that is proving to be a place of great temptation?

Paul clearly lays out that Yahweh's will is for us to live sanctified lives. *"For this is the will of God, your sanctification: that you should abstain from sexual immorality; 4 that each of you should know how to possess his own vessel in sanctification and honor, 5 not in passion of lust, like the Gentiles who do not know God;"* (1 Thessalonians 4:3-5). Our Heavenly Father is expecting us to know how to possess, in other words, control our own bodies. He says that those who do not know Yahweh are the ones who allow their passion for lust to control them. What controls you?

We have all found ourselves in the valley of decision, conflicted, debating in our minds whether to follow our fleshly desires or obey the will of Yahweh. We are tempted to lie, steal, cheat, kill, fornicate, abuse alcohol and the list goes on. To our shame we have all sinned and fallen short of the glory of God, according to Romans 3:23.

Self- control is one of the more challenging fruits to develop because it requires a complete change in our mindsets. Most of us want love, joy, peace, gentleness, goodness, faith, meekness. We definitely don't want longsuffering, but we don't have a choice in that; life just happens, we get the sunshine mixed in with the rain. But, when it comes to self-control, everyone seems to set their own guidelines of what self-control looks like in their lives.

There are many who believe that as long as you're not hurting anyone else, you should do whatever makes you feel good, whether Yahweh approves or disapproves. For example, should I partake in the distribution or abuse of substances that alters how I feel? Should I be involved in sexual acts that Scripture condemns? Should I condone the killing of babies based on whether they are located inside or outside the body? If my mind is Christ centered my desires are focused on pleasing

Him and not my flesh. As of 2016, amongst those who call themselves believers and followers of Christ, there does not seem to be a consensus on what boundaries we should set for ourselves. Remember, Yahweh laid out all of the boundaries in His Word for our safety and the safety of others, yet many in Christendom have chosen to disagree with or disregard Yahweh's guidelines and principles. Is your lifestyle aligned with Yahweh's Word? Have you become comfortable with "going along to get along" even when doing so compromises Yahweh's Word? If you want to live in the fullness of His Word, I encourage you to stop right here, repent and change.

King Solomon describes it perfectly in Proverbs 25:28, *"Whoever has no rule over his own spirit, is like a city broken down, without walls."* If a city has no protection it is vulnerable to its enemies. When we do not control ourselves we have given the enemy of our souls an open invitation. Apostle Peter encourages us in 1 Peter 1:13-16, *"Therefore <u>gird up the loins of your mind, be sober</u>, and rest your hope fully upon the grace that is to be brought to you at the revelation of Jesus Christ; ¹⁴ as obedient children, not conforming yourselves to the former lusts, as in your ignorance; ¹⁵ but as He who called you is holy, you also be holy in all your conduct, ¹⁶ because it is written, "Be holy, for I am holy."* May I encourage you to not make excuses for your lust issues and unholy living? Before you accepted Christ, you did not know better. Now each of us are without excuse, no matter what is taught from a pulpit, we all are responsible to read Yahweh's Word for ourselves and understand that we are required to live obediently, holy unto the Lord in **every area of our lives**. Even husbands and wives are not to deprive each other of sexual intimacy because of the temptation the devil will bring. Paul writes, *"Do not deprive one another except with consent for a time, that you may give yourselves to fasting and prayer; and come together again so that Satan does not tempt you <u>because of your lack of self-</u>*

<u>control."</u> (1 Corinthians 7:5)

Self-control is the ability to control our desires and passions. It is the disciplined state of the human, mind, body and emotions. We must exercise self-control in our finances, speech, eating, temper, and every other area of our lives. It is vital that we allow the Spirit of Yahweh to lead us into self-control, because without Him, we will be controlled by the sinful nature. We are called by Yahweh to exercise self-control. The Apostle Paul explains in Romans 8:5-17: <u>*For those who live according to the flesh*</u> ***set their minds on the things of the flesh***, *but* <u>*those who live according to the Spirit*</u>, ***the things of the Spirit.*** **⁶ *For to be carnally minded is death*,** *but* ***to be spiritually minded is life and peace.*** ⁷ *Because* <u>*the carnal mind is enmity against God*</u>; *for it is not subject to the law of God, nor indeed can be.* ⁸ *So then,* <u>*those who are in the flesh cannot please God.*</u> **⁹ But you are not in the flesh but in the Spirit, if indeed the Spirit of God dwells in you. Now if anyone does not have the Spirit of Christ, he is not His.** ¹⁰ *And if Christ is in you, the body is dead because of sin, but the Spirit is life because of righteousness.* ¹¹ *But if the Spirit of Him who raised Jesus from the dead dwells in you, He who raised Christ from the dead will also give life to your mortal bodies through His Spirit who dwells in you* **¹² Therefore, brethren, we are debtors—not to the flesh, to live according to the flesh. ¹³ For if you live according to the flesh you will die; but if by the Spirit you put to death the deeds of the body, you will live. ¹⁴ For as many as are led by the Spirit of God, these are sons of God. ¹⁵ For you did not receive the spirit of bondage again to fear, but you received the Spirit of adoption by whom we cry out, "Abba, Father."** ¹⁶ *The Spirit Himself bears witness with our spirit that we are children of God,* ¹⁷ *and if children, then heirs—heirs of God and joint heirs with Christ, if indeed we suffer with Him, that we may also be glorified together.*

This passage clarifies why I believe this fruit has everything to do with our mindsets. Every morning we wake up, we must decide what we will set our mind on.

CARNAL MIND	SPIRITUAL MIND
Lives according to the flesh	Lives according to the Spirit
Death	Life and Peace
Enmity against God	Dead to sin
Not subject to the law of God	Spirit is life because of righteousness
Cannot please God	Gives life to our mortal bodies
Does not belong to Christ	Put to death the deeds of the body, you will live
You will die	Led by the Spirit of God, makes you a son of God through the Spirit of adoption
Bondage to fear	We have a witness
	Children of God, Heirs of God, joint heirs with Christ
	We suffer with Him that we may be glorified together

Please note that the carnal mind represents spiritual bondage to fear, while the Spirit led mind is our confirmation that we have received the Spirit of adoption and are children of Yahweh. In 2 Timothy 1:7, Paul says, *"For God has not given us the spirit of fear, but of power, and of love, and of a sound mind."* Yahweh's Sprit is a Spirit of Power of Love and Sound Mind!

As a side note, I am aware that there are individuals in other religions who seem to have mastered the art of controlling their body, emotions, and even the elements around them. I would like to issue a warning against this. It is not the will of Yahweh that we combine other methods and belief systems, such as Buddhism, Hinduism, Reiki, Meditations to balance Chakras and any other techniques with our Christian faith. I assure you, in love for you and love for those who practice these ways, that these things are being done through another spirit.

So what is the difference between the Fruit of the Spirit called SELF-CONTROL and the self-control that comes from another religion? The first story that comes to mind is that of Moses. Remember when Aaron threw his staff down before Pharaoh in Exodus 7 and it became a serpent? The Egyptian magicians did the same thing with their magic! But something phenomenal happened, Aaron's staff swallowed up their staffs. The enemy of our soul will always try to replicate what God does but the self-control that comes from the Spirit of God is a greater fruit than that which comes from the world! We must allow Christ's love to control as He did Paul in 2 Corinthians 5:14.

Leaders of Christ's church and their spouses are called to live lives of temperance, self-control.

A bishop then must be blameless, the husband of one wife, temperate, sober-minded, of good behavior, hospitable, able to teach; - 1 Timothy 3:2

Likewise, their wives must be reverent, not slanderers, temperate, faithful in all things. - 1 Timothy 3:11

that the older men be sober, reverent, temperate, sound in faith, in love, in patience; - Titus 2:2

Please understand that it is very important for you to examine the fruit of your life and the life of your spiritual leaders. Do not allow yourself to be deceived because someone is giving you doctrine that makes you comfortable in your sins. Let us heed the warning given in 2 Peter 2:1-3, *"But there were also false prophets among the people, even as there will be false teachers among you, who will secretly bring in destructive heresies, even denying the Lord who bought them, and bring on themselves swift destruction. 2 And many will follow their destructive ways, because of whom the way of truth will be blasphemed. 3 By covetousness they will exploit you with deceptive words; for a long time their judgment has not been idle, and their destruction does not slumber."*

As parents, teachers, and leaders we must teach children self-control. Apostle Paul tells Timothy in 2 Timothy 3:15, *"and that from childhood you have known the Holy Scriptures, which are able to make you wise for salvation through faith which is in Christ Jesus."* We cannot be satisfied with a generation of youth growing up thinking they can do whatever feels right, whether it is against the law of God or not.

King Solomon says it best...

My son, do not despise the chastening of the LORD, nor detest His correction; 12 for whom the LORD loves He corrects, just as a father the son in whom he delights. - Proverbs 3:11-12

He who spares his rod hates his son, but he who loves him disciplines him promptly. - Proverbs 13:24

Foolishness is bound up in the heart of a child; the rod of correction will drive it far from him. - Proverbs 22:15

Do not withhold correction from a child, For if you beat him with a rod, he will not die. - Proverbs 23:13

The rod and rebuke give wisdom, but a child left to himself brings shame to his mother. - Proverbs 29:15

Correct your son, and he will give you rest; yes, he will give delight to your soul. - Proverbs 29:17

Apostle Paul teaches that the last days will be perilous times. He describes the fruit of men in these coming or present times. As you review the list, can you identify with any of those traits?

PERILOUS LAST DAYS, MEN WILL BE...
2 Timothy 3:1-5

Lovers of Self	Money Lovers
Proud	Blasphemers
Unthankful	Unholy
Unforgiving	Slanderers
Traitors	Unloving
Brutal	Despisers of Good
Without Self-Control	Disobedient to Parents
Headstrong	Haughty
Love Pleasure Rather than God	Form of Godliness, Denying its Power
Boasters	

Apostle Paul warned in 2 Timothy 3:6-7 that these men are those who
- Creep into Households.
- Make captives of gullible women who are:
    - Loaded down with sins.
    - Led away by various lusts.
    - Always learning and never able to come to the knowledge of the truth.

Do you have any similarities to these gullible women? Are you loaded down with sins? Led away by various lusts? Are you always learning and never able to come to the knowledge of the truth about Yahshua and the freedom He brings when we accept and obey Him? 2

Peter 1:3-11 teaches us how to get and maintain our self-control, through Christ's divine power.

"as His divine power has given to us all things that pertain to life and godliness, <u>through the knowledge of Him who called us by glory and virtue</u>, 4 by which have been given to us exceedingly great and precious promises, that through these you may be partakers of the divine nature, having escaped the corruption that is in the world through lust. 5 But also for this very reason, giving all diligence, add to your faith virtue, to virtue knowledge, 6 <u>to knowledge self-control, to self-control perseverance,</u> to perseverance godliness, 7 to godliness brotherly kindness, and to brotherly kindness love. 8 <u>For if these things are yours and abound, you will be neither barren nor unfruitful in the knowledge of our Lord Jesus Christ.</u> 9 For he who lacks these things is shortsighted, even to blindness, and has forgotten that he was cleansed from his old sins. 10 Therefore, brethren, be even more diligent to make your call and election sure, for if you do these things you will never stumble; 11 for so an entrance will be supplied to you abundantly into the everlasting kingdom of our Lord and Savior Jesus Christ."

Peter tells us we must add self-control to knowledge. You have to have a revelation and understanding, to be able to walk in the freedom Yahshua brings. In Psalm 32:8-9 the Lord says through David, *"I will instruct you and teach you in the way you should go; I will guide you with My eye. 9 Do not be like the horse or like the mule, which have no understanding, which must be harnessed with bit and bridle, else they will not come near you."* The Lord is inviting us to come near Him and be taught by Him. He wants to give us understanding. Let's accept His invitation so we will not be considered an ignorant mule.

2 Peter 2:19-20, states, *"While they promise them liberty, they themselves are slaves of corruption; <u>for by whom a</u>*

person is overcome, by him also he is brought into bondage. ²⁰ *For if, after they have escaped the pollutions of the world through the knowledge of the Lord and Savior Jesus Christ, they are again entangled in them and overcome, the latter end is worse for them than the beginning.* We are slaves to anyone and anything that controls us. I plead with you by the Spirit of Yahweh, DO NOT LET SIN CONTROL YOU, you must rule over it! Genesis 4:7 - If you do well, will you not be accepted? And if you do not do well, sin lies at the door. And its desire is for you, but you should rule over it."

Psalm 19:12-14 - Who can understand his errors? Cleanse me from secret faults.¹³ Keep back Your servant also from presumptuous sins; Let them not have dominion over me. Then I shall be blameless, and I shall be innocent of great transgression. ¹⁴ Let the words of my mouth and the meditation of my heart be acceptable in Your sight, O LORD, my strength and my Redeemer.

Proverbs 5:21-23 - For the ways of man are before the eyes of the LORD, and He ponders all his paths. ²² His own iniquities entrap the wicked man, and he is caught in the cords of his sin. ²³ He shall die for lack of instruction, and in the greatness of his folly he shall go astray.

Romans 6:12 - Therefore do not let sin reign in your mortal body, that you should obey it in its lusts.

Romans 7:5 - For when we were in the flesh, the sinful passions which were aroused by the law were at work in our members to bear fruit to death.

1Corinthians 3:3 - for you are still carnal. For here there are envy, strife, and divisions among you, are you not carnal and behaving like mere men?

We must learn to control our emotions. Solomon writes in Proverbs 16:32, *"He who is slow to anger is better than the mighty, and he who rules his spirit than he who takes a city."* It is more beneficial to have control over yourself than to have control over others. It is more valuable to control yourself than to control cities and nations. It is very normal to get angry, unfortunately when we do get angry, most times we do not handle it in the way Yahweh has taught. We allow our anger to control our thoughts, words and actions, instead of us controlling it. Solomon says in Proverbs 14:29, *"He who is slow to wrath has great understanding, but he who is impulsive exalts folly."* Having understanding helps us to control ourselves. Our impulsivity will cause us to do and say foolish things. Solomon warns in Ecclesiastes 7:9, *"Do not hasten in your spirit to be angry, for anger rests in the bosom of fools."* How did David, Solomon's dad, define a fool? In Psalm 14:1, David said, *"The fool has said in his heart, "There is no God." They are corrupt, they have done abominable works, there is none who does good."* His description reminds me of those who are controlled by a carnal mind. Do not chose to be a fool, chose to be a sensible person. Solomon said in Proverbs 19:11, *"The discretion of a man makes him slow to anger, and his glory is to overlook a transgression."*

Are you willing to overlook transgressions? This sounds like forgiveness to me. David sings, in Psalm 4:4, *"Be angry, and do not sin. Meditate within your heart on your bed, and be still. Selah"* When we get angry, we need to relax by laying down and becoming very still in the presence of our Almighty Father and process our emotions in His presence, until there is peace within us. The Apostle Paul adds, *"Be angry, and do not sin": do not let the sun go down on your wrath, nor give place to the devil."* (Ephesians 4:26-27). When you let anger control you, you are like the city with no walls, giving your enemy a foothold.

<u>We must learn to control our tongues</u>. James teaches that our religion is useless and we have deceived ourselves if we do not control our tongues. *"If anyone among you thinks he is religious, and does not bridle his tongue but deceives his own heart, this one's*

religion is useless." (James 1:26) He further explains that whoever controls their tongue, is able to control their whole body. *"For we all stumble in many things. If anyone does not stumble in word, he is a perfect man, able also to bridle the whole body."* (James 3:2) Solomon warned in Proverbs 13:3, *"He who guards his mouth preserves his life, but he who opens wide his lips shall have destruction."* It seems next to impossible to control our words on our own, so we cry out like David in Psalm 141:3, *"Set a guard, O LORD, over my mouth; Keep watch over the door of my lips."*

This fruit of self-control looks like complete obedience to Yahweh in our lifestyles. The presence of it exemplifies that we are students of the Most High God, who hear His Word with understanding and live it out in our physical bodies. The lack of it brings us into disobedience and magnifies ignorance.

CHAPTER FOURTEEN
Developing: Righteousness

Those who are wise shall shine like the brightness of the firmament, and those who turn many to righteousness like the stars forever and ever. Daniel 12:3

If you have not tried a star fruit, I would like to encourage you to taste this delicious sweet, sometimes sour fruit. All parts of it are edible; when choosing, the more yellow this fruit is, the sweeter it will be. Think of the scripture above, those who turn many to righteousness shine like the stars forever. The brighter we are, the tastier we are in the lives of others. In Matthew 13:43, Yahshua tells us, *"Then the righteous will shine forth as the sun in the kingdom of their Father. He who has ears to hear, let him hear!"*

When I started writing this book in 2005, it was out of my desire to learn how to cultivate the Fruit of the Spirit in my own life and share it with others. I knew that I lacked understanding and wanted to mature in my walk with Christ. It was not until 2009 that He placed in my heart that we are to be a reflection in the Earth of the Tree of Life in Heaven, which bears 12 crops of fruit each month. Through prayer I searched the scriptures to see if He had classified any more of His characteristics as fruit. The first one that stood out was RIGHTEOUSNESS.

Solomon teaches in Proverbs 11:30, *"The fruit of the righteous is a tree of life, and he who wins souls is wise."* We offer people eternal life in Christ by the purity of the fruit seen in our lives. The Lord calls us Trees of

Righteousness in Isaiah 61:3, *"... that they may be called trees of righteousness, the planting of the L*ORD*, that He may be glorified."*

In Amos 6:12 the Prophet Amos writes, *"Do horses run on rocks? Does one plow there with oxen? Yet you have turned justice into gall, and the **fruit of righteousness** into wormwood,"* Apostle Paul writes in Philippians 1:11, *"Being filled with the **fruits of righteousness** which are by Jesus Christ, to the glory and praise of God."* In Isaiah 45:8, Yahweh declares, *"Rain down, you heavens, from above, and let the skies pour down righteousness; let the earth open, **let them bring forth salvation, and let the righteousness spring up together**. I the Lord, have created it."* In Hebrews 12:11 we are told, *"Now no chastening seems to be joyful for the present, but painful; nevertheless, afterward it yields the **peaceable fruit of righteousness** to those who have been trained by it."* James 3:18 teaches, *"Now the **fruit of righteousness** is sown in peace by those who make peace."*

As can be seen by the above passages, righteousness is not only a fruit but it is the name of our tree. By now, we should all be bearing fruit, yet we may still have hidden patches of soil in our hearts, that we do not want Yahweh to interfere with. These places are called the fallow grounds; they are the uncultivated parts of our heart that bears no crops. Let us be brave enough to invite Holy Spirit to help us to daily break up the fallow ground of our hearts, and rain God's righteousness on us. Hosea 10:12 states, **"Sow for yourselves righteousness; reap in mercy**; *break up your fallow ground, for it is time to seek the Lord, till He comes and rains righteousness on you."* Please note that the seeds of righteousness will reap a fruit called mercy, we will discuss this more in Chapter 16.

Let's pray.

Heavenly Father, I realize there are still some areas in my life that I have not surrendered to you. I am afraid to let go of some things from my past, some people who you have not appointed to my life and my present inhibitions. I need your help to break up the fallow ground of my heart, give me your peace to replace my fear. Please give me your courage to let go of my comfort zones and step out into your plans for my life. Please forgive me from holding back from you, I give you my all today, be glorified through my life, please rain your righteousness on me, in Yahshua's name, Amen.

In Malachi 3:18 we are taught how to discern the righteous from the wicked, *"Then you shall again discern between the righteous and the wicked, between <u>one who serves God and one who does not serve Him</u>."* **The line of demarcation is, do you serve Yahweh?** Before Yahshua's death and resurrection, Yahweh's people had to abide by the Laws of God to be made righteous whereas now, it is through faith in Yahshua that we are made righteous. The Apostle Paul in Romans 3:21-26, writes, *"But now the righteousness of God without the law is manifested, being witnessed by the law and the prophets; 22 Even the righteousness of God which is by faith of Jesus Christ unto all and upon all them that believe: for there is no difference: 23 For all have sinned, and come short of the glory of God; 24 Being justified freely by his grace through the redemption that is in Christ Jesus: 25 Whom God hath set forth to be a propitiation through faith in his blood, <u>to declare his righteousness for the remission of sins that are past</u>, through the forbearance of God; 26 To declare, I say, at this time his righteousness: that he might be just, and the justifier of him which believeth in Jesus.*

Thank you Father for Yahshua! In Matthew 5:20 Yahshua says, *"For I say to you, that unless your righteousness exceeds the righteousness of the scribes and Pharisees, you will by no means enter the kingdom of heaven."* These were those who perceived themselves as righteous. Matthew 23 is filled with Yahshua rebuking the Pharisees, in verses 27-28, He says, *"Woe to you, scribes and Pharisees, hypocrites! For you are like whitewashed tombs which indeed appear beautiful outwardly, but inside are full of dead men's bones and all uncleanness. 28 Even so you also outwardly appear righteous to men, but inside you are full of hypocrisy and lawlessness."*

Yahweh never changes. He always looks at the heart of men and women, the part of us that people cannot see, such as our thoughts, desires and the life we live when we think no one is watching, yet He is always watching. In Luke 16:14-15 Yahshua corrected the Pharisees again, *"Now the Pharisees, who were lovers of money, also heard all these things, and they derided Him. 15 And He said to them, "You are those who justify yourselves before men, but <u>God knows your hearts</u>. For what is highly esteemed among men is an abomination in the sight of God."*

This fruit is developed from the inside out. Isaiah prayed for Jerusalem in Isaiah 62:1, *"For Zion's sake I will not hold my peace, and for Jerusalem's sake I will not rest, until her **righteousness goes forth as brightness**, and her salvation as a lamp that burns."* I want to shine for Yahshua, I hunger and thirst for Yahweh's righteousness to be visible in every area of my life. Yahshua tells us in Matthew 5:6, *"Blessed are those who hunger and thirst for righteousness, for they shall be filled."* Just tell the Lord right now, *"Father I am hungry and thirsty for your righteousness, please fill me according to Your Word."*

The Apostle Paul explains in Romans 5:17-21, *"For if by the one man's offense death reigned through the one, much more those who receive abundance of grace and of <u>the gift of righteousness</u> will reign in life through the One,*

Jesus Christ.) ¹⁸Therefore, as through one man's offense judgment came to all men, resulting in condemnation, even so through one Man's righteous act the free gift came to all men, resulting in justification of life. ¹⁹ For as by one man's disobedience many were made sinners, so also by one Man's obedience many will be made righteous. ²⁰ Moreover the law entered that the offense might abound. But where sin abounded, grace abounded much more, ²¹ so that as sin reigned in death, even so grace might reign through righteousness to eternal life through Jesus Christ our Lord."

RESULTS OF ADAM	RESULTS OF YAHSHUA
Death reigned through his **offense**	**Life** reigned through **Grace & Righteousness**.
Judgment came to **all men** through **his offense**, resulting in **condemnation**.	**Free gift** came to **all men**, through **His righteous act**, resulting in **justification of life**.
Many were **made sinners** because of his disobedience.	Many will be **made righteous** through His **obedience**.

Sin abounded because it was impossible for any person to live without breaking one of Yahweh's laws. Thank Yahweh, for Yahshua stepping into earth. His grace abounds more than sin! In the lives of those not committed to Christ, sin is king and the kingdom they live in, is death, but for those in Christ, grace is king, through Righteousness, and the kingdom we live in, is Eternal Life! Through Christ's obedience we were made righteous!

"I will greatly rejoice in the L<small>ORD</small>*, my soul shall be joyful in my God; for He has clothed me with the garments of salvation,* <u>*He has covered me with the robe of*</u>

righteousness, *as a bridegroom decks himself with ornaments, and as a bride adorns herself with her jewels.* ¹¹ *For as the earth brings forth its bud, as the garden causes the things that are sown in it to spring forth,* <u>*so the Lord* GOD *will cause righteousness and praise to spring forth before all the nations.*</u>" (Isaiah 61:10-11)

The Lord covers us in a robe of righteousness. It is our faith in Christ that is accredited to us as righteousness.
<u>Romans 4:22-25</u> - And therefore "it was accounted to him for righteousness." ²³ Now it was not written for his sake alone that it was imputed to him, ²⁴ but also for us. It shall be imputed to us who believe in Him who raised up Jesus our Lord from the dead,
²⁵ who was delivered up because of our offenses, and was raised because of our justification.
<u>Galatians 5:5-6</u> - For we through the Spirit eagerly wait for the hope of righteousness by faith. ⁶ For in Christ Jesus neither circumcision nor uncircumcision avails anything, but faith working through love.
<u>Hebrews 11:4</u> - By faith Abel offered to God a more excellent sacrifice than Cain, through which he obtained witness that he was righteous, God testifying of his gifts; and through it he being dead still speaks.
<u>Hebrews 11:7</u> - By faith Noah, being divinely warned of things not yet seen, moved with godly fear, prepared an ark for the saving of his household, by which he condemned the world and became heir of the righteousness which is according to faith.
<u>James 2:23</u> - And the Scripture was fulfilled which says, "Abraham believed God, and it was accounted to him for righteousness." And he was called the friend of God.
<u>Philippians 3:8-9</u> - Yet indeed I also count all things loss for the excellence of the knowledge of Christ Jesus my Lord, for whom I have suffered the loss of all things, and count them as rubbish, that I may gain Christ ⁹ and be

found in Him, not having my own righteousness, which is from the law, but that which is through faith in Christ, the righteousness which is from God by faith;

Yahweh exchanged our filthy garments, with His Robe of Righteousness. From everlasting to everlasting, His righteousness will remain!

Psalm 36:6 - Your righteousness is like the great mountains; Your judgments are a great deep; O Lord, You preserve man and beast.

Psalm 71:19 - Also Your righteousness, O God, is very high, You who have done great things; O God, who is like You?

Psalm 97:6 - The heavens declare His righteousness, and all the peoples see His glory.

Psalm 98:2 - The LORD has made known His salvation; His righteousness He has revealed in the sight of the nations.

Psalm 111:3 - His work is honorable and glorious, and His righteousness endures forever.

Psalm 145:17 - The LORD is righteous in all His ways, gracious in all His works.

Isaiah 42:21 - The LORD is well pleased for His righteousness' sake; He will exalt the law and make it honorable.

Isaiah 51:6-8 - Lift up your eyes to the heavens, and look on the earth beneath. For the heavens will vanish away like smoke, the earth will grow old like a garment, and those who dwell in it will die in like manner; but My salvation will be forever, and My righteousness will not be abolished. "Listen to Me, you who know righteousness, you people in whose heart is My law: Do not fear the reproach of men, nor be afraid of their insults. 8 For the moth will eat them up like a garment, and the worm will eat them like wool; but My righteousness will be forever, and My salvation from generation to generation."

Just as faith without works is dead, when Yahweh makes us righteous, the fruit of that, or should I say, the proof of that is in the actions of righteous living. Yahweh expects us to do righteous and just acts and to train our children to do the same from generation to generation. There are many benefits to our personal lives and our neighbors, when we chose to live righteous lives. In Genesis 18:19, Yahweh says of Abraham, *"For I have known him, in order that he may <u>command his children and his household after him, that they keep the way of the* L<small>ORD</small>*, to do righteousness and justice</u>, that the Lord may bring to Abraham what He has spoken to him."* Then our Heavenly Father disclosed His plans for Sodom and Gomorra to Abraham. Abraham was concerned that when God issued His judgment against Sodom and Gomorra that the righteous would be destroyed with the wicked, and He reminded Yahweh that He is a Just God. He asked God if there were 50, then 45, or 30, 20 and finally 10 righteous in the city, would He still destroy the city, and Yahweh said He would not. There is a benefit to those in our families and communities, when we live righteous lives. Abraham was a mighty intercessor. James 5:16 tells us, *"Confess your trespasses to one another, and pray for one another, that you may be healed. The effective, fervent prayer of a righteous man avails much."* Unfortunately, the sins of these cities, were so grave and had corrupted so many that God removed the few righteous before destroying the city. Solomon tells us in Proverbs 15:29, *"The Lord is far from the wicked, but He hears the prayer of the righteous."*

As we move into Genesis 19, two angels arrive at Lot's home, and instruct him to take his family and leave Sodom. Lot, his wife and their two daughters were escorted out by the angels. The husbands of the daughters were left behind because they did not take Lot seriously when he told them to leave. Ponder on this for a minute, do you realize that Yahweh would not have destroyed the city for ten righteous, but he only found 4? And then it became three, when Lot's wife disobeyed, looked back and became a pillar of salt. **Are you like Lot's wife? Each time Yahweh delivers you from an environment filled with sin, filth, and shame, do you look back because you miss it and end up going right back to where you came from? Are you like Lot's son-in-laws, you receive warnings from Yahweh, but you laugh, your heart fills with unbelief, and another area of your life is destroyed?**

2 Peter 2:20-22 says, *"For if, after they have escaped the pollutions of the world through the knowledge of the Lord and Savior Jesus Christ, they are again entangled in them and overcome, the latter end is worse for them than the beginning. 21 For it would have been better for them not to have known the way of righteousness, than having known it, to turn from the holy commandment delivered to them. 22 But it has happened to them according to the true proverb: "A dog returns to his own vomit," and, "a sow, having washed, to her wallowing in the mire."*

Paul instructs us not to be unequally yoked with unbelievers, because our bodies are the temple of God.

HE ASKS WHAT FELOWSHIP HAS...
2 Corinthians 6:14-16

Righteousness with	Lawlessness
Light with	Darkness
Christ with	Belial
A Believer with	An Unbeliever
The Temple of God with	Idols

In 2 Corinthians 6:16-18, he explains, *"...For you are the temple of the living God. As God has said: "I will dwell in them and walk among them. I will be their God, and they shall be My people." 17 Therefore "Come out from among them and be separate, says the Lord. Do not touch what is unclean, and I will receive you." 18 "I will*

be a Father to you, and you shall be My sons and daughters, says the LORD Almighty."

We must obey our Heavenly Father; Lot's wife would not have died, had she only obeyed. Deuteronomy 6:24-25 states, *"And the LORD commanded us to observe all these statutes, to fear the LORD our God, for our good always, that He might preserve us alive, as it is this day. 25 Then it will be righteousness for us, if we are careful to observe all these commandments before the LORD our God, as He has commanded us."*

Can you hear God's heart cry in Isaiah 48:18, *"Oh, that you had heeded My commandments! Then your peace would have been like a river, and your righteousness like the waves of the sea."*

We need to ask God for the same conviction of the writer of Psalm 119:106, *"I have sworn and confirmed that I will keep Your righteous judgments."*

In Matthew 25:31-46 Yahshua details that when He comes in His glory, He will set the sheep, who are classified as the righteous to His right and the goats will be set to His left. What does Christ use as His measuring rod? Let's take a listen.
Then the King will say to those on His right hand, 'Come, you blessed of My Father, inherit the kingdom prepared for you from the foundation of the world: 35 for I was hungry and you gave Me food; I was thirsty and you gave Me drink; I was a stranger and you took Me in; 36 I was naked and you clothed Me; I was sick and you visited Me; I was in prison and you came to Me.' 37 **"Then the righteous will answer Him***, saying, 'Lord, when did we see You hungry and feed You, or thirsty and give You drink? 38 When did we see You a stranger and take You in, or naked and clothe You? 39 Or when did we see You sick, or in prison, and come to You?' 40 And the King will answer and say to them,*

'Assuredly, I say to you, inasmuch as you did it to one of the least of these My brethren, you did it to Me.' (Matthew 25:34-40)

Do you see Yahweh's theme throughout scripture? We are supposed to take care of one another, this is the RIGHT thing to do, when we do this, we do it unto Him. *"Then He will also say to those on the left hand, 'Depart from Me, you cursed, into the everlasting fire prepared for the devil and his angels:* <u>*42 for I was hungry and you gave Me no food; I was thirsty and you gave Me no drink; 43 I was a stranger and you did not take Me in, naked and you did not clothe Me, sick and in prison and you did not visit Me.'*</u> *44 "Then they also will answer Him, saying, 'Lord, when did we see You hungry or thirsty or a stranger or naked or sick or in prison, and did not minister to You?' 45 Then He will answer them, saying,* <u>*'Assuredly, I say to you, inasmuch as you did not do it to one of the least of these, you did not do it to Me.'*</u> *46 And these will go away into everlasting punishment,* **but the righteous into eternal life.***"* (Matthew 25:41-46)

Paul tells us in Romans 1:18-32 that Yahweh's wrath is revealed from heaven against ungodliness and unrighteousness. As we read through the description of the ungodly, you will find that they are the complete opposite of the fruit of the spirit Yahweh is expecting from our lives.

For the wrath of God is revealed from heaven against all ungodliness and unrighteousness of men, who suppress the truth in unrighteousness, 19 because what may be known of God is manifest in them, for God has shown it to them. 20 For since the creation of the world His invisible attributes are clearly seen, being understood by the things that are made, even His eternal power and Godhead, so that they are without excuse, 21 because, <u>*although they knew God, they did not glorify Him as God, nor were thankful, but became futile in their thoughts, and their foolish hearts were darkened*</u> *22 Professing to* be wise, they became fools, ²³ and changed the glory of the incorruptible God into an image made like corruptible man—and birds and four-footed animals and creeping things. ²⁴ <u>Therefore God also gave them up to uncleanness, in the lusts of their hearts, to dishonor their bodies among themselves,</u> ²⁵ <u>who exchanged the truth of God for the lie, and worshiped and served the creature rather than the Creator, who is blessed forever. Amen.</u>²⁶ <u>For this reason God gave them up to vile passions. For even their women exchanged the natural use for what is against nature.</u> ²⁷ <u>Likewise also the men, leaving the natural use of the woman, burned in their lust for one another, men with men committing what is shameful, and receiving in themselves the penalty of their error which was due.</u> ²⁸ <u>And even as they did not like to retain God in their knowledge, God gave them over to a debased mind, to do those things which are not fitting;</u> ²⁹ being filled with all unrighteousness, sexual immorality, wickedness, covetousness, maliciousness; full of envy, murder, strife, deceit, evil-mindedness; they are whisperers, ³⁰ backbiters, haters of God, violent, proud, boasters, inventors of evil things, disobedient to parents, ³¹ undiscerning, untrustworthy, unloving, unforgiving, unmerciful; ³² who, <u>knowing the righteous judgment of God, that those who practice such things are deserving of death, not only do the same but also approve of those who practice them</u>.

Yahweh says in Ezekiel 18:23-26, *"Do I have any pleasure at all that the wicked should die?" says the Lord G*OD*, "and not that he should turn from his ways and live?* ²⁴ *"But when a righteous man turns away from his righteousness and commits iniquity, and does according to all the abominations that the wicked man does, shall he live? All the righteousness which he has done shall not be remembered; because of the unfaithfulness of which he is guilty and the sin which he has committed, because of them he shall die.* ²⁵ <u>*"Yet you say, 'The way of the Lord is not fair.' Hear now, O house*</u>

of Israel, is it not My way which is fair, and your ways which are not fair? ²⁶ When a righteous man turns away from his righteousness, commits iniquity, and dies in it, it is because of the iniquity which he has done that he dies.

In Romans 2:5-10, Paul elaborates, *"But in accordance with your hardness and your impenitent heart you are treasuring up for yourself wrath in the day of wrath and revelation of the righteous judgment of God, ⁶ who "will render to each one according to his deeds": ⁷ eternal life to those who by patient continuance in doing good seek for glory, honor, and immortality; ⁸ but to those who are self-seeking and do not obey the truth, but obey unrighteousness —indignation and wrath, ⁹ tribulation and anguish, on every soul of man who does evil, of the Jew first and also of the Greek; ¹⁰ but glory, honor, and peace to everyone who works what is good, to the Jew first and also to the Greek."*

At first glance, it seems like the consequence of eternal punishment is too extreme for those classified as goats, the ungodly and the unrighteous. Yet 1 John 3:7-12 clarifies, *"**Little children, let no one deceive you. He who practices righteousness is righteous, just as He is righteous.** ⁸ He who sins is of the devil, for the devil has sinned from the beginning. For this purpose the Son of God was manifested, that He might destroy the works of the devil. ⁹ Whoever has been born of God does not sin, for His seed remains in him; and he cannot sin, because he has been born of God. ¹⁰ In this the children of God and the children of the devil are manifest: **Whoever does not practice righteousness is not of God, nor is he who does not love his brother.** ¹¹ For this is the message that you heard from the beginning, that we should love one another, ¹² not as Cain who was of the wicked one and murdered his brother. And why did he murder him? Because his works were evil and **his brother's righteous.**"* John drew another demarcation, dividing those who are of Yahweh and those who are of the devil. What's the difference? **The practice of righteous living.**

We serve a merciful Father and He desires for all to be saved, so He gives all the opportunity to believe in Yahshua and to serve Him. He has made the way for us all to be saved. The consequence of iniquity results from choosing not to accept the Way. 1 John 2:1 encourages us, *"My little children, these things I write to you, so that you may not sin. And if anyone sins, we have an Advocate with the Father, Jesus Christ the righteous."* Grace is not an excuse to live in sin. Why would we choose to stay in sin, when we can receive, in Yahshua's name, Yahweh's forgiveness and strength in every area of our life?

Yahweh makes RIGHTEOUS JUDGEMENTS and Yahshua is our RIGHTEOUS JUDGE.
Deuteronomy 4:8 - And what great nation is there that has such statutes and righteous judgments as are in all this law which I set before you this day?
Psalm 119:7 - I will praise You with uprightness of heart, when I learn Your righteous judgments.
Isaiah 11:3-5 - His delight is in the fear of the LORD, and He shall not judge by the sight of His eyes, nor decide by the hearing of His ears; ⁴ But with righteousness He shall judge the poor, and decide with equity for the meek of the earth; He shall strike the earth with the rod of His mouth, and with the breath of His lips He shall slay the wicked. ⁵ Righteousness shall be the belt of His loins, and faithfulness the belt of His waist.
Jeremiah 9:24 - "But let him who glories glory in this, that he understands and knows Me, that I am the LORD, exercising loving kindness, judgment, and righteousness in the earth. For in these I delight," says the LORD."
Jeremiah 23:5-6 - "Behold, the days are coming," says the LORD, "That I will raise to David a Branch of

righteousness; A King shall reign and prosper, and execute judgment and righteousness in the earth. ⁶ In His days Judah will be saved, and Israel will dwell safely; now this is His name by which He will be called:
THE LORD OUR RIGHTEOUSNESS.
Revelation 19:11 - Now I saw heaven opened, and behold, a white horse. And He who sat on him was called Faithful and True, and in righteousness He judges and makes war.

We must present our bodies as instruments of righteousness to a righteous God. Let's take a few minutes and meditate on Romans 6:12-23.
Therefore do not let sin reign in your mortal body, that you should obey it in its lusts. ¹³ And do not present your members as instruments of unrighteousness to sin, but present yourselves to God as being alive from the dead, and your members as instruments of righteousness to God. ¹⁴ For sin shall not have dominion over you, for you are not under law but under grace. ¹⁵ What then? Shall we sin because we are not under law but under grace? Certainly not! ¹⁶ <u>Do you not know that to whom you present yourselves slaves to obey, you are that one's slaves whom you obey, whether of sin leading to death, or of obedience leading to righteousness?</u> ¹⁷ But God be thanked that though you were slaves of sin, yet you obeyed from the heart that form of doctrine to which you were delivered. ¹⁸ <u>And having been set free from sin, you became slaves of righteousness.</u> ¹⁹I speak in human terms because of the weakness of your flesh. For just as you presented your members as slaves of uncleanness, and of lawlessness leading to more lawlessness, so now present your members as slaves of righteousness for holiness. ²⁰ For when you were slaves of sin, you were free in regard to righteousness. ²¹ **What fruit did you have then in the things of which you are now ashamed?** *For the end of those things is death. ²² But now having been set free from sin, and having become slaves of God,* **you have your fruit to holiness, and**

the end, everlasting life. ²³ *For the wages of sin is death, but the gift of God is eternal life in Christ Jesus our Lord.*

We often, read Bible verses too quickly. We are in a hurry to finish our quiet time with the Lord, so we can move on to the busier parts of our day. I know I have said this before, but it is important that you take your time to read through this book. It is your opportunity to examine yourself, reflect, repent, change and grow. Do not rush through what Yahweh wants to do in you, through you and for you.

Ask yourself this question, "Whose slave am I?" Take out your notepad and make a list of all the unclean things that control you. Once you have completed this list ask Yahshua to set you free, and to surround you with the right support system so that you can come into the realization that being a slave to Yahweh's righteousness makes you free from sin.

Apostle Paul explains in Ephesians 4:24-32, "**and that you put on the new man which was created according to God, in true righteousness and holiness.** ²⁵ *Therefore, putting away lying, "Let each one of you speak truth with his neighbor," for we are members of one another. ²⁶ "Be angry, and do not sin": do not let the sun go down on your wrath, ²⁷ nor give place to the devil. ²⁸ Let him who stole steal no longer, but rather let him labor, working with his hands what is good, that he may have something to give him who has need. ²⁹ Let no corrupt word proceed out of your mouth, but what is good for necessary edification, that it may impart grace to the hearers. ³⁰ And do not grieve the Holy Spirit of God, by whom you were sealed for the day of redemption. ³¹ Let all bitterness, wrath, anger, clamor, and evil speaking be put away from you, with all malice. ³² And be kind to one another, tenderhearted, forgiving one another, even as God in Christ forgave you.*

Paul tells us to put on the new man which was created according to God, in true righteousness and holiness. What does this new, righteous man look like? Let's see...

Does not lie, but is Truthful.
"*A righteous man hates lying, but a wicked man is loathsome and comes to shame.*" Proverbs 13: 5

"*Righteous lips are the delight of kings, and they love him who speaks what is right.*" Proverbs 16:13

Does not sin when angry.
"*for the wrath of man does not produce the righteousness of God.*" James 1:20

Does not steal.
"*Better is a little with righteousness, than vast revenues without justice.*" Proverbs 16:8

Works hard to have something to give to others.
The desire of the lazy man kills him, for his hands refuse to labor. ^{26} *He covets greedily all day long, but the righteous gives and does not spare. Proverbs 21:25-26*

Does not speak corrupt and evil words.
"*And you shall take no bribe, for a bribe blinds the discerning and perverts the words of the righteous.*" *Exodus 23:8*

Speaks words that are edifying and impart grace to the hearers.
The heart of the righteous studies how to answer, but the mouth of the wicked pours forth evil. Proverbs 15:28

Does not grieve the Holy Spirit.

Not bitter, full of wrath and malicious.

Beloved, do not avenge yourselves, but rather give place to wrath; for it is written, "Vengeance is Mine, I will repay," says the Lord. Romans 12:19

Kind to others.
"He has dispersed abroad; He has given to the poor; His righteousness endures forever; His horn will be exalted with honor." Psalm 112:9

Tenderhearted.
"Because I delivered the poor who cried out, the fatherless and the one who had no helper. 13 The blessing of a perishing man came upon me, and I caused the widow's heart to sing for joy. 14 I put on righteousness, and it clothed me; my justice was like a robe and a turban. 15 I was eyes to the blind, and I was feet to the lame. 16 I was a father to the poor, and I searched out the case that I did not know." Job 29:12-16

Forgiving as God in Christ, forgave us.

Apostle Paul speaks of an armor of righteousness in 2 Corinthians 6:7, *"by the word of truth, by the power of God, by <u>the armor of righteousness on the right hand and on the left</u>,"* What is this righteous armor? He writes in Ephesians 6:10-18, *"Finally, my brethren, <u>be strong in the Lord and in the power of His might.</u> 11 <u>Put on the whole armor of God, that you may be able to stand against the wiles of the devil.</u> 12 For we do not wrestle against flesh and blood, but against principalities, against powers, against the rulers of the darkness of this age, against spiritual hosts of wickedness in the heavenly places. 13 Therefore take up the whole armor of God, that you may be able to withstand in the evil day, and having done all, to stand. 14 Stand therefore, <u>having girded your waist with truth, having put on the breastplate of righteousness, 15 and having shod your feet with the preparation of the gospel of peace;</u> 16 <u>above all, taking the shield of faith with which you will be able</u>*

to quench all the fiery darts of the wicked one. ¹⁷ *And take the helmet of salvation, and the sword of the Spirit, which is the word of God;* ¹⁸ *praying always with all prayer and supplication in the Spirit, being watchful to this end with all perseverance and supplication for all the saints.*

Where did Paul get the idea of the armor from? From Holy Spirit, of course, but check out what Isaiah 59:16-17, speaks of Yahweh, *"He saw that there was no man, and wondered that there was no intercessor; therefore His own arm brought salvation for Him; and His own righteousness, it sustained Him.* ¹⁷ *For He put on righteousness as a breastplate, and a helmet of salvation on His head; He put on the garments of vengeance for clothing, and was clad with zeal as a cloak."* Since the Lord himself put on righteousness as His breastplate and the helmet of salvation on His head, we should do the same. Our righteous armor will one day be traded in for a crown, *"Finally, there is laid up for me the crown of righteousness, which the Lord, the righteous Judge, will give to me on that Day, and not to me only but also to all who have loved His appearing."* 2 Timothy 4:8

In Matthew 6:33, Yahshua tells us, *"But seek first the kingdom of God and His righteousness, and all these things shall be added to you."* Our priorities must be His Kingdom and His Righteousness. Paul explains in Romans 14:17, "for the kingdom of God is not eating and drinking, but righteousness, peace and joy in the Holy Spirit." If we don't choose to live righteous lives filled with peace and joy, then we have chosen to live outside of the Kingdom, where we are consumed by the worries of life. Isaiah 32:17-18 declares, *"The work of righteousness will be peace, and the effect of righteousness, quietness and assurance forever."* ¹⁸ *My people will dwell in a peaceful habitation, in secure dwellings, and in quiet resting places,"* Yahweh promises so much to His righteous children in His Word.

YAHWEH'S PROMISES

Psalm 34:15-21 - The eyes of the LORD are on the righteous, and His ears are open to their cry. 17 The righteous cry out, and the LORD hears, and delivers them out of all their troubles. 19 Many are the afflictions of the righteous, But the LORD delivers him out of them all. 20 He guards all his bones; not one of them is broken. 21 Evil shall slay the wicked, and those who hate the righteous shall be condemned.

Psalm 112:1-8 - Praise the LORD! Blessed is the man who fears the LORD, Who delights greatly in His commandments. 2 His descendants will be mighty on earth; the generation of the upright will be blessed. 3 Wealth and riches will be in his house, and his righteousness endures forever. 4 Unto the upright there arises light in the darkness; He is gracious, and full of compassion, and righteous. 5A good man deals graciously and lends; He will guide his affairs with discretion. 6 Surely he will never be shaken; the righteous will be in everlasting remembrance. 7 He will not be afraid of evil tidings; his heart is steadfast, trusting in the LORD. 8 His heart is established; he will not be afraid, until he sees his desire upon his enemies.

Isaiah 33:15-16 - He who walks righteously and speaks uprightly, he who despises the gain of oppressions, who gestures with his hands, refusing bribes, who stops his ears from hearing of bloodshed, and shuts his eyes from seeing evil: 16 He will dwell on high; his place of defense will be the fortress of rocks; bread will be given him, His water will be sure.

Proverbs 11:4 - Riches do not profit in the day of wrath, but righteousness delivers from death.

Proverbs 11:5-6 - The righteousness of the blameless will direct his way aright, but the wicked will fall by his own wickedness. 6 The righteousness of the upright will deliver them, but the unfaithful will be caught by their lust.

Proverbs 11:8-10 - The righteous is delivered from trouble, and it comes to the wicked instead. 9The hypocrite with his mouth destroys his neighbor, but through knowledge the righteous will be delivered. ¹⁰ When it goes well with the righteous, the city rejoices; and when the wicked perish, there is jubilation.

Proverbs 11:18-19 - The wicked man does deceptive work, but he who sows righteousness will have a sure reward. ¹⁹ As righteousness leads to life, so he who pursues evil pursues it to his own death.

Proverbs 11:21, 23, 28 - ²¹ Though they join forces, the wicked will not go unpunished; but the posterity of the righteous will be delivered. ²³ The desire of the righteous is only good, but the expectation of the wicked is wrath. ²⁸ He who trusts in his riches will fall, but the righteous will flourish like foliage.

Proverbs 13:6 - Righteousness guards him whose way is blameless, but wickedness overthrows the sinner.

Proverbs 13:9 - The light of the righteous rejoices, but the lamp of the wicked will be put out.

Proverbs 13:21 - Evil pursues sinners, but to the righteous, good shall be repaid.

Proverbs 13:25 - The righteous eats to the satisfying of his soul, But the stomach of the wicked shall be in want.

Proverbs 21:21 - He who follows righteousness and mercy finds life, righteousness, and honor.

Proverbs 29:6 - By transgression an evil man is snared, but the righteous sings and rejoices.

Malachi 4:2 - But to you who fear My Name the Sun of Righteousness shall arise with healing in His wings; and you shall go out and grow fat like stall-fed calves.

Peter 3:13 - Nevertheless we, according to His
promise look for new heavens and a new earth in which righteousness dwells.

Hallelujah! Everything we need to live in this life will be added to us as we allow His righteousness to shine through us. Solomon tells us in Proverbs 21:3, *"To do righteousness and justice is more acceptable to the* L ORD *than sacrifice."* Yahweh desires justice and righteous living from each of us; Amos 5:24 instructs, *"But let justice run down like water, and righteousness like a mighty stream."* Are you ready to do both? The foundation of Yahweh's throne is righteousness and justice.

"<u>Righteousness and justice are the foundation of Your throne</u>; Mercy and truth go before Your face.
15 Blessed are the people who know the joyful sound! They walk, O LORD, in the light of Your countenance.
16 In Your name they rejoice all day long, and in Your righteousness they are exalted."
Psalm 89:14-16

CHAPTER FIFTEEN
Developing: JUSTICE
Thus says the LORD: "Keep justice, and do righteousness, for My salvation is about to come, and My righteousness to be revealed." Isaiah 56:1

Do you know of a fruit that is considered the ruler of all others? Interestingly, the Mango has been labeled, "King of Fruits" in India. Mangoes are the world's most consumed fruit, with more than 400 possibly over a thousand varieties! Finding their origin in India, India continues to be the largest mango producer in the world. The mango pulp is consumed in countless ways and the seed is powdered in order to partake of its many benefits. Filled with all the vitamins and minerals needed to keep your immune system strong, it is rich in iron and potassium, aids in lowering cholesterol, helps your eyesight, while the antioxidants it contains helps to protect the body against certain types of cancer.

Justice paints pictures in my mind of individuals, groups and even nations demanding fair treatment from their leaders. King David's last words are recorded in 2 Samuel 23. In verses 2-3 he wrote, *"The Spirit of the LORD spoke by me, and His word was on my tongue. ³ The God of Israel said, The Rock of Israel spoke to me:* <u>*'He who rules over men must be just, ruling in the fear of*</u>

God." On the Queen of Sheba's first visit to King Solomon she rejoiced, *"Blessed be the LORD your God, who delighted in you, setting you on the throne of Israel! Because the LORD has loved Israel forever, therefore He made you king, to do justice and righteousness."* (1 Kings 10:9) Kings, Queens, Presidents, Prime Ministers, all leaders should rule with justice and righteousness. The Lord rebukes those who are not, such as in Ezekiel 45:9, *'Thus says the Lord GOD: "Enough, O princes of Israel! Remove violence and plundering, execute justice and righteousness, and stop dispossessing My people," says the Lord GOD.* This message extends to all of us in our own spheres of influence, no matter how small or large it may be.

We are the plants in Yahweh's vineyard and He searches for the fruit of justice and righteousness, Isaiah 5:7 states, *"For the vineyard of the LORD of hosts is the house of Israel, and the men of Judah are His pleasant plant. He looked for justice, but behold, oppression; for righteousness, but behold, a cry for help."* We have to be very careful. Examine your heart and motives, don't let it be that Yahweh finds us oppressing others instead of treating them fairly. When Yahshua ascended He sent us precious Holy Spirit. Isaiah 32:15-18, prophesied *"Until the Spirit is poured upon us from on high, and the wilderness becomes a fruitful field, and the fruitful field is counted as a forest. ¹⁶ Then justice will dwell in the wilderness, and righteousness remain in the fruitful field."* We need Holy Spirit to produce in us the crop of justice and righteousness the Lord is requiring of us.

As you read through the Greek and Hebrew translations of Scripture, you find that there are some words that are translated interchangeably depending on the context of the sentence. Righteousness and Justice are two of these words. Because of this, it is important to differentiate between the two. The Lord says in Isaiah 28:16-17, *"Therefore thus says the Lord GOD: "Behold, I lay in Zion a stone for a foundation, a tried stone, a precious cornerstone, a sure foundation; whoever believes will not act hastily.* ¹⁷ *Also I will make <u>justice the measuring line, and righteousness the plummet;</u> the hail will sweep away the refuge of lies, and the waters will overflow the hiding place.* Justice is Yahweh's measuring tool, while righteousness is His leveling tool. The foundation of Yahweh's throne is righteousness and justice, *"Clouds and darkness surround Him; Righteousness and Justice are the foundation of His throne." (Psalm 97:2)*

Righteousness, as you already know from the previous chapter, has to do with living your life correctly before Yahweh and men. Justice has this same element in that you are doing what is right towards other by treating them fairly, being impartial.

Our Heavenly Father loves justice!
Psalm 33:5 - He loves righteousness and justice; the earth is full of the goodness of the LORD.
Psalm 37:28 - For the LORD loves justice, and does not forsake His saints; they are preserved forever, but the descendants of the wicked shall be cut off.
Psalm 99:4 - The King's strength also loves justice; You have established equity; You have executed justice and righteousness in Jacob.
Isaiah 61:8 - "For I, the LORD, love justice; I hate robbery for burnt offering; I will direct their work in truth, and will make with them an everlasting covenant.

We worship a King who is abundant in Justice.
Deuteronomy 32:4 - He is the Rock, His work is perfect; for all His ways are justice, a God of truth and without injustice; righteous and upright is He.
Psalm 111:7 - The works of His hands are verity and justice; all His precepts are sure.
Psalm 103:6 - The LORD executes righteousness and justice for all who are oppressed.

Isaiah 9:7 - Of the increase of His government and peace there will be no end, upon the throne of David and over His kingdom, to order it and establish it with judgment and justice from that time forward, even forever. The zeal of the LORD of hosts will perform this.
Zechariah 9:9 - "Rejoice greatly, O daughter of Zion! Shout, O daughter of Jerusalem! Behold, your King is coming to you; He is just and having salvation, Lowly and riding on a donkey, a colt, the foal of a donkey.
Zephaniah 3:5 - The LORD is righteous in her midst, He will do no unrighteousness. Every morning He brings His justice to light; He never fails, but the unjust knows no shame.

Yahweh gives justice to the orphans, widows, oppressed and the poor.
Deuteronomy 10:18 - He administers justice for the fatherless and the widow, and loves the stranger, giving him food and clothing.
Psalm 10:18 - To do justice to the fatherless and the oppressed, that the man of the earth may oppress no more.
Psalm 72:4 - He will bring justice to the poor of the people; He will save the children of the needy, and will break in pieces the oppressor.
Psalm 140:12 - I know that the LORD will maintain the cause of the afflicted, and justice for the poor.
Psalm 103:6 - The LORD executes righteousness and justice for all who are oppressed.
Psalm 146:7 - Who executes justice for the oppressed, who gives food to the hungry. The LORD gives freedom to the prisoners.

Solomon tells us in Proverbs 28:5, *"Evil men do not understand justice, but those who seek the LORD understand all."* To get understanding we must seek the Lord. Our Heavenly Father is pleased when we ask for hearts to discern justice as seen in His response to Solomon in 1 Kings 3:11-12, *"Then God said to him:*

"Because you have asked this thing, and have not asked long life for yourself, nor have asked riches for yourself, nor have asked the life of your enemies, but have asked for yourself understanding to discern justice, 12 behold, I have done according to your words; see, I have given you a wise and understanding heart, so that there has not been anyone like you before you, nor shall any like you arise after you." Yahweh's wisdom is needed to be able to execute justice. He is the source of all knowledge and understanding. Isaiah 40:14 asks, *"With whom did He take counsel, and who instructed Him, and taught Him in the path of justice? Who taught Him knowledge, and showed Him the way of understanding?"*

<u>1 Kings 3:28</u> - And all Israel heard of the judgment which the king had rendered; and they feared the king, for they saw that the wisdom of God was in him to administer justice.

<u>Psalm 37:30</u> - The mouth of the righteous speaks wisdom, and his tongue talks of justice.

<u>Proverbs 2:6-9</u> - For the LORD gives wisdom; from His mouth come knowledge and understanding; 7 He stores up sound wisdom for the upright; He is a shield to those who walk uprightly; 8 He guards the paths of justice, and preserves the way of His saints. 9 Then you will understand righteousness and justice, Equity and every good path.

<u>Proverbs 8:12, 15-17, 20-21</u> - "I, wisdom, dwell with prudence, and find out knowledge and discretion. 15 By me kings reign, and rulers decree justice. 16 By me princes rule, and nobles, all the judges of the earth. 17 I love those who love me, and those who seek me diligently will find me. 20 I traverse the way of righteousness, in the midst of the paths of justice, 21 that I may cause those who love me to inherit wealth, that I may fill their treasuries.

<u>Proverbs 9:9</u> - Give instruction to a wise man, and he will be still wiser; teach a just man, and he will increase in learning.

In turn, we are to train our children in Yahweh's righteousness and justice. Solomon teaches us in Proverbs 21:3, *"To do righteousness and justice is more acceptable to the LORD than sacrifice."* In Genesis 18:19, Yahweh says to Abraham, *"For I have known him, in order that he may command his children and his household after him, that they keep the way of the LORD, to do righteousness and justice, that the LORD may bring to Abraham what He has spoken to him."* Yahweh trained Abraham so that he in turn would be able to train the great nation that would come from him. When we cultivate the right seed in our children it will become a generational blessing that is passed down the family line. Since our children tend to quickly model what we do before applying what we say, it is important that when we discipline them, that it is done through justice and not in our anger. Jeremiah cried to the Lord, *"O LORD, correct me, but with justice; not in Your anger, lest You bring me to nothing."* (Jeremiah 10:24) Yahweh comforts him with these words to Israel and Judah in Jeremiah 30:11, *"For I am with you,' says the LORD, 'to save you; though I make a full end of all nations where I have scattered you, yet I will not make a complete end of you. <u>But I will correct you in justice, and will not let you go altogether unpunished.</u>'*

There is a blessing in living just lives. Proverbs 21:15 states, *"It is a joy for the just to do justice, but destruction will come to the workers of iniquity"*.
<u>Deuteronomy 16:20</u> - You shall follow what is altogether just, that you may live and inherit the land which the LORD your God is giving you.
<u>Zephaniah 2:3</u> - Seek the LORD, all you meek of the earth, who have upheld His justice. Seek righteousness, seek humility. It may be that you will be hidden in the day of the LORD's anger.
<u>Psalm 106:3</u> - Blessed are those who keep justice, and he who does righteousness at all times!

<u>Isaiah 1:27</u> - Zion shall be redeemed with justice, and her penitents with righteousness.

There are however, moments when we have been treated unfairly, judged wrongly and cried out for justice. David declares in Psalm 37:12-15, *"The wicked plots against the just, and gnashes at him with his teeth. ¹³ The Lord laughs at him, for He sees that his day is coming. ¹⁴ The wicked have drawn the sword and have bent their bow, to cast down the poor and needy, to slay those who are of upright conduct. ¹⁵ Their sword shall enter their own heart, and their bows shall be broken."* When people fail to treat you justly, do not get discouraged, as you know, Christ, our Savior was treated unjustly, instead rejoice because our justice comes from the Lord, Proverbs 29:26 tells us, *"Many seek the ruler's favor, but justice for man comes from the LORD."* We cry out as David did in Psalm 17:1, *"Hear a just cause, O LORD, attend to my cry; give ear to my prayer which is not from deceitful lips."* There are moments that our cry sounds more like Habakkuk 1:2-4, because justice seems like it has been delayed for too long. *"O LORD, how long shall I cry, and You will not hear? Even cry out to You, "Violence!" and You will not save. ³ Why do You show me iniquity, and cause me to see trouble? For plundering and violence are before me; there is strife, and contention arises. ⁴ Therefore the law is powerless, and justice never goes forth. For the wicked surround the righteous; therefore, perverse judgment proceeds."* When the Lord answered him, it still did not silence him, because he cannot understand how the Lord can look upon the wicked doing evil and not issue immediate judgment. The Lord's response is incredible. He tells Habakkuk to write the vision down and make it plain enough for others to run with it and although it may tarry, He says to wait for it. Apostle Paul recites the latter part of Habakkuk 2:4 a few times in his letters, *"Behold the proud, His soul is not upright in him; <u>but the just shall live by his faith</u>."* Yahweh is telling us to wait on His justice, wait on His promise, we who cry out for justice, need to be just ourselves. Therefore we must live believing that what Yahweh said He will do will certainly manifest in due time. In Isaiah 30:18, we are encouraged, *"Therefore the LORD will wait, that He may be gracious to you; and therefore He will be exalted, that He may have mercy on you. For the LORD is a God of justice; blessed are all those who wait for Him."*

The Psalmist declares that the Word of Yahweh is a light unto His path. Yahweh refers to His justice as a light as well, in Isaiah 51:4, *"Listen to Me, My people; and give ear to Me, O My nation: for law will proceed from Me, and I will make <u>My justice rest as a light of the peoples</u>."* In Psalm 37:5-6 David tells us to, *"Commit your way to the LORD, trust also in Him, and He shall bring it to pass. ⁶ He shall bring forth your righteousness as the light, and your justice as the noonday."*

Where there is no justice there is only darkness. Isaiah 59:9 states, *"Therefore justice is far from us, nor does righteousness overtake us; we look for light, but there is darkness! For brightness, but we walk in blackness!"*

Yahshua calls us the light of the world in Matthew 5, in verse 16, he commissions us to, *"Let your light so shine before men, that they may see your good works and glorify your Father in heaven."*

The justice that permeates from our lives is a part of the light that we are to shine before men.

We are not permitted to ignore, neglect, or pervert justice.
When there are starving people anywhere in the world, it is a result of injustice. <u>Proverbs 13:23</u> tells us, *"Much food is in the fallow ground of the poor, and for lack of justice there is waste."* Remember fallow ground is uncultivated ground, so who is stopping the poor from

planting seed to reap a harvest? Solomon is letting us know there is more than enough to feed the poor but we waste so much and for this we must repent.

Amos 5:12-15 - For I know your manifold transgressions and your mighty sins: afflicting the just and taking bribes; diverting the poor *from justice* at the gate. 13 Therefore the prudent keep silent at that time, for it is an evil time. 14 Seek good and not evil, that you may live; so the LORD God of hosts will be with you, as you have spoken. 15 Hate evil, love good; establish justice in the gate. It may be that the LORD God of hosts will be gracious to the remnant of Joseph.

Exodus 23:2 - You shall not follow a crowd to do evil; nor shall you testify in a dispute so as to turn aside after many to pervert justice.

Leviticus 19:15 - You shall do no injustice in judgment. You shall not be partial to the poor, nor honor the person of the mighty. In righteousness you shall judge your neighbor.

Deuteronomy 16:18-19 - "You shall appoint judges and officers in all your gates, which the LORD your God gives you, according to your tribes, and they shall judge the people with just judgment. 19 You shall not pervert justice; you shall not show partiality, nor take a bribe, for a bribe blinds the eyes of the wise and twists the words of the righteous.

Deuteronomy 27:19 - 'Cursed is the one who perverts the justice due the stranger, the fatherless, and widow.' "And all the people shall say, 'Amen!'

Isaiah 10:1-4 - "Woe to those who decree unrighteous decrees, who write misfortune, which they have prescribed 2 To rob the needy of justice, and to take what is right from the poor of My people, that widows may be their prey, and that they may rob the fatherless. 3 What will you do in the day of punishment, and in the desolation which will come from afar? To whom will you flee for help? And where will you leave your glory? 4 Without Me they shall bow down among the prisoners, and they shall fall among the slain." For all this His

anger is not turned away, but His hand is stretched out still.
Lamentations 3:34-36 - To crush under one's feet all the prisoners of the earth, 35 To turn aside the justice due a man Before the face of the Most High, 36 Or subvert a man in his cause - The Lord does not approve.
2 Chronicles 19:7 - Now therefore, let the fear of the LORD be upon you; take care and do it, for there is no iniquity with the LORD our God, no partiality, nor taking of bribes.
Proverbs 17:23 - A wicked man accepts a bribe behind the back to pervert the ways of justice.
Proverbs 19:28 - A disreputable witness scorns justice, and the mouth of the wicked devours iniquity.
Proverbs 21:7 - The violence of the wicked will destroy them, because they refuse to do justice.
Proverbs 29:4 - The king establishes the land by justice, but he who receives bribes overthrows it.
Amos 5:6-7 - Seek the LORD and live, lest He break out like fire in the house of Joseph, and devour it, with no one to quench it in Bethel— 7 You who turn justice to wormwood, and lay righteousness to rest in the earth!"
Micah 7:3 - That they may successfully do evil with both hands - the prince asks for gifts, the judge seeks a bribe, and the great man utters his evil desire; so they scheme together.
Matthew 23:23 - "Woe to you, scribes and Pharisees, hypocrites! For you pay tithe of mint and anise and cummin, and have neglected the weightier matters of the law: justice and mercy and faith. These you ought to have done, without leaving the others undone.

Have you treated anyone harshly lately? Have you abused your power, by causing distress, discomfort, or anxiety to your subordinates? If you have, then you have oppressed another. Read with me what God says in Zechariah 7:9-10 about oppressing others. "Thus says the LORD of hosts: *'Execute true justice, show mercy and compassion everyone to his brother. Do not oppress the widow or the fatherless, the alien or the poor. Let none of you plan evil in his heart against his brother."* Rather we are to, *"These are the things you shall do: Speak each man the truth to his neighbor; give judgment in your gates for truth, justice, and peace;* ¹⁷ *Let none of you think evil in your heart against your neighbor; and do not love a false oath. For all these are things that I hate,' Says the LORD."* (Zechariah 8:16-17)

How often have you or I:

- Looked down on a struggling single mom or dad of three or more children and asked the question in our mind, haven't they heard of birth control?
- Not wanted to be approached by the homeless mom with her unclean child asking for money?
- Not wanted our child to associate with an orphan or foster child for fear of him/her being a bad influence?
- Got angry at someone from a different nationality than our own, and judged an entire nation of people from a foreign land based on a negative encounter we had with a few individuals from the same country?
- Maybe we're compassionate for the homeless and embrace the opportunity to feed them on a field trip, but how would you treat the unbathed homeless person sitting next to you in church every Sunday, would you hold their hand or greet them with a hug?

James 1:26-27 reinforces what acceptable religion is, "If anyone among you thinks he is religious, and does not bridle his tongue but deceives his own heart, this one's religion is useless. Pure and undefiled religion before God and the Father is this: to visit orphans and widows in their trouble, and to keep oneself unspotted from the world".

What is true religion?

True Religion Is To:	We Are NOT to:
Execute True Justice (Judge Fairly)	Oppress Widows
Show Mercy to One Another	Oppress Fatherless/Orphans
Show Compassion to One Another	Oppress Foreigners
Bridle/Control our Tongue	Oppress the Poor
Visit orphans and widows in their trouble	Plan evil in our heart/Scheme Against Each Other
Keep ourselves unspotted from the world/don't let the world corrupt you	

We have to get better as children of Yahweh; He is not pleased with the conditions of our hearts. We have to be *willing* to change, *do something* to change, and *give Yahshua permission* to change us. Our Heavenly Father is a Just Judge, He is Merciful, Compassionate and Kind and has always required us to do the same. Let's repent and change.

Father God, we humbly come to you, ashamed of the negative thoughts and schemes of our hearts, please forgive us. We repent for mistreating others and giving your name a bad reputation. Please give me a heart that will judge fairly, show mercy and compassion to others, and care for widows and orphans. I ask that you bridle my tongue and keep me from becoming corrupted by things in this world that would pull my focus and destiny from you. Thank you Father, in Yahshua's Mighty Name I pray, Amen.

CHAPTER SIXTEEN
Developing: MERCY
I will sing of mercy and justice; to You, O LORD, I will sing praises. Psalm 101:1

This deliciously sweet tropical fruit is rich in energy, dietary fiber, minerals and vitamins. By looking on the outside of this fruit, you would never guess that it contained dozens of yellowish edible bulbs individually enclosing a seed. It is closely related to two of the fruits we discussed, the fig and the breadfruit. Like the breadfruit, jackfruit is being researched as an answer to starvation! Jackfruit is the largest fruit that is grown on a tree. It can reach the size of 80 pounds, almost 3 feet in length with an almost 1 ½ foot diameter! Its outer surface is covered with blunt thorn-like projection which soften when the fruit becomes ripe. Its seeds are dried, roasted or boiled in stews. I should give you a fair warning, things might get a little sticky while separating the bulbs, since it oozes latex, so rub your hands lightly with some type of cooking oil, for easier handling.

In this chapter we will peel back the skin of mercy to enjoy what lies beneath. Mercy is the compassion shown to your offender, enemy or any person in your power. According to Micah 6:8 there are three things that Yahweh requires of us, "*He has shown you, O man, what is good; and what does the* LORD *require of you but to do justly, to love mercy, and to walk humbly with your God?"* He wants us to **love mercy**. We all love to receive mercy but the challenge is, do we love showing mercy to others? In Zechariah 7:9, we are further instructed, *"Thus says the LORD of hosts: 'Execute true justice, show mercy and compassion everyone to his brother."* We are to show mercy in the community of believers, as well as to our neighbors as can be seen in the parable classified as the Good Samaritan. In Luke 10:37 Yahshua tells us we are to demonstrate the same mercy as this man did to assist his neighbor. Because it takes the grace of Yahweh over our lives, to display His mercy to others, the application can prove to be challenging, yet Paul says in Romans 12:8 that we are to show mercy with cheerfulness.

Hosea 4:1 declares, *"Hear the word of the LORD, You children of Israel, for the LORD brings a charge against the inhabitants of the land: "There is no truth or mercy or knowledge of God in the land."* When Yahweh examines the fruit of your life, will He find truth, mercy and the knowledge of Him? He is such a loving Father that He promises to give us our hearts' desires. Do we love Him enough to satisfy His heart's desire? In Hosea 6:6 Yahweh says, **"For I desire mercy** *and not sacrifice,* **and the knowledge of God** *more than burnt offerings."* He desires to see us walk in mercy. As people we tend to become more focused on our religious routines, requirements, rules and regulations than on building relationships. We notice the faults, weaknesses and shortcomings of others, before we answer their silent cry for love.

Yahweh desires that we KNOW Him. There is a difference in knowing His commandments and knowing Him. We think our religious acts satisfies His desire to spend time with us, but it does not. When we know Him deeply, there is a Holy fear that arises in us that drives us to be like our Heavenly Father. In Matthew 12:7,

Yahshua says, *"But if you had known what this means, 'I desire mercy and not sacrifice,' you would not have condemned the guiltless."* In Matthew 23:23 Yahshua warns, *"Woe to you, scribes and Pharisees, hypocrites! For you pay tithe of mint and anise and cummin, and* **have neglected the weightier matters of the law: justice and mercy and faith.** *These you ought to have done, without leaving the others undone."* Yahshua is not implying that we should stop following all of His precepts. If we are missing the weightiest portions of His law, then we have missed the whole point. Yahweh consistently models for us what He requires of us, yet often times we're too stubborn to show justice and mercy, and too afraid to trust Him wholeheartedly with blind faith.

Unfortunately, we become like Jonah to all those we think are not "worthy" and are "undeserving" of our forgiveness, let alone Yahweh's forgiveness. Our Heavenly Father is Merciful and Compassionate. Throughout Yahweh's Word, we read story after story of men and women who deserved the righteous judgment of God, but He extended His arm of mercy to them. This is clearly seen in the Book of Jonah. Jonah was furious with Yahweh for showing mercy to the Ninevites, because he believed they should be destroyed for their sinful ways. Yet when confronted with the word that they would be destroyed by God in 40 days, they chose to repent, change their ways and were forgiven. Jonah 4:1-3 records, *"But it displeased Jonah exceedingly, and he became angry. So he prayed to the* LORD, *and said, "Ah,* LORD, *was not this what I said when I was still in my country? Therefore I fled previously to Tarshish; for I know that You are a gracious and merciful God, slow to anger and abundant in lovingkindness, One who relents from doing harm. Therefore now, O* LORD, *please take my life from me, for it is better for me to die than to live!"*

Can you imagine the audacity of Jonah? He's telling Yahweh to kill him because death is better than the experience of God's mercy on his enemies (sinful people). Who in your life, is the worst of sinners? Will you show him/her mercy? Yahshua says in Matthew 5:7, *"Blessed are the merciful, for they shall obtain mercy."* Each time we give mercy we sew a seed to reap Yahweh's mercy. Think of it this way, for each piece of jackfruit you share, its seed will be planted, in a lifetime you'll grow several thousand mercy trees. James 2:13, warns, *"For judgment is without mercy to the one who has shown no mercy. Mercy triumphs over judgment."* I need all of the mercy I can get, how about you?

Growing up, my parents did an excellent job of disciplining me. I do remember the time, however, that I hid in my closet as a 16-year-old girl, sitting on the ground with my arms wrapped tightly around my knees leaning against my chest. As I rocked back and forth with tears streaming from my eyes, I sang <u>Jesus Loves Me</u>, a song I learned in Sunday school as a little girl. My mother and I had just returned from the gynecologist who informed us that I was three months pregnant. My father was banging down the front door, about to learn the news. My cry was that of Habakkuk 3:2, *"... in wrath remember mercy."* I needed both Yahweh's mercy and my parents' mercy.

Repentance and confession grants us mercy. Solomon teaches that when we try to hide our sins, we will not prosper, but we will find mercy when we confess and forsake our sins (Proverbs 28:13). I was trying to hide my sin of fornication. I remember the day months before, my father asked me, if I had lost my virginity to my boyfriend and I lied. It was through my repentance that mercy came. Isaiah 55:7 says, *"Let the wicked forsake his way, and the unrighteous man his thoughts; let him return to the LORD, and He will have mercy on him; and to our God, for He will abundantly pardon."*

After David sinned with Bathsheba, he cried out in Psalm 51:1, *"Have mercy upon me, O God, according to Your lovingkindness; according to the multitude of Your tender mercies, blot out my transgressions."*

Apostle Paul had murdered and imprisoned many followers of Christ, before His Damascus Road experience, yet God had great mercy on him, he writes in 1 Timothy 1:12-13, *"And I thank Christ Jesus our Lord who has enabled me, because He counted me faithful, putting me into the ministry, 13 although I was formerly a blasphemer, a persecutor, and an insolent man; but I obtained mercy because I did it ignorantly in unbelief."*

Hebrews 4:14-16 tells us, *"Seeing then that we have a great High Priest who has passed through the heavens, Jesus the Son of God, let us hold fast our confession. 15For we do not have a High Priest who cannot sympathize with our weaknesses, but was in all points tempted as we are, yet without sin. <u>16 Let us therefore come boldly to the throne of grace, that we may obtain mercy and find grace to help in time of need</u>."*

Thank Yahweh that we can come boldly before Him through Yahshua and obtain the mercy and grace that we need daily.

<u>Daniel 9:18</u> - "O my God, incline Your ear and hear; open Your eyes and see our desolations, and the city which is called by Your name; for we do not present our supplications before You because of our righteous deeds, but because of Your great mercies."

<u>Titus 3:5</u> - not by works of righteousness which we have done, but according to His mercy He saved us, through the washing of regeneration and renewing of the Holy Spirit,

<u>Jude 21</u> - keep yourselves in the love of God, looking for the mercy of our Lord Jesus Christ unto eternal life.

<u>1 Peter 2:9-10</u> - But you are a chosen generation, a royal priesthood, a holy nation, His own special people, that

you may proclaim the praises of Him who called you out of darkness into His marvelous light; ¹⁰ who once were not a people but are now the people of God, who had not obtained mercy but now have obtained mercy.

1 Peter 1:3 - Blessed be the God and Father of our Lord Jesus Christ, who according to His abundant mercy has begotten us again to a living hope through the resurrection of Jesus Christ from the dead,

There are other moments in our life when we call on God for His mercy in our health, deliverance and safety. He proves Himself to be merciful.

Psalm 57:1 - Be merciful to me, O God, be merciful to me! For my soul trusts in You; and in the shadow of Your wings I will make my refuge, until these calamities have passed by.

Psalm 9:13 - Have mercy on me, O LORD! Consider my trouble from those who hate me, you who lift me up from the gates of death,

Psalm 25:16 - Turn Yourself to me, and have mercy on me, for I am desolate and afflicted.

Psalm 31:9 - Have mercy on me, O LORD, for I am in trouble; my eye wastes away with grief, yes, my soul and my body!

Psalm 119:132 - Look upon me and be merciful to me, as Your custom is toward those who love Your name.

Psalm 123:1-3 - Unto You I lift up my eyes, O You who dwell in the heavens. ² Behold, as the eyes of servants look to the hand of their masters, as the eyes of a maid to the hand of her mistress, so our eyes look to the LORD our God, until He has mercy on us. ³ Have mercy on us, O LORD, have mercy on us! For we are exceedingly filled with contempt.

YAHWEH IS MERCIFUL

Nehemiah 9:27-28 - Therefore You delivered them into the hand of their enemies, who oppressed them; and in the time of their trouble, when they cried to You, You heard from heaven; and according to Your abundant mercies You gave them deliverers who saved them from the hand of their enemies. ²⁸ "But after they had rest, they again did evil before You. Therefore You left them in the hand of their enemies, so that they had dominion over them; yet when they returned and cried out to You, You heard from heaven; And many times You delivered them according to Your mercies,

Exodus 34:6 - And the LORD passed before him and proclaimed, "The LORD, the LORD God, merciful and gracious, longsuffering, and abounding in goodness and truth,

Nehemiah 9:19 - Yet in Your manifold mercies You did not forsake them in the wilderness. The pillar of the cloud did not depart from them by day, to lead them on the road; nor the pillar of fire by night, to show them light, and the way they should go.

Nehemiah 9:31 - Nevertheless in Your great mercy You did not utterly consume them nor forsake them; For You are God, gracious and merciful. God you are!

Psalm 86:15 - But You, O Lord, are a God full of compassion, and gracious, longsuffering and abundant in mercy and truth.

Psalm 69:16 - Hear me, O LORD, for Your lovingkindness is good; turn to me according to the multitude of Your tender mercies.

Psalm 119:156 - Great are Your tender mercies, O LORD; revive me according to Your judgments.

Isaiah 49:10 - They shall neither hunger nor thirst, neither heat nor sun shall strike them; for He who has mercy on them will lead them, even by the springs of water He will guide them.

Luke 1:50 - And His mercy is on those who fear Him from generation to generation.

Ephesians 2:4 - But God, who is rich in mercy, because of His great love with which He loved us,

James 5:11 - Indeed we count them blessed who endure. You have heard of the perseverance of Job and seen the end intended by the Lord—that the Lord is very compassionate and merciful.

HE IS MERCIFUL TO HEAL

<u>Psalm 41:4</u> - I said, "LORD, be merciful to me; heal my soul, for I have sinned against You."

<u>Matthew 9:27</u> - When Jesus departed from there, two blind men followed Him, crying out and saying, "Son of David, have mercy on us!"

<u>Matthew 15:22</u> - And behold, a woman of Canaan came from that region and cried out to Him, saying, "Have mercy on me, O Lord, Son of David! My daughter is severely demon-possessed."

<u>Matthew 17:15</u> - "Lord, have mercy on my son, for he is an epileptic and suffers severely; for he often falls into the fire and often into the water.

<u>Matthew 20:30</u> - And behold, two blind men sitting by the road, when they heard that Jesus was passing by, cried out, saying, "Have mercy on us, O Lord, Son of David!"

<u>Luke 17:13</u> (Jesus heals ten lepers) - And they lifted up their voices and said, "Jesus, Master, have mercy on us!"

<u>Philippians 2:25-27</u> - Yet I considered it necessary to send to you Epaphroditus, my brother, fellow worker, and fellow soldier, but your messenger and the one who ministered to my need; 26 since he was longing for you all, and was distressed because you had heard that he was sick. 27 For indeed he was sick almost unto death; but God had mercy on him, and not only on him but on me also, lest I should have sorrow upon sorrow.

According to Psalm 25:10, *"All the paths of the LORD are mercy and truth, to such as keep His covenant and His testimonies."* Are you keeping His covenant and testimonies from a pure heart? Psalm 89:14 tells us that mercy and truth go before Him. I love the way Yahweh works, he embodied His Pathway, through Yahshua. *"Jesus said to him, "I am <u>the way</u>, <u>the truth</u>, and <u>the life</u>. No one comes to the Father except through Me."* (John 14:6) Proverbs 16:6 says that it is in mercy and truth that atonement is provided for iniquity. Yahshua provided the atonement for our sins. Isaiah 16:5 prophesied, *"In mercy the throne will be established; and One will sit on it in truth, in the tabernacle of David, judging and seeking justice and hastening righteousness."* Psalm 57:3 explains that it is God's mercy and truth that rescues us, *"He shall send from heaven and save me; He reproaches the one who would swallow me up. Selah God shall send forth His mercy and His truth."* We rejoice and sing Psalm 115:1, *"Not unto us, O LORD, not unto us, but to Your name give glory, because of Your mercy, because of Your truth."*

<u>Psalm 57:10</u> - For Your mercy reaches unto the heavens, and Your truth unto the clouds.

<u>Psalm 100:5</u> - For the LORD is good; His mercy is everlasting, and His truth endures to all generations.

<u>Psalm 108:4</u> - For Your mercy is great above the heavens, and Your truth reaches to the clouds.

Through Yahshua we are able to walk in mercy and truth. Proverbs 14:22 tells us mercy and truth belong to those of us who plan to do what is good. Proverbs 3:3-4 instructs, *"Let not mercy and truth forsake you; bind them around your neck, write them on the tablet of your heart, ⁴ and so find favor and high esteem in the sight of God and man."* The Lord wants mercy and truth to be so ingrained in us, that we will not forget them. With them we gain favor and our lives are preserved (Psalm 61:7). Yahweh says in Isaiah 60:10, *"...But in My favor I have had mercy on you."*

> *But the wisdom that is from above is first pure, then peaceable, gentle, willing to yield,*
> **<u>full of mercy and good fruits</u>**,
> *without partiality and without hypocrisy.*
> *James 3:17*

CHAPTER SEVENTEEN
CONCLUSION

I can't believe it, we've reached the end! I pray you are stronger than when you first picked up this book. I pray that you have matured in the Lord and are actively applying all we have meditated on in His Word. The seed which is the WORD of GOD has been planted into the soil (LOVE of GOD) of our souls, and nourished by Holy Spirit. Let's take a moment and reexamine the soil of our souls.

WHAT TYPE OF SOIL ARE YOU NOW?
(Matthew 13:18-23)

<u>Good Ground</u>	*Hears & understands the Word; bears fruit & produces: some a hundredfold, some sixty, some thirty*
Wayside	*Hears the Word & does not understand it, the wicked one comes & snatches away what was sown in his heart.*
Stony Places	*Hears the Word & immediately receives it with joy; yet he has no root, endures only for a while. When tribulation or persecution arises because of the Word, immediately he stumbles.*
Thorns	*Hears the Word, & the cares of this world & the deceitfulness of riches choke the Word, and he becomes unfruitful.*

John 12:23-25, records *"But Jesus answered them, saying, "The hour has come that the Son of Man should*

be glorified. ²⁴ *Most assuredly, I say to you, unless a grain of wheat falls into the ground and dies, it remains alone; but if it dies, it produces much grain. ²⁵ He who loves his life will lose it, and he who hates his life in this world will keep it for eternal life."* We know that Yahshua is the WORD of YAHWEH, and through His death and resurrection came our salvation. Now, by us dying to our flesh, we produce much fruit. Our spiritual growth is evidenced by the development of the Fruit of the Spirit. It is how others are ministered to through our lives. Anyone should be able to pick of the fruit at any time and give all Glory to Yahweh. When we come out of the presence of God (spending time with Him) we should smell like the fresh aroma of heaven to others.

WHAT FRUIT ARE YOU DEVELOPING NOW?
Galatians 5:16-26

FRUIT OF THE SPIRIT	FRUIT OF THE SINFUL NATURE
Love	Adultery
Joy	Fornication
Peace	Uncleanness
Longsuffering/Patience	Lewdness
Kindness	Idolatry
Goodness	Sorcery
Faithfulness	Hatred
Gentleness/Meekness	Contentions
Self-Control	Jealousies
Righteousness	Outbursts of Wrath
Justice	Selfish Ambitions
Mercy	Dissensions
	Heresies
	Envy
	Murders
	Drunkenness
	Revelries

In John 17, Yahshua prayed to the Father, *"I have given them Your word; and the world has hated them because they are not of the world, just as I am not of the world. ¹⁵ I do not pray that You should take them out of the world, but that You should keep them from the evil one. ¹⁶ They are not of the world, just as I am not of the world. ¹⁷ Sanctify them by Your truth. Your word is truth. ¹⁸ As You sent Me into the world, I also have sent them into the world. ¹⁹ And for their sakes I sanctify Myself, that they also may be sanctified by the truth.* **²⁰ "I do not pray for these alone, but also for those who will believe in Me through their word**; *²¹ that they all may be one, as You, Father, are in Me, and I in You; that they also may be one in Us, that the world may believe that You sent Me. ²² And the glory which You gave Me I have given them, that they may be one just as We are one: ²³ I in them, and You in Me; that they may be made perfect in one, and that the world may know that You have sent Me, and have loved them as You have loved Me.* **²⁴ "Father, I desire that they also whom You gave Me may be with Me where I am, that they may behold My glory which You have given Me; for You loved Me before the foundation of the world.** *²⁵ O righteous Father! The world has not known You, but I have known You; and these have known that You sent Me. ²⁶ And I have declared to them Your name, and will declare it, that the love with which You loved Me may be in them, and I in them."*

Yahshua's heart's desire is for us to be with Him, where He is and for us to behold His glory. He said in Revelation 2:7, *"He who has an ear, let him hear what the Spirit says to the churches. To him who overcomes I will give to eat from the tree of life, which is in the midst of the Paradise of God."'* In Revelation 22:1-5 John describes what the angel showed him, *"And he showed me a pure river of water of life, clear as crystal, proceeding from the throne of God and of the Lamb. ² In the middle of its street, and on either side of the river, was the tree of life, which bore twelve fruits, each tree yielding its fruit every month. The leaves of the tree were for the healing of the nations. 3 And there shall be no more curse, but the throne of God and of the Lamb shall be in it, and His servants shall serve Him. 4 They shall see His face, and His name shall be on their foreheads. 5 There shall be no night there: They need no lamp nor light of the sun, for the Lord God gives them light. And they shall reign forever and ever."* This is the same tree Ezekiel 47:12 records, *"Along the bank of the river, on this side and that, will grow all kinds of trees used for food; their leaves will not wither, and their fruit will not fail. They will bear fruit every month, because their water flows from the sanctuary. Their fruit will be for food, and their leaves for medicine."* John tells us in Revelation 22:14, *"Blessed are those who do His commandments, that they may have the right to the tree of life, and may enter through the gates into the city."*

Notice John said, blessed are those who do the Lord's commandments? One of the themes that were clearly seen as we discussed each fruit, was the element of OBEDIENCE. Every attribute requires us to obey Yahweh in every area of our lives. Remember it is our obedience that proves our love to Him.

In 2 Peter 1:5-11, Christ makes us partakers of the divine nature, making it possible for us to never stumble and to remain fruitful, if we abound in the following:

ABOUND IN THESE AND NEVER STUMBLE

Add to Your FAITH	VIRTUE
Add to Your VIRTUE	KNOWLEDGE
Add to Your KNOWLEDGE	SELF-CONTROL
Add to Your SELF- CONTROL	PERSEVERANCE
Add to Your PERSEVERANCE	GODLINESS
Add to Your GODLINESS	BROTHERLY LOVE

Another theme we experienced is the necessity of having Godly wisdom. I encourage you to do a study on the book of Proverbs as you daily ask the Lord to increase your wisdom. Wisdom is described as a tree of life in Proverbs 3:18-20, *"She is a tree of life to those who take hold of her, and happy are all who retain her. 19 The LORD by wisdom founded the earth; by understanding He established the heavens; 20 by His knowledge the depths were broken up, and clouds drop down the dew."* Since wisdom is likened to a tree of life, we cannot be fruitful without Yahweh's wisdom. Let's be the reflection of the Tree of Life in Heaven, in the earth.

WISDOM FROM ABOVE James 3:13-17
Pure
Peaceable
Gentle
Willing to Yield
Full of Mercy and Good Fruits
Without Partiality

"For this reason we also, since the day we heard it, do not cease to pray for you, and to ask that you may be filled with the knowledge of His will in all wisdom and spiritual understanding; 10 that you may walk worthy of the Lord, fully pleasing Him, being fruitful in every good work and increasing in the knowledge of God; 11 strengthened with all might, according to His glorious power, for all patience and longsuffering with joy; 12 giving thanks to the Father who has qualified us to be partakers of the inheritance of the saints in the light. 13 He has delivered us from the power of darkness and conveyed us into the kingdom of the Son of His love, 14 in whom we have redemption through His blood, the forgiveness of sins." Colossians 1:9-14

WALK WORTHY OF THE CALLING WITH ALL... Ephesians 4:1-3
Lowliness
Gentleness
Longsuffering
Bearing with one another in Love
Keep the unity of the Spirit in the bond of Peace

PURSUE 1 Timothy 6:11	PURSUE 2 Timothy 2:22
Righteousness	Righteous Living
Godliness	Faithfulness
Faith	Love
Love	Peace
Patience	
Gentleness	

Let's review.

THE FRUIT OF LOVE (Page 38)
When cultivating a garden at home, your productivity and crop quality is based on the health of your soil. The soil must be fertilized. Our SOUL is the SOIL, the WORD of Yahweh is the SEED and LOVE is the FERTILIZER (Luke 13:8) needed for all other fruits to grow. **EVERY FRUIT OF THE SPIRIT IS DEVELOPED IN LOVE.** For the Word to be fruitful and multiply, it must be planted in healthy ground. That good ground represents those whose *understanding of the WORD causes them to apply it in their lives* (Matthews 13:23). We must ask our Heavenly Father, to root and ground us in His love, so we will be filled with His fullness, through our faith in Yahshua as in Ephesians 3:17-19, *"that Christ may dwell in your hearts through faith;* **that you, being rooted and grounded in love**, [18] *may be able to comprehend with all the saints what is the width and length and depth and height—* [19] *to know the love of*

Christ which passes knowledge; that you may be filled with all the fullness of God."

LOVE...
1 Corinthians 13:4-7

Suffers Long	Is Kind	Does Not Envy
Does Not Parade Itself (Boastful)	Is Not Puffed Up (Proud)	Does Not Behave Rudely
Does Not Seek Its Own	Is Not Provoked	Thinks No Evil
Does Not Rejoice in Iniquity	Rejoices in Truth	Bears All Things
Believes All Things	Hopes All Things	Endures All Things

THE FRUIT OF JOY- (PAGE 57)
Our joy comes in knowing that we have eternal life in Christ sealed with the gift of Precious Holy Spirit. If we **focus on what is eternal** and **not on what is temporary** then we never have to lose our joy. Joy should not be based on material things in this life, but rooted in our eternal hope. When the foundation of our joy is correct nothing can shake it. **Joy should be continual not conditional.**

THE FRUIT OF PEACE (PAGE 87)
Peace is developed in our lives when we set our mind on the things of the Spirit. The Apostle Paul tells us in Romans 8:6, *"For to be carnally minded is death, but to be spiritually minded is life and peace."* What we think about and meditate on controls the direction and quality of our lives. Isaiah 26:3 explains, *"You will keep him in perfect peace, whose mind is stayed on You, because he trusts in You."* When a negative thought

pops in your mind, do not meditate on it, expel it by replacing it with Yahweh's truth from His Word.

FIX YOUR THOUGHTS ON THESE THINGS (Philippians 4:8)
Whatever is TRUE
Whatever is HONORABLE
Whatever is RIGHT
Whatever is PURE
Whatever is LOVELY
Whatever is ADMIRABLE
Whatever is EXCELLENT
Whatever is WORTHY OF PRAISE

THE FRUIT OF LONGSUFFERING (PAGE 111)
James 1:2-4 explains, *"My brethren, count it all joy when you fall into various trials, ³ knowing that the testing of your faith produces patience.* **⁴ But let patience have its perfect work, that you may be perfect and complete, lacking nothing**.*"* Do not run in fear from the process, allow the Lord to complete the work He started in you.

WE GLORY IN TRIBULATIONS KNOWING THAT... Romans 5:3-5
TRIBULATION Produces PERSEVERANCE
PERSEVERANCE Produces CHARACTER
CHARACTER Produces HOPE

THE FRUIT OF KINDNESS (PAGE 115)
Thank you Father for Your great kindness and love! Even when I do not deserve it, you see fit to bless me anyway! Luke 6:35 speaks of Yahweh, *"...For He is kind to the unthankful and evil"*. Job 6:14 tells, *"To him who is afflicted, kindness should be shown by his friend, even though he forsakes the fear of the Almighty."* The kindness that we show others should not be contingent on how they treat us, but on how Yahweh treats us. Paul instructs us in Romans 12:10 to, *"Be kindly*

affectionate to one another with brotherly love, in honor giving preference to one another;" 2 Peter 1:7 urges, *"to godliness brotherly kindness, and to brotherly kindness love."*

THE FRUIT OF GOODNESS (PAGE 122)
Yahweh gives us a clear definition of what He defines as good in Micah 6:8, *"He has shown you, O man, what is good; and what does the L<small>ORD</small> require of you but to <u>do justly, to love mercy, and to walk humbly with your God</u>?"* We must understand that doing good is something we learn, which also means it is something that must be taught. Isaiah 1:17 tells us, **"Learn to do good**; *Seek justice, Rebuke the oppressor; Defend the fatherless, Plead for the widow."* Titus 3:14 encourages, *"And let our people also* **learn to maintain good works**, *to meet urgent needs, that they may not be unfruitful."*

THE FRUIT OF FAITHFULNESS (PAGE 168)
Let this be our motto, *"I have been crucified with Christ; it is no longer I who live, but Christ lives in me; and the life which I now live in the flesh* **I live by faith in the Son of God**, *who loved me and gave Himself for me. (Galatians 2:20)"* Our faith in Yahshua gives us VICTORY to overcome the world! He is the author and finisher of our faith (Hebrews 12:2). I John 5:3-5 tells us, *"For this is the love of God, that we keep His commandments. And His commandments are not burdensome. ⁴ For whatever is born of God overcomes the world.* **And this is the victory that has overcome the world—our faith.** ⁵ *Who is he who overcomes the world, but he who believes that Jesus is the Son of God?"*

THE FRUIT OF GENTLENESS (PAGE 172)
Gentleness is likened to a nursing mother cherishing her children. It is an affection that is acted out selflessly. Paul writes in 1 Thessalonians 2:4-9, *"But as we have been approved by God to be entrusted with the*

gospel, even so we speak, not as pleasing men, but God who tests our hearts. ⁵ For neither at any time did we use flattering words, as you know, nor a cloak for covetousness—God is witness. ⁶ Nor did we seek glory from men, either from you or from others, when we might have made demands as apostles of Christ. ⁷ <u>But we were gentle among you, just as a nursing mother cherishes her own children. ⁸ So, affectionately longing for you, we were well pleased to impart to you not only the gospel of God, but also our own lives, because you had become dear to us.</u> ⁹ For you remember, brethren, our labor and toil; for laboring night and day, that we might not be a burden to any of you, we preached to you the gospel of God."

THE FRUIT OF SELF CONTROL (PAGE 192)
This fruit of self-control looks like complete obedience to Yahweh in our lifestyles. The presence of it exemplifies that we are students of the Most High God, who hear His Word with understanding and live it out in our physical bodies. The lack of it magnifies ignorance and brings us into disobedience.

PROVE OURSELVES **2 Corinthians 6:6**	**BE AN EXAMPLE** **1 Timothy 4:12**
By our Purity	In what you SAY
By our Understanding	In the way you LIVE
By our Patience	In your LOVE
By our Kindness	In your FAITH
By the Holy Spirit	In your PURITY
By our Sincere Love	

THE FRUIT OF RIGHTEOUSNESS *(PAGE 200)*
Just as faith without works is dead, when Yahweh makes us righteous, the fruit of that, or should I say, the proof of that is in the actions of righteous living. Yahweh expects us to do righteous and just acts and to train our children to do the same from generation to generation. There are many benefits to our personal

lives and our neighbors, when we chose to live righteous lives. In Genesis 18:19, Yahweh says of Abraham, *"For I have known him, in order that he may <u>command his children and his household after him, that they keep the way of the LORD, to do righteousness and justice</u>, that the Lord may bring to Abraham what He has spoken to him."*

Yahweh has His own clothing line, there is a spiritual wardrobe that we wear in Christ. There should never be a day that we are without our garment. We are clothed in the righteousness of God and must wear the whole armor of God.

SPIRITUAL GARMENT Colossians 3:12-15	ARMOR OF GOD Ephesians 6:10-17
Tender Mercies	Gird your waste with truth
Kindness	Breastplate of Righteousness
Humility	Shod Your feet with the preparation of the Gospel of peace
Meekness	Shield of Faith
Longsuffering	Helmet of Salvation
Love	Sword of the Spirit (the WORD)

<u>THE FRUIT OF JUSTICE</u> (PAGE 216)
We are the plants in Yahweh's vineyard and He searches for the fruit of justice and righteousness, Isaiah 5:7 states, *"For the vineyard of the LORD of hosts is the house of Israel, and the men of Judah are His pleasant plant. <u>He looked for justice, but behold, oppression; for righteousness, but behold, a cry for help."</u>* We have to be very careful. Examine our heart and motives, don't let it be that Yahweh finds us oppressing others instead of treating them fairly. When Yahshua ascended He sent us precious Holy Spirit. Isaiah 32:15-18, prophesied *"Until the Spirit is poured upon us from on high, and the*

wilderness becomes a fruitful field, and the fruitful field is counted as a forest. ¹⁶ Then justice will dwell in the wilderness, and righteousness remain in the fruitful field." We need Holy Spirit to produce in us the crop of justice and righteousness the Lord is requiring of us.

True Religion Is to: James 1:26-27
Execute True Justice (Judge Fairly)
Show Mercy to One Another
Show Compassion to One Another
Bridle/Control our Tongue
Visit orphans and widows in their trouble
Keep ourselves unspotted from the world/don't let the world corrupt you

THE FRUIT OF MERCY (PAGE 228)
Hosea 4:1 declares, *"Hear the word of the LORD, You children of Israel, for the LORD brings a charge against the inhabitants of the land: "There is no truth or mercy or knowledge of God in the land."* When Yahweh examines the fruit of your life, will He find truth, mercy and the knowledge of Him? He is such a loving Father that He promises to give us our hearts' desires. Do we love Him enough to satisfy His heart's desire? In Hosea 6:6 Yahweh says, **"For I desire mercy** *and not sacrifice,* **and the knowledge of God** *more than burnt offerings."* He desires to see us walk in mercy. As people we tend to become more focused on our religious routines, requirements, rules and regulations than on building relationships. We notice the faults, weaknesses and shortcomings of others, before we answer their silent cry for love.

Our Heavenly Father will continue to nurture His Fruit in us, as we allow Him. Be excited that you have stepped out of your worldly thinking and have embraced the mind of Christ. Remember, it's ok to forgive your offenders, its ok to say hello and show kindness to a stranger, it's ok to rejoice during times of suffering. It may not be the world's normal, thankfully, Yahweh's ways and thoughts are higher than ours. Have faith in Yahshua and let nothing hold you back from your destiny in Him! You are special and valuable to His Kingdom. *Be courageous as you walk humbly in the gifts that He has planted in you.*

BE FRUITFUL AND MULTIPLY SOULS INTO HIS KINGDOM!

www.ingramcontent.com/pod-product-compliance
Lightning Source LLC
LaVergne TN
LVHW051547070426
835507LV00021B/2460